LEO. W. YODER
625 N. E. 78th AVE.
PORTLAND 16, ORE.
LI. 5501

David Lee Crane
1324 N. E. 81st Avenue
Portland 13, Oregon

THE
BEST
FROM
PULPIT
DIGEST

PULPIT DIGEST PUBLISHING CO.
Great Neck, New York

Manufactured in the United States of America
by The Haddon Craftsmen, Inc., Scranton, Pa.

This selection of some of the material which, during the fifteen years of Pulpit Digest's publication, has evoked the greatest response from our readers is affectionately dedicated to the thousands of ministers who have made Pulpit Digest possible. Their interest, their loyalty, and their constructive criticism have always been both an inspiration and a challenge to produce a professional journal for the Protestant ministry which is worthy of their trust.

Table of Contents

Preaching from the Bible

BY HALFORD E. LUCCOCK

Professor of Homiletics, Yale Divinity School

ONE of the most effective demonstrations—all the more effective because wholly unintentional—of what preaching from a Biblical narrative may be, as a message to the contemporary world, is found in a chapter in a book, published his spring, *One World or None*, edited by Dexter Matthres and Katherine Way, chapters written by the leading atomic scientists. In one chapter Professor Phillip Morrison, of Cornell University, who worked on the atomic project at Los Alamos, N.M., describes his visit to Hiroshima to investigate the effects of the explosion of the first atomic bomb. He was one of the first observers and is extremely eager to make the whole thing vivid to Americans. So, after a short description of the devastation at Hiroshima, he moves the whole catastrophe to New York City. He writes:—

The streets and buildings of Hiroshima are unfamiliar to Americans. Even from pictures of the damage, realization is

7

abstract and remote. A clearer and truer understanding can be gained from thinking of the bomb as falling on a city which Americans know well. The diversity of the awful experience which I saw at Hiroshima—I shall project on an American target.

There, in these words, "project on an American target" —is one secret of effective preaching from the Bible. It projects the truth that is in the Bible on to "an American target." It tells the Biblical story and then moves it into the familiar scenes of everyday life. That is exactly what Professor Morrison does with the atom bomb. He moves it from Japan to New York. He shows in terms of exact measurements and descriptions of what happened at Hiroshima, what would have happened had the same bomb dropped on Gramercy Park, New York City. The whole thing comes terribly alive.

Now take a parallel illustration from preaching. Here is the way in which Dr. Charles W. Gilkey, of the University of Chicago, moved the story of the Good Samaritan from Palestine to an American college campus:

A certain Freshman went from home to college and she fell among critics who said that she had no style, that her manners were awkward and that she had an unattractive personality. Then they stripped her of her self-confidence, her enthusiasm and her courage, and departed, leaving her hurt and lonely and half dead.

And when the seniors saw it they were amused, saying, "What a good job the sophomores are doing on that freshman," and they passed on the other side.

In like manner, the Juniors also, when they saw it, smiled and said, "Yea, verily, for she hath not the makings of a good sorority girl." And they passed by on the other side.

But a certain special student, as she went about, came where the freshman was, and when she saw the freshman she was moved with compassion, and came to her and bound up her wounds, pouring on sympathy and understanding. And she took the freshman to her room and set her on her feet again, and brought her unto her own circle and was a friend to her.

Which of these, thinkest thou, proved neighbor to her that fell among the critics? Go thou and do likewise!

Such preaching brings the truth into our present life with a feeling of nearness and challenge which were in the words which Jesus used at Nazareth, "This day is this scripture fulfilled in your ears." True expository preaching is a great bridge across the gulf of the centuries, over which spiritual traffic may pass from 1000 B.C. to 30 A.D. to 1946 A.D.

This does not mean the violent and unhistorical process of "modernizing Jesus" or reading back into His mind ideas that were completely foreign to Him. We have had quite enough of that grotesque distortion of Jesus. It is simply to make vivid the contemporary application of the truth of His words, just as He, Himself, in every quotation He used from the Old Testament, showed a meaning in it for His day, and to the situation in which He found Himself.

There are many signs of an increased place for Biblical preaching. A generation ago was the hey-day of topical preaching. Among the reasons for that was a revolt against the domination of expository preaching; there was also the emergence of new interests such as stress on the social aspects of Christianity, the psychology of religion, and the newly grasped realization of the effectiveness of life-situation preaching. There was also a strong feeling of the weakness of much that passed under the name of "Biblical preaching," which often degenerated into a lazy preacher's paradise, in which the sermon was mainly a vague rehash of a Biblical passage, accomplishing little more than to take great poetry and imagination and turn it into leaden, heavy-footed prose.

Recent years have brought many influences leading to a revaluation of Bible-centered preaching. Among these have been the bankruptcy of secular optimism and the recovery of a God-centered theology. Another strong influence has been a growing sense among many preachers of the thinness of continuous topical preaching. Dr. Gordon Poteat, in his book, *We Preach Not Ourselves*, has put this forcefully:

> Up to date topical preaching, while timely, may lack the element of timeliness. It is too easily detached from Christian traditions, and thus cut off from any deep roots . . . Another weakness in topical preaching is a tendency to monopoly in the handling of the themes. When the preacher approaches his sermon primarily from the problem angle, he does not preach very long before he has compassed most of the possible themes.
>
> The weakness of the tradition-detached non-Biblical preaching is felt by many. The people in the pews want something more, something different from what they get in editorials. For many preachers with sensitive consciences it has become more and more difficult to ascend the pulpit "on their own." They realize that the expectation of the people exceeds their meagre fare.

All these influences have called for a new type of Biblical preaching, vital and closely related to everyday life. There has been a fresh discovery of the Bible as an incomparable source of preaching.

1. *The Bible is the most dramatic material the preacher*

will ever find. The man who pitches the Bible out of the study window might as well pitch himself along with it. That, indeed, is exactly what he does, for he renounces what the sermon desperately needs: life, action, color and concreteness. In a hundred Bible stories there is a real incarnation; the Word becomes flesh and walks among us. Much of the Bible is marked by the same genius which appears in the Elizabethan dramatists, the personification of abstract qualities, not in the wooden manner of the Miracle Play, or in a formal allegory, but in the creative way of a drama. The word "ambition" becomes flesh in *Macbeth*, "jealousy" in *Othello*, "youth" in *Romeo and Juliet*.

2. *One of the Bible's greatest gifts is the sheer power of narrative.* Can anyone doubt the need of much preaching for more narrative? Abstract generalizations in excess do for a sermon what a flat tire does for a car—they stop movement. Familiarity with the Bible to the extent that it gets into the very bones of a preacher, gives him the saving power of the concrete. The preacher's danger, which does so easily beset him, is similar to that of the Maine farmer who was shingling his house on a foggy day and shingled right off into the fog. That is an easy thing to do in the pulpit. Think over the multitude of concrete things in the speech of Jesus as recorded in the synoptic gospels:

> He talked of the grass and wind and rain,
> And fig trees and fair weather.
> He spoke of lilies, vines and corn,
> The sparrow and the raven,
> And yeast and bread and flax and cloth
> And eggs and fish and candles.

It is the concrete, so abundantly found in narrative, which

gives traction for the mind, as sand gives traction for wheels on an icy road.

3. *Another great resource of the Bible for preaching is its amazing variety.* The longer a man preaches, the higher, I think, he will rate variety. In the days of youth when the evil days come not, one is not terribly worried over variety. The beginner in the pulpit always seems new to himself, and there is often a freshness about youth that makes even a twice-told tale seem new to others. But a man in what H. G. Wells calls "deep middle age" (a disturbing phrase, suggestive of being stuck in the mud!) realizes that no man has many main ideas. Left to himself he stresses them to the point of weariness to the congregation. The Bible brings a whole gallery of fresh ideas and suggestions. A student leaves the theological seminary with about four sermons, as a rule. Being young, he has one on "Youth Building a New World." He usually has one on "Tension Points in the Modern World" including race, industry, and war (all in one sermon!). Then he has one which is a tribute to Jesus. Then, usually there is a blistering sermon on "What's Wrong with the Church?" Then the question arises, "Where do we go from here?" *He had better go to the Bible!*

4. One great advantage of Biblical preaching is that *it is the material already accepted* by the majority of the hearers. The preacher can go on from there. There is no need of a dynamiting process to get an idea into the mind of the hearer—it is already there in terms of Scripture, so that he starts with a great advantage. He can clarify and enforce. He does not bring a strange novelty leading the people to look up and say: "Jesus I know, and Paul I know, but who are you?"

It would not be too much to call this kind of Biblical preaching "journalistic preaching" in the best sense. That may have a superficial sound, but it means simply bringing truth to bear on a particular situation for a specific purpose. Bernard Shaw has said with much truth that nothing which did not originate as journalism ever endured as great literature. The gospels originated as "journalism." They were "good news" for the particular audience to which they were brought. Mr. Shaw writes:

> The prophets railed or prophesied or comforted because they wanted to reach the hearts of the children of Israel, not because they wanted to utter beautiful words. St. Paul wanted to convert the inhabitants of Greece and Asia Minor, not to write beautiful letters. And the more passionately they wanted to do these things, the more journalistically they wrote and spoke; such passages as the thirteenth Chapter of First Corinthians and the exhortations beginning, "Comfort ye, comfort ye, my people" being the result.

An instance of this kind of preaching is the sermon of Rabbi Isserman of St. Louis, who in trying to bring the message of Amos close to today, imagined Amos preaching at Atlantic City during the Easter Parade. The goal is to enable people to see themselves in the Bible story. Preaching shares one important truth with historical fiction. It is successful if the reader can live in it; if he feels that it is about him. Both historical fiction and expository preaching are unsuccessful if they remind the reader or hearer that it is about another time than ours. History is about the past. But in a work of imagination, and in effective preaching, the scenes and customs and issues must be translated into modern terms.

To do this calls sternly for the preacher *to live with the Bible*. If the world came down in ruins tomorrow, it ought to find the preacher working on some portion of the Bible, not for next Sunday but because it is a lifelong process with him, passing in review before his mind the whole parade of people and truth in the Bible. That is a counsel of perfection, but it can be approximated. For any theme on which a man is preaching, providing that it is a vital issue of life, there is a word in the Bible which was fore-ordained from the foundation of the world for that sermon. But there is a "catch" in it! You must know where that word is, and you will not know it without continuous exploration. The most vital sermons are not those prepared for a special occasion, on the spur of the day or the week. They are those which are glimpsed when one is reading the Bible without reference to occasion, just allowing it to speak to his imagination and conscience. Then, when the occasion arises later, what he has met in his study and regular meditation will come again to him as the theme and word for that time.

One very homely instance of this truth is to be found in the occurrence in a "treasure hunt" conducted by a group of young people at a summer camp. One of the things which they were required to bring in was a snake. Now a snake is a rather hard thing to find when one is out looking for it. One boy, however, brought in a snake, the only person in the group who found one. It was a dead snake, but a snake. When asked how he ever found a snake, he modestly replied, "I saw it yesterday."

That is good advice for the preacher: "See your snakes yesterday." That is, get your idea and themes out of a regular, life-long habit of reading the Bible. Then you will have the "treasure" to bring in when it is required. It is a preaching version of some good advice given a long time ago: "Cast your bread upon the waters and it will come back to you after many days."

Now it may be of some suggestiveness to conclude with a few samples of the fruitfulness of the Bible as a source of preaching pointed at the contemporary person and scene. These are taken at random from here and there, with no purpose except as samples.

Just look at the Old Testament for a moment. If you want to get away from a sweet and sappy religion that turns inward exclusively and away from evils that ride roughshod over the earth, you will find iron and fire in many places in the Old Testament.

There is stern judgement on a religion that does not face actual evil. Such a religion can easily become a sort of cathedral close, a walled-in garden. Take the whole fourth Chapter of Amos: "Go on, multiply your sacrifices, announce your gifts, you are far from God," etc. There is Isaiah: "I am sick of your worship," and Hosea: "Love and not sacrifice."

In the prophets there is devastating deflation of our modern confidence and achievement. The prophets say: "You have great pride and satisfaction, but the Eternal hath said . . ." There is much challenge to a humanistic substitution of ethics for religion. Isaiah, for instance: "Ye that bring good tidings to Zion, get thee up on a high mountain." There is no other source of permanent good news than in God. The whole ethical conception of life is tied in with faith in God.

There is hope in the prophetic conception of the Messianic Kingdom. Its central affirmation is God acting in history. The note of expectation in both the Old and New Testament is something that has sadly dropped out of much contemporary Christianity. The characteristic "messianic hope" of our world today is a tawdry thing, the hope of a marvellous place which man will create with invention and industrial advance—a sort of plastic heaven. We look for a day of a paradise of chromium and ceramics, of helicopters and refrigerators, egg-shaped autos and layer-cake houses, glass skyscrapers and clothing made from soy beans. We have no need for a day of the Lord—General Motors will take care of all that! What a trade—heaven for earth, God for gadgets! So the Old and New Testament expectation of the action of God has immense meaning for our day.

So many themes of great timeliness spring up, when we allow the Bible to speak to us, when we are in an unhurried and inquiring meditation on it. Such themes as: the preservation of religion in an alien culture (the Hebrews in Babylon); the recovery of the inner life against a quantitative civilization; the need for an ancient wisdom for a lifetime rather then a new prudence for every hour. Take the old question, for instance: "Shall I give the fruit of my body for the sin of my soul?" Is that not an exact description of war, our sins of omission today bringing the human sacrifice of tomorrow?

Take the wonderful picture of Nehemiah looking out at night over the devastated Jerusalem—what a starting point for treating the theme of a ruined civilization waiting to be rebuilt! Or think of the 5th chapter of 1st Samuel: "And they took Dagon and set him in his place again"—the setting up of an old idol, which is going on in a hundred places in our post-war world, the old idols of nationalism, power politics, the lust of profits though the country swirls into a ruinous inflation—Dagon set up in his place again!

Or take some texts which are frankly pictures. It should be made clear that the preacher is not trying to read back modern meanings into the old situation. Let an honest exegesis be given, with the best critical help possible. Then the suggestive truth in the picture can be given. For instance, take the words said to Jesus when he was brought to the house where a little girl had died. "Lay thine hands upon her and she will live." What a word for a tremendous truth, that what we allow Jesus to lay His hands upon, does live! The sex instinct, which can destroy terribly, can live as love and family devotion if we allow Jesus to lay his hands on it; ambition, another deadly force, can live as service; even sorrow can live, and has lived, when it is under Jesus' hand.

What a text for Armistice or Memorial day this is, from the words said to Jesus as he stood by the grave of Lazarus: "Lord, if thou hadst been here, my brother had not died." True, in the largest sense! Or take the new meaning which the atomic bomb has put into the words of the 23rd Psalm: "The valley of the shadow of death." That is what humanity will be walking in from now till the end of time. Or take the suggestion of the most momentous journey in the world, the journey from a question mark to an exclamation point; the question, asked in doubt: "Art thou he that cometh or look we for another?" and the exclamation point: "Hosanna, Blessed is He that cometh in the name of the Lord!"

Or the words in the story of the preparation of the room for the Last Supper: "They found it as He said it unto them." Simple words, having no other meaning than description of the preparation of the room. But how they gleam as a record of history for nineteen centuries! Men have found that life works out as Jesus said it would. Our society today is conclusive proof on that point!

Here is the sermon of one preacher on the text "My Father worketh." He spoke of the sign so frequently seen on the roads: "Men at Work." In how many places we ought to see the sign, "*God* at work." The sermon was on some places in our life, both as individuals and society, where God is at work and where we may cooperate with Him.

Or take the new fresh meaning these days have brought to the first word of Jesus' ministry: "Repent." That means: "Get a new mind. There is a new order at hand. Adjust yourself to it." How profoundly true that is now! Another text with a very simple meaning, Judges 4:14: "Up, up, for this is the day," will serve to convey many Christian challenges to our time.

So one might go on forever. That is the preacher's hope—that this kind of receptivity to the word will go on as long as life lasts, a well of water springing up to everlasting life.

—*from* PULPIT DIGEST *for July, 1946*

Building God's House

BY ELBERT M. CONOVER

Director of the Interdenominational Bureau of Architecture

FROM the "Rule Book" of one denomination:

Let our church buildings be designed in keeping with the lofty purposes of providing for divine worship, or the administration of the Holy Sacraments, and for the ministries of preaching, religious education, and fellowship and service. Funds devoted to the erection and equipment of church property should be most judiciously and effectively administered and building projects should become religious and spiritual advances in the life of the congregation.

A building enterprise should engage the varied talents of the entire congregation, and it should proceed slowly, steadily, and comprehensively. As the leader, it is the pastor who must bear the ultimate responsibility for its success.

The kind of organization here suggested makes it possible to enlist the services and talents of a large group. It avoids antagonizing or hurting the feelings of interested members of the congregation who are not on the so-called "building committee." The larger the group of workers en-

19

gaged in the preliminary activities, the greater the unity, the enthusiasm, and the understanding of problems, and incidentally the greater the financial support. Religious values of tremendous significance in the life of the congregation may thus be developed.

Approved denominational procedure will govern the establishment of the organization, or the group selected to enlist and assemble the organization.

An inspirational meeting may be arranged, to be attended by all invited to enlist for committee work. A written statement of the duties and responsibilities of each committee and of the entire organization should be presented to the meeting. All items that will need attention may be mentioned, and then assigned to the several committees.

The following is a typical plan of organization. Each church will need to modify it to suit its own particular requirements, and at the same time work out in specific detail the duties of all committees and sub-committees.

The Church Building Council or the Forward Movement Council, including the members of all committees. Don't appoint a Building Committee at the beginning of the program. Don't assign to a Board of Trustees the task of leading the project.

The Executive Committee, acting for the church as the church may direct. May be composed of the chairmen of the working committees and chairman of the Council. The pastor should be ex-officio a member of all committees. The chairman of each committee may have an advisory relation to the Executive Committee and should regularly report to it.

The Survey Committee: Conduct a religious census and

a community survey. Make a thorough study of religious affiliations of the population in the "responsibility field." Locate on map present membership and constituents and prospects. Study public school locations and, where possible, religious affiliations of pupils. Confer with utility companies and others regarding possible population trends. Consider industrial and other situations that may affect population movements. Recommend future location of the church. Estimate numbers to be provided for in each department of church work.

Committee on Worship and Religious Arts: Study trends and effective programs in Worship. Training in Worship. Recommend facilities and arrangements for sanctuary, choir, and auxiliary rooms. The chapel. Children's chapel. The organ. Study and recommend glass, decoration, color schemes, selection of pictures, symbols, etc., for entire building. Study exterior design. Confer with Committee on Christian Education. Read some of the many splendid books on worship and religious arts.

Committee on Christian Education: See publications of the International Council of Religious Education, 203 North Wabash Avenue, Chicago, Illinois, and denominational agencies. Sub-divide for studies of Christian Education for children, for youth, for young adults, adult Christian Education, week-day and vacation Church Schools. Confer with committee on Worship and the Religious Arts and Committee on Fellowship and Recreation. Help estimate, on basis of surveys, future possible church school constituency. Present list of rooms and equipment required, characteristics of rooms, floor areas, ceiling heights, built-in features, etc.

Committee on Fellowship and Recreation: The social and recreational life of the church must be integrated with the work of Christian Education and Evangelism and the spiritual strengthening of the church. Consider moving pictures, games, craft shop, summer and outdoor activities, music, dramatics, and pageantry. Dining hall, kitchen, parlor, and kitchenette facilities. Confer with denominational and interdenominational workers. List rooms, equipment needed, floor areas, ceiling heights, etc.

Plans and Construction Committee: This may be called the Building Committee. Investigate and recommend contractors. Study, in conference with architects, materials, mechanical equipment, etc., suitable for church work. After the Building Program has been written, and as directed by the Executive Committee, the congregation, or the official church body, secure and exhibit tentative plans and estimates of cost, have them revised, and secure construction drawings and specifications. Arrange for erection of the building. Check closely with Finance and Promotion Committee, in addition to being guided by Executive Committee. Have *one person* to transmit *in writing* all instructions to the architect and through the architect to the builders. Have sub-committee on landscaping.

Committee on Finance and Promotion: It may be well to appoint *two* committees for the work herein described, a Finance Committee and a Promotional and Publicity Committee. After careful study and planning, conduct campaigns of promotion and fund raising, as directed by the Executive Committee. Prepare publicity material. Arrange for newspaper publicity. Give special attention to religious values in connection with the promotional program. Seek to cultivate a religious interest on the part of the entire church, church school, and community. Help plan participation in the building program such as having young people gather rocks for a fireplace, help plan symbolism to be used, etc. Excellent and varied talent can be enlisted for this work.

Committee on Women's Work: Confer with Committees on Fellowship and Recreation and Christian Education. Recommend program of building and equipment for dining hall and kitchen facilities, parlors, work rooms, etc. Plan for good church housekeeping.

Committee on Furnishings and Equipment: Cooperate with the Committees on Worship, Christian Education, and Fellowship and Recreation. Investigate sources of supply, prices, samples, etc., of all furnishings and equipment. Cooperate closely with the architect. Perform work as assigned by Executive Committee.

Committee on Administration and Special Facilities: This Committee will recommend adequate church offices, pastor's conference room, and rooms for staff workers, and seek to guard against any desirable items being overlooked. This committee would do well to visit other churches.

After the pastor has arranged for the work of fact-finding and program-building he will be faced with the task of assembling the statement of needs. This statement should not be prepared by the Plans and Construction Committee or by a Building Committee, but should be carried out by the pastor himself or by an independent committee. A complete list of all the rooms and facilities needed for the work of the church should be prepared, and it should be done without regard to the form which the building plans may take. The total need should be stated and religiously considered, regardless of what amounts of money may have been budgeted for use either currently or in the future.

Many building projects have failed of success because of entanglement of the program with preconceived ideas about building plans and designs.

—*from* PULPIT DIGEST *for October, 1946*

The Worship of
the Average Church

BY ANDREW W. BLACKWOOD

Chairman of the Practical Department,
The Princeton Theological Seminary

THE average church" here stands for the most important place on earth, apart from Christian homes. It means a congregation where the minister has no full-time paid assistants other than the sexton. Most of the books and articles about public worship deal with large churches, which have needs and problems more or less their own. The vast majority of ministers labor in smaller bodies. These men should feel thankful for the thesis that appears in the following sentence.

By the blessing of God the leader of worship in a church of average size can make his part of the service as uplifting and helpful as that of any vast congregation. For obvious reasons we shall think only about the work of the pastor, and not about such related concerns as architecture. Also we shall take for granted the guidance of the Holy Spirit, in

25

response to prayer. Nowhere does the man of God more need to follow the apostolic injunction: "Pray without ceasing." Now let us look at some of the ways in which our thesis works.

I. The pastor's choice of hymns may prove as helpful and uplifting as in the Brick Presbyterian Church of New York City. There at time the music has become known for its beauty and helpfulness. Under God, such an effect depends largely on care and skill in the choice of hymns. And yet sometimes a friendly observer of churches feels that ministers have learned almost everything about hymns except how to choose three of them for an hour of worship.

The ideal appears in the preface of a book, *University Hymns*, which the Deans of Religion at Yale and Princeton Universities prepared for use in chapel. The following excerpt has to do with the words, not the tunes. If the hour of worship begins with a few words of song, do not include them in the list that follows:

> The more objective type of hymn, expressing adoration, praise, or thanksgiving, appropriate for the beginning, forms one group. The more introspective and subjective type of hymn, appropriate for the central part of the service, is a second group. Hymns appropriate for the climax of the service are grouped according to the emphasis on confidence, on consecration [dedication], on service, or on social appeal. The seasonal hymns for the church year and for special occasions follow in a group by themselves.

Here let us think only about the three types of hymns for a regular service. Take an example of the first kind: "Our God, our help in ages past." Of the second, "Love divine, all loves excelling" or "Spirit of God, descend upon my heart." Of the third, in two aspects, one personal and the other collective: "Jesus, I my cross have taken," or "Lead on, O King Eternal."

Now look over your church bulletins for the past six months and see whether or not you have carried out these ideals. Remember that they have little to do with the size of the congregation, except that a man ought to choose hymns that he has trained the people to sing.

Why have three full hymns at every regular service? Partly because you wish to lead a singing church. If so, let the people sing! Also because you wish to have them voice three kinds of needs, ever present in hearts today. In a vast congregation not far distant, the worshipers almost never join in any kind of hymns save the objective, which include the noblest of all our songs on earth. In another sanctuary equally large and thronged, they seldom have anything but subjective hymns. In an occasional house of worship the people sing little but hymns of action. The choir marches in singing "Stand up, stand up, for Jesus." At the middle of the service they have "Fight the good fight," and near the end, "The Son of God goes forth to war." Three closing hymns!

Elsewhere the people have no third hymn, or it may be no congregational singing at the center of the service. Consequently, they ignore large sections of the hymnal. Who must accept the major portion of the blame? The minister. He in turn may point to the divinity school, and to books about public worship. How many readers while in the seminary had any adequate teaching about the way to choose three hymns? As a rule classes in church music deal with almost everything else. Why do not the books about worship stress the importance of choosing hymns, and then tell a man how? Perhaps because that would call for the use of brains on the part of the author, or teacher. A man finds it easier to compile from books.

II. The pastor of a small church can make his public use of the Scriptures as memorable as in the Chapel of Princeton University. For example, the dean emeritus, Dr. R. R. Wicks, used always to read the Scriptures with distinction, and his successor does much the same. Sometimes the hour of worship calls for a responsive reading. If so, the people stand, as they do whenever they sing. Under the right sort of minister, with a little training of the lay leaders, a responsive reading can bring out the majestic music of the old King James. The pastor must know how to choose the selections, and how to enlist the choir, or somebody else, to lead in the congregational responses.

In our semininary the other day a professor met with a class of a hundred men and a dozen women. He asked this question: "How many of you have come from home churches that use responsive readings in the morning service?" Seventy-five percent of the hands went up. That proportion seemed to him high, as he had found that approximately half of our better churches, in the way of public worship, do not have responsive readings regularly. Then he asked another question: "How many of you look back on that part of public worship as effective?" Only a few hands went up. More than three-fourths of those who joined in responsive readings back at home look on that part of public worship as more or less futile. Here again, the blame must rest with the pastors, and back of them, with the seminaries and the books about worship. How many of you readers had any such training or guidance?

Think too about the public reading of the Scriptures. Many of us look on such lessons as the most important thing we do in God's house, except when we administer the sacraments. With reference to Scripture reading we must note a fact that defies explanation. If a body where the minister does not hold a high theory of Inspiration, he may read the Book with distinction. In many churches where pastors accept what the Bible says about itself as the Written Word of God, they mumble words of Holy Writ so as to make them seem insipid. John Wesley used to say about certain "orthodox" clergymen that people ought to pay them to refrain from reading the Bible in public.

III. You can also make the prayers of a wayside chapel as uplifting and helpful as Spurgeon used to do in the vast London Tabernacle. A certain American professor of preaching, who looked on Spurgeon as the mightiest pulpit master since the Apostle Paul, used to say that the London divine excelled even more in his public prayers. Spurgeon's way of approach to the mercy seat would not fit the needs of any church today. If he were living now he would not pray so long, and he might introduce more of form. He would surely have his ministerial admirers learn to excel in public prayer, as the most difficult thing they ever do for God.

An old book long out of print suggests a kind of acrostic that will help any man check up on his public prayers. Beginning with the words ACTSS, the author calls for five elements, and in this order: Adoration, Confession, Thanksgiving, Supplication, and Submission. The supplications ought to include Petitions for those present, and Intercessions for others near and far. As for Submission, that sounds too passive. With it blend the idea of dedication to Service. Now look back over your public prayers last Sunday morning. Did you voice these five needs of human hearts, and in this order? Better still, do you plan for such a service on the coming Lord's Day?

In this connection Dr. Ernest F. Tittle of the First Methodist Church at Evanston, Ill., makes a fruitful suggestion. He believes in the use of collects and other classic forms of devotion. He also pleads for more emphasis on what we used to call the pastoral prayer. In an article for ministers, he deplores the tendency to ignore the needs of hearts whose feelings the minister should voice when he brings them to the mercy seat. Dr. Tittle would agree with Joseph Parker at the City Temple in London. This man, famed as a pulpit orator, used to declare that in every pew the minister could find at least one broken heart. That still holds true everywhere save when pews stand empty. But no person would gain such an impression after following many a so-called pastoral prayer. It seems as remote, as cold, as inhuman as one of Greenland's icy mountains. Yet we wonder about those empty pews! People's hearts these days feel starved.

IV. The pastor of a small church can make his sermons as interesting and helpful as those at the Riverside Church in New York City. Why refer to the sermon in an article about worship? Partly because this portion of the hour in church may become far from worshipful. Let us think of public worship in terms of revelation and response. Through the reading of the Scriptures and the message from the pulpit, God reveals His will for men and women here and now.

In other parts of worship they respond to God's revelation of Himself in Christ. Hence the time of worship ought to include every minute from the beginning of the prelude, and even before, until the friends have departed from the house of God.

All of this applies especially to the introduction of a sermon. Take an extreme example. On a Lord's Day in March of the present year, in a large sanctuary that must remain nameless, the first half of the morning hour brought every heart close to God. In praise and prayer, as in lessons from the Book, the waiting throng moved silently along mystic slopes that brought them face to face with the Living Christ. Just before the sermon they arose to sing a hymn that fitted its place in such a God-centered service.

Instead of starting with a text, or something else distinctly Christian, the "sermon" began with a personal anecdote, which would have seemed out of place at a dinner party or in a gathering of ladies and gentlemen. The minister told about a Vermont farmer spitting tobacco while he explained about his boy trying to shoe a mule, which "kicked him to God and back." Apart from this reference to the Almighty, the anecdote had nothing to do with religion, or with what had preceded the sermon. The rest of the discourse, however, moved on a worthy level. It related to God in Christ and to human needs here and now.

Why does a man of ability, a believer in Christ, start to "preach" this way? Perhaps because someone has taught him to "begin with people where they are." Amen! Why not do the same with all the rest of the hour in worship? Either those people did not follow the praises, the prayers, and the readings, or else they felt ready also for a religious

introduction to the sermon. Our most skillful living master
of homiletics always plans to put into the first sentence or
two the gist of what he expects to say during the rest of the
sermon. Who follows in his train? Only the man who does
not fear anyone in the pew!

We must allow some leeway for exceptions. As a rule,
the fault lies not with the pew but with the pulpit, or rather
with the man in the study. He ought to know that when
people come to church these days they want religion. They
need God. They may not object to a touch of humor once in
a while, but they often feel that a dislocated love of horse-
play belongs with the jawbone of an ass. As Dr. A. J. Gossip
says, not one minister in a hundred knows how to handle
humor reverently in the pulpit. If not reverent, keep it out!
On the mountain top let the people do nothing but worship God.

V. The pastor of an average church can likewise make
the order of service as uplifting and helpful as in the Euclid
Avenue Methodist Church of Cleveland. The ways of worship there would not fit the rural church at Cream Ridge.
Partly for this reason it is unwise for pastors of average
congregations to receive all their seminary training under
men who have had no experience other than in vast congregations; and to read nothing but books by able men who
know little about the small church or one of average size.

Within any denomination the pastor can do no better
than follow the order of worship he finds in his Book of
Worship, whatever the title. Unfortunately, when a man
becomes concerned about this subject, he may begin to
experiment. By way of "enriching the service" he introduces irrelevant and distracting elements, which run counter

feels that the early portions of worship have anticipated the message from the pulpit. At such an hour, as at the dinner table in a parsonage, the one in charge plans to meet the needs of the persons present. Needless to say, only a man of ability can plan this kind of service, but why should a man without such ability undertake to lead in the public worship of God?

VI. At an average church the pastor can make his part in the celebration of the sacraments as uplifting and helpful as in the largest Lutheran or Episcopalian church. The same holds true at a funeral, or at a marriage, which almost deserves a place with the two Christian sacraments. In such a service the value depends on the grace of God the Giver, on the faith of the receiver, and on the skill of the minister. All of this holds true of baptism. According to Bishop Stephen E. Keeler, of the Protestant Episcopal Church, the New Testament contains more about baptism than about the Lord's Supper. As for the latter, hear Dr. Arthur J. Gossip of Glasgow. He is addressing candidates for the parish ministry:

> One day you will stand in Christ's stead at His Table, and be His hand wherewith He gives to needy souls the bread that is His body. 'Prayer time,' says Faber, 'is God's punishment time.' Then our disloyalties come home to roost. Our sins never seem so ghastly as when we seem to soil the vessels with our touch, and are afraid lest we block the rush of God's grace into the hearts of His people.

Looking back over the trail, anyone can see that all of these things belong together. The pastor of an average church, or a small one, should take these matters to heart now more than ever before. Whenever he leads in worship

to the history of worship, and fail to meet the n
today. Under such "leadership" the people m
how to diagnose the trouble, but still they bec
By way of improvement let us think about tw
services, each of them good in its place. Do no
the two!

In a special service, let everything accord with
of the day. On Easter, or at Thanksgiving, only
would introduce any dominant note other than tl
the hour. Such a special service may lead through
valleys, with more than one vista opening out
mensities. A minister with a love of God and a
drama can plan for an hour in which every porti
have to do with one central theme. On the other hand
a preacher of ability flounders as leader of worship
high day of the Christian Year. Most of our churche
too many special days. We could make them glow
more luster if we observed only about eight or nine.

At a regular service why not proceed differently? N
an hour of special worship seem unique by having a ser
closely unified. If you always planned this way, the w
might suffer from monotony. If you never prepared fo
closely unified service, you might not meet the needs
human hearts today. Note the stress on meeting the ne
of hearts today. As a rule, many of them need somethin
other than the specific message in the sermon. If you hav
eight special services, each of them closely unified, why no
plan for two score hours of regular morning worship, with
each hour as varied as one of Beethoven's symphonies?

In such an hour of uplift every part follows naturally
after all that has gone before, but no friend in the pew ever

he must compete with metropolitan divines who speak over the radio, perhaps with television. If the local pastor knows his business as a leader of worship, including the sermon, he need not fear any such unseen competition. On the other hand, if he never has learned how to do this part of the Lord's work, he ought to start now.

The pastor of an average church may develop an inferiority complex. Privately or even in the presence of the people he may say with a sigh: "If we had a staff of workers, a huge budget, and up-to-date equipment we could make our worship worthy of the God whom we represent." Perhaps so, but why does he not prove it by making the most of what he has? In the Early Church, with a single exception, believers had to worship God in private homes. They lacked almost everything that we today count essential for a church. And yet Friedrich Heiler insists that never in history so far has Christian worship moved on such a lofty level as in those days of simplicity.

VII. Let us suppose that the young reader wishes to start a home course of self-improvement as a leader in public worship. Where should he begin? If he wishes something relatively easy, he may start with the bulletin. In a church of average size, or in a small one, the pastor can lead indirectly to a bulletin as interesting and helpful as one at the First Congregational Church in Los Angeles. When at length he works out plans for a first-class bulletin he may discover that he has toned up the entire hour of worship. In teaching a course on the subject a man finds that almost every practical problem emerges in connection with the weekly bulletin, or calendar.

No one expects the friends at a wayside chapel to have

the sort of bulletin that people use in a large metropolitan church. Fortunately, the value of such printed matter, or of mimeographed materials, depends much more on content and arrangement, with neatness, than on the cost of the paper and the printing. The minister himself should not do the mechanical part of the work. At least indirectly, he should guide in the general policy. William Allen White did so with the Emporia Gazette. For the people of that town and county in Kansas he made the local paper more interesting than any other journal on earth. How? Read one of the various biographies and see that he used brains. He stressed the use of facts, as they concerned the people in that community. The same plan works with a bulletin.

Also use brains with the order of service. If you have two regular hours of worship on the Lord's Day, dignify the second service by putting the order at the top of its page. In any case give a descriptive title to each hymn and to each prayer. Plan for a variety of benedictions. In San Antonio, Texas, the pastor of a leading Methodist church has made a long list of benedictions, both from the Scriptures and from church history. Without knowing anything of his other work, a distant observer hazards the guess that the pastor's special study of benedictions has helped to tone up the entire hour of worship. From the beginning of the prelude he should wish it all to prepare for the blessing of the Triune God. Did you ever preach four sermons, at intervals, about the major benedictions in the Bible?

So we might go on, but we have already laid out enough work to keep a man profitably employed in the study four or five hours every week. This part of his studies a minister either enjoys or endures. He may approach such things with dread or with delight. Fortunately, a man begins to enjoy what he keeps doing well. He also learns to do well whatever he enjoys. All of this holds true when a minister carries out the will of the Lord. If anyone finds such things a bother and a bore year after year, let him search his heart and discover why.

Suffer another word of caution, and one of encouragement. The warning comes from James Denney, of Glasgow, master theologian of yesterday. He bids the leader of worship beware of showmanship: "No man can bear witness to Christ and to himself at the same time. . . . No man is being blessed by the Holy Spirit when his hearers say, 'What an able sermon!' " (or, what an able prayer!)

The word of cheer and hope comes from the Bible, and there from a book that tells much about public worship in its upper reaches. The promise from the living Christ relates to the reading of God's Written Word, but the same principle holds true in every other part of public worship. His promise comes to the leader in every church, whether it be small, large, or of medium size:

Blessed is he who reads aloud the words of this prophecy, and blessed are they who hear, and who keep what is written therein. (Rev. 1:3, R.S.V.)

—*from* PULPIT DIGEST *for June, 1949*

Evangelism and the

Ecumenical Movement

BY EDWIN T. DAHLBERG

Pastor of Delmar Baptist Church, Saint Louis, Missouri

ONE of the striking features of the Amsterdam Assembly of the World Council of Churches in 1948 was the decorative scheme employed in the great *Concertgebouw*. In addition to the masses of flowers on the platform, beautiful white fish nets were looped over the entire length of the balcony. Placed there as a symbol of the fishing industry of the Netherlands, they were also an eloquent reminder of the fact that our main business as Christians is to be fishers of men.

A happy coincidence is found also in the fact that the name of the Executive Secretary of the World Council of Churches, Visser 't Hooft, literally means "The Chief Fisher."

If the ecumenical movement is to succeed, it is extremely important to remember that the Christian churches must

38

not only be re-united but re-born. That is what makes the
United Evangelistic Advance of the Federal Council of
Churches so significant. It is a reminder that the religion
of America, at the grass roots, must come alive.

Soren Kierkegaard, the great Danish theologian, once
suggested that the Church address itself to this question:
"How can a person become a Christian who already is
one?" The United Evangelistic Advance is an attempt not
only to answer this question for people already in the
churches, but to inspire other people to become Christians
who are today completely outside Christ.

Sparked by its dynamic chairman, Dr. Homrighausen,
and correlating the evangelistic personnel, literature, and
methods of forty denominations—27 of them members of
the Federal Council and 13 of them outside the Council—
the United Evangelistic Advance promises to be one of the
most challenging demonstrations of ecumenical Christianity
in action that has ever been manifest on this continent. It
seeks to embody in its program all the majesty, depth, and
New Testament vigor of evangelism as defined by the
Madras Conference in 1938:

> By evangelism . . . we understand that the church universal in
> all its branches and through the service of all its members,
> must so present Christ Jesus to the world in the power of the
> Holy Spirit that men shall come to put their trust in God
> through him, accept him as their Saviour and service him as
> their Lord in the fellowship of his church.

We need not go into detail as to the over-all program of
the United Evangelistic Advance on the national level.
Plenty of material on the national plans is going to ministers
all over America relative to the National Preaching Mis-

sions, the National Teaching Missions, the University Missions, Bible Conference Missions, and other large-scale projects. Suffice it to say that the cooperation already evident on the part of our most distinguished pulpit leaders, and on the part of liberal and conservative theological seminaries alike, is heartening beyond measure. The important thing now is that as pastors and lay workers in the local communities we should have a clear understanding of the part our own churches and congregations will play.

First of all, it is imperative that we should all as individual followers of Christ re-capture the evangelistic passion.

Many pastors have lost faith in evangelism. This is true not only because of the fantastic commercialism and sensationalism of certain evangelists a generation ago, but also because of the superficial emphasis on mechanical techniques today. Of what value the addition of many members to the Church if there is no real transformation of life, and no sense of meaning to Christian discipleship?

I must confess that I myself am not by nature an evangelist. Except for the fine evangelical influence of a godly home, and a childhood spent in a little Swedish Baptist church from my infancy to the age of ten, all my background has been non-evangelistic. I was baptized and ordained in a college church where evangelism was rarely mentioned. My education was in one of our largest state universities, and in one of our most liberal seminaries. Most of my pastorates have been in student centers where the emphasis was strongly educational and cultural rather than evangelistic. The result was that much of our familiar evangelistic vocabulary such as "salvation," "personal work," "prayer lists," became distasteful to me. Even today it takes a great deal of courage for me to give an altar call, though I do so at practically every service.

Nothing is more needed in our time than a fresh, sparkling language of evangelism that will make it possible to preach "the faith of our fathers in the language of our children." I have discovered as the years have gone on that it is perfectly possible to attract a person to Christ without any of the stock evangelistic phrases, so long as we believe in the loving grace of God, and are willing to bow humbly before Him in supplication for the troubled person kneeling at our side.

In the second place, we should employ all the cooperative resources of the local community in an effort to make the whole population Christ-conscious and Church-conscious.

World-wide Communion Sunday, October 2, gives us a matchless opportunity to do this. That is the day that has been set apart all over the nation as the day for launching the United Evangelistic Advance, which will then go on for fifteen months, to the close of the year 1950.

The national committee is endeavoring to arrange for a nation-wide radio presentation of the Advance, on Saturday evening, October 1, when religious leaders of world stature will bring a message to the American people in behalf of all Protestantism. From there on, the procedure is a major responsibility of local churches, state and local council of churches, denominational and inter-denominational committees in every city, town, and cross-roads hamlet from coast to coast.

Where possible, a united community approach in keeping with the spirit of World Communion Sunday is by all means to be encouraged, with all the churches, all the pastors, and all the men's, women's, and youth groups working in concert. Such an ecumenical approach not only means a building up of the body of Christ, but makes a profound impression on the secular mind as a result of the radio and newspaper publicity always available for such a simultaneous cooperative enterprise. Many of the public schools, luncheon clubs, factories, and other civic groups will be open to the Christian message on such a basis, where a one-church or a denominational approach would not even get a hearing.

The ministers' associations and local church councils, including our Christian education groups, should be the responsible agencies in waking up the total Christian community to the possibilities of a far-reaching ecumenical revival. There should be local evangelistic and preaching missions, directed toward a verdict.

Near-by seminary professors and Bible department teachers from our denominational schools should be invited to conduct Bible conferences on some of the great themes of the gospel, such as the nature and being of God, the lordship of Jesus Christ, the person and work of the Holy Spirit, the experience of the Christian in prayer, the place of the Bible in everyday life, the Christian calling and vocation of the believer, the contribution of the Church to the modern world, and the processes by which the kingdom of God shall come, whether within history or from beyond history.

Church school workers might well arrange a systematic visitation of the parents of all Sunday School and weekday school pupils in the area, with a view to presenting the claims of Christ upon the home. Certainly there should be a thorough training of lay workers in the art of personal visitation, so that they can witness intelligently and helpfully to their faith, as they call upon the homes listed on the responsibility roll of the church.

This responsibility roll should contain the names of all parents, brothers and sisters, and friends of members of all the church groups, who have never made a commitment to Christ. In the larger city churches, many names can be added to such a responsibility roll by taking an attendance registration of all those present at church services on the Sundays between World-wide Communion Sunday and Thanksgiving Day.

Undergirding all this effort there should by all means be a thoughtful fellowship of prayer and intercession, with little groups meeting together in homes and in church gatherings for meditation and self-examination. Young people, married couples, fathers and mothers, men of similar vocations and professions, should come together in cell groups of eight or ten to study the Bible, and to pray for further light on their personal problems and for guidance in all areas of their relationship to God and their fellow men. There is no purpose in having an evangelistic advance unless there is more *depth*. We must discover "that the big things are big, and the little things are little, before it is too late."

If the local churches have not reached a degree of community mindedness to make a united approach practicable, or if denominational programs conflict with such a simultaneous effort, every church should go into the Advance on its own, at such a time and in such a way as seems most effective. In the last analysis, the key to the religious future of America is in the zeal and initiative of the individual church and the individual pastor. No matter what happens in Amsterdam or in New York on the ecumenical level, there will never be a national revival without God-inspired men and women in the pulpit and in the pew.

Although the United Evangelistic Advance is a national movement, it can not be stressed strongly enough that the outworkings of it will depend altogether on the originality and devotion of local people. Ample resource material in the way of inspirational literature, as well as instruction in method, can be secured through the Executive Secretary of the Department of Evangelism of the Federal Council of Churches, Dr. Jesse M. Bader, at 297 Fourth Avenue, New York. State and national secretaries of evangelism in the various denominations also stand ready to aid. Make full use of them.

If we bend every effort in this United Evangelistic Advance to present Christ in all his authoritative glory to the people of America, who knows what new revelations of the Spirit may not come to us through our obedience to the will of God?

Already some fine pioneering work is done. One of the finest television programs in the nation, with one of the highest Hooper ratings, is now being carried on by Dr. Harold Geistweit of the Lakeshore Baptist Church of Oakland, California. In addition to the music of an excellent male quartette, Dr. Geistweit presents for fifteen minutes each Sunday evening a fascinating interpretation of the gospel, from a thoroughly modern, intelligent point of view.

One evening last spring, for instance, while he expounded

Christ's parable of the man who kept building bigger barns, an able chalk-talk artist sketched the outlines of the story in picture form, so that the television audience in taverns, hotels, and homes as far away as Las Vegas, Nevada, saw the building of the barns before their eyes, in all the modern setting of tractors and farm machinery. This is good social gospel as well as evangelistic gospel.

One pastor in Illinois takes pictures of all his church school groups on Rally Day, Children's Day, Christmas, and Thanksgiving, combining motion picture films with sound effects: children's choirs, religious drama, processions, and the like. These films he then takes to the homes, saying to the parents: "I would like to show you a movie in which your child has a part."

The father and mother are entranced. When the film is over, the pastor says: "Now you have seen what the church school is trying to do for the Christian life of your child. But we cannot do it alone. We need the help of the home." On the basis of as simple an appeal as that, he has won thirty young married people to Christ and the Church in one year.

A Seventh Day Adventist church has a physician on its staff who is definitely a minister of the Church. He is a medical missionary in the American community just as other men are medical missionaries in the African or Chinese community. This is not socialized medicine in the usual sense of the word. It is Christianized medicine, in the employ of the Church. Other churches have psychiatric ministers, and marriage counsellors, who open the way into a full realization of Christian personality.

However it is done, the United Evangelistic Advance in

the local community is primarily a matter of preaching the gospel from the pulpit, and person-to-person sharing of the Christian faith between Sundays. No matter what the method may be, we must sharpen up the message of Christianity, and penetrate to the very heart and conscience of the American people.

The times are urgent. Every morning and evening we read of devastating moral tragedies in every part of the United States—murders and robberies, young people cast into prison, fathers and mothers wrecking their homes, children mutilated and deserted, to say nothing of the larger social and economic disasters on a world scale. As the Red Cross throws its disaster squads into action when floods, fires, and earthquakes come, so the Christian Church must throw its disaster squads into moral and spiritual action now.

That Christian will surely be held accountable before God who does not throw the weight of his faith and testimony against the breaking levees of our civilization. If the first half of the twentieth century has brought only bloodshed and destruction, can we not so redeem it in the next half century that the year 2000 A.D. will dawn upon a world where the shadows have fled away?

—*from* PULPIT DIGEST *for October, 1949*

Ministry to the Sick

BY RUSSELL L. DICKS

Professor of Pastoral Care, The Divinity School, Duke University

THE pastor's effective ministry to the sick turns upon his own attitude and state of mind.

The sickroom is an emotionally charged situation, and many little things, some of which are intangible, affect the course of the patient's recovery. Life under any circumstances is full of emotion, but the sickroom is especially so. The pastor, like the nurse, physician, relative, or friend, affects the patient by his attitude as soon as he enters the sickroom. He may contribute to the patient's welfare or he may detract from it.

The pastor's first principle in ministry to the sick should be: *do no harm.*

This principle he holds in common with the physician. The doctor knows that if he can avoid killing his patients through the use of surgery or drugs most of them will get well. He knows also that some will not get well as quickly as if he treats them, that some will suffer unnecessarily

47

unless he treats them, and that some will not get well at all unless he treats them. This latter group he searches for constantly, for it is to them that he makes his greatest contribution. But always he is careful to avoid doing harm.

The pastor must follow the same procedure as the doctor. He too must recognize that there are some people who will not get well *spiritually* unless he ministers to them; there are some whose recovery *spiritually* will be delayed, and there are others who will suffer tremendously, *spiritually*, unless the pastor helps them.

I emphasize the term *spiritual* here because the minister is not concerned primarily with the physical recovery of the patient; that is his secondary interest, for it is primarily the job of the physician. In many instances—how many we are unable to say—the recovery of health is greatly aided through the pastor's work, just as, in many instances, the spiritual condition of a patient is greatly aided by the work of the physician. This latter situation is far more common than the former, yet the doctor does not claim that he is treating the soul of his patient, even though he recognizes that he is.

The physical care of the sick cannot be separated from the spiritual care. Both pastor and physician ought to recognize that fact.

Actually in many cases it is neither the doctor nor the minister who makes the greatest contribution to both the patient's recovery of health and his spiritual growth, but the nurse, who goes quietly on her way, unspoiled and uninhibited by involved discussions and ethical arguments as to whose patient a given person is and who shall do what. He is her patient and she takes care of him as best she can, whether he has a sick gall-bladder or a sick soul. It is that simple.

The person who is sick is a complicated creature, and the machinery and ritual that the doctor and his assistant have evolved to take care of the sick is equally complicated. Our modern society has many intricate institutions, but none more so than its hospitals. There is a greater concentration of skilled professions, complex machines, and involved rituals in the modern hospital than in any other institution the mind of man has concocted.

The minister, who has had little or no preparation or orientation either in understanding sickness or in the workings of a hospital, is expected to be able to enter a sickroom and make a major contribution to the patient's recovery. Is it any wonder that easily 90 percent of all calls made upon the sick by pastors, especially in the hospital during the acute phases of an illness, actually do not help? It is a safe guess, in fact, that probably 50 percent do actual harm. These are only estimates, but I am sure they are conservative figures.

It is impossible to estimate the number of calls made in hospitals as compared to those made by pastors in homes. The growing tendency is to go to the hospital when one is ill. This practice is the result of increased hospitalization plans, small homes where it is difficult to take care of a sick person, increasingly complicated scientific machinery needed for the diagnosis and treatment of disease, and the doctor's reluctance to treat patients at home where that equipment is not available.

We may expect more and more people to go to hospitals as more hospitals are built. Therefore, the pastor must expect increasingly to carry on his ministry to the actually ill in hospitals.

For the same reasons, more and more people will die in hospitals. It is becoming the practice to permit the admission of persons to the hospital for the sole purpose of dying even when it is recognized that their lives cannot be prolonged by hospital care. This is contrary to the practices followed by hospitals and doctors a short time ago, when great efforts were made to get patients home if they were going to die so that the hospital records would show a low morbidity rate. This was both inhuman and un-Christian. There is much that can be done in a hospital for a dying person to make him comfortable that cannot be done in a home, however comfortable the home may be otherwise.

If the minister is to carry on some of his most important pastoral duties in the hospital he should know what his environment there is going to be like.

In the first place he should know how to get to a patient's room. It is really quite simple. Go to the information desk, place your calling card in front of the attendant, and inquire if your parishioner is in the hospital and in what room.

Every hospital admits clergymen out of visiting hours. If there is some hospital which does not, call upon the administrator of the hospital and find out why. Most hospital administrators know that the clergyman should make his call outside of visiting hours; otherwise he runs into rooms filled with the patient's friends and family.

When there are others present, if they are not the patient's family and if they do not offer to leave when the minister arrives, he should stay only long enough to say "hello" and then leave. More than two people in a sickroom is a crowd, and the sickroom is no place for a crowd.

The one exception where the clergyman is not admitted out of visiting hours is the obstetrical department, when the babies are with the mothers. Then no one is admitted, not even the doctor. The minister can easily ascertain what hours the babies are with the mothers and plan his work so as to avoid calling during those hours. Frequently, I come across the story of a minister who has raised a howl because of the rules that prevent him from being admitted to see a mother when he is called. To complain about such a rule is to mark oneself as a fool, and whenever possible we would be well advised to avoid revealing ourselves as more foolish than we really are. People find it out soon enough anyway.

When the pastor comes to the floor where his parishioner has his room he should go to the head nurse, place his card in front of her, and explain, "I am Mr. Blank's pastor, I wonder if it is all right to see him now?" Thus the nurse will know who you are and why the regular visiting hours do not apply to you. If he is sleeping, or if he is seriously ill, she will be able to tell you and thus help you avoid doing harm through waking him up when he has had a hard time getting to sleep.

The "No Visitors" sign on the door does not mean a patient should not be seen by his pastor, but it does mean that the pastor should inquire what the sign means before he pushes in. It may mean that the patient should not be seen even by his pastor, and we would be wise to inquire, for the patient's whole family may become antagonized at the pastor if they feel he is too aggressive. If you are not satisfied with the nurse's explanation, then call the doctor; remember that the nurse just works there, she does not make the rules.

Once you are in the patient's room, conduct yourself according to his desires, not yours. If he is lonely and wants you to stay and visit, do so. If he wants you to sit down he will ask you to; if he does not ask you to sit down or to take off your coat, or does not encourage you in any other way to stay, don't do it. Most persons are polite. As patients they will not ask you to leave, however much they might want you to, but if you have not been urged to stay it is a reasonable conclusion that they will be helped more by a brief call than by a long one.

A few general statements and questions are sufficient, such as: "I just wanted to drop by for a moment to let you know we are thinking about you and pulling for you."

"You're in a good hospital. Who is your doctor?"

"Did you sleep well last night?"

"How long have you been sick?"

"How long will you have to be here?"

"How are things going?"

Do not use all of these. Any two or three will express your interest. If none of these questions are followed up by the parishioner you should let it go at that, and make your exit.

Do not ask a patient about his diagnosis. If he wants you to know what is the matter with him he will tell you.

The question must be considered: shall you pray or not? With your own parishioners (not the non-church people you will also call upon during the course of every week) the ideal you should hold to is to pray, at least the first time you call upon them during their illness. Whether you pray in subsequent calls will be determined by their response to your first prayer. If they are receptive, pleased, and seem to be helped, then you will pray upon later calls. If not, then you will be well advised not to pray the next time. You have demonstrated your willingness to pray; they know of your eagerness to pray; they will ask for it if they desire further prayer.

Those persons who are not parishioners present something of a problem. These are people the minister calls upon at the request of their physicians, families, or friends. The rule I follow is to pray if they express any interest in religion, such as: "I'm so glad to see a minister;" or "I used to go to church quite regularly but I got away from it. I wish I hadn't;" or "What you have is what I need now."

If there is no such statement and only a cool expression of interest in the fact that you have called, then do not pray; but call again and again, as the opportunity presents itself. Thus you continue to show your interest and the interest of the church. Many a person comes to appreciate such an interest, and ultimately turns to the church for strength, just because the pastor gave him attention but did not push him or try to take advantage of him during his illness.

The length of a prayer in the sickroom should not exceed the number of phrases in the Twenty-Third Psalm. Our younger clergy are apt to err on the side of making their prayers too brief, while our older clergy make their prayers too long. (This is likely to be true in public prayer as well as in the sickroom.)

Here is a typical prayer for the sick which is general enough to apply to most situations:

> Eternal God, Father of us all, we come to Thee in quietness and confidence, thanking Thee for the gift of life and the strength of faith; we thank Thee for the strength of the Everlasting Arms that support us, and that bear us up at all times; We thank Thee for those who serve Thee through the healing ministries: doctors and nurses, and all who assist the healing forces. Bless this one through these days, and return him unto health; bless his loved ones and strengthen them for the day's task; through Jesus Christ, Our Lord, in Whose Name we pray. Amen.

The Lord's Prayer may be used effectively with many persons, and parts of the Twenty-Third Psalm are also especially helpful in ministering to the sick. Both have the advantage of being familiar, which is especially desirable in that phrases of these prayers will return to the parishioner's mind after you have left.

One further word upon the subject of ministry to the sick, and that is that our first and major responsibility is to our own parishioners. The hospital is not a hunting ground. When the minister goes to a hospital he should call upon his own parishioners and, except on specific invitation, no one else. He has no right to push into rooms and go around speaking to patients he does not know. Any minister who does should be prohibited from coming to the hospital.

—*from* PULPIT DIGEST *for October, 1948*

Getting the Most
Out of Church Films

BY HARRY J. KREIDER

Pastor of St. James Lutheran Church, Ozone Park, New York City

A^T A previewing session at which we are showing the new films on the Life of Paul, one of the teachers sighed with more than usual feeling: "If only we had had these in Sunday School when we were children!" Possessing a good religious training and having taught for twenty years, she sensed deeply the value of films like these. For one thing, such films can portray the religious experiences of a man like Paul far more vividly than words alone can do. But more than that, the vivid portrayal can readily lead the audience into their own religious experiences.

When we use a film, we want our people to get the most out of it. We shall do that when we proceed with the film in the same way that we do with a sermon or a lesson. We may prepare a wonderful sermon, but if we want our hearers to get the most out of it we must present it well.

55

The same is true of a film. A good film has had a lot of thought and work put into it. Then it comes into our hands, and to get the most out of it we must use it skilfully.

A skilful use of the film is much more than a mere "showing" of it. Even when we do our best in presenting it, we may still not accomplish all we hope. Several years ago at St. James Church, of which the writer is pastor, we used the excellent stewardship film "And Now I See." The film is the story of the Church's work, a work so important that it merits our best support.

In the film there is a dramatic incident of a missionary inspiring a little crippled girl with courage to learn to walk again. The incident was designed, obviously, to make more forceful the greatness of the Church's ministry of healing.

The pulpit message preceding the film was well prepared, I thought. But after the service, all the comments of the congregation seemed to be upon that one touching scene, and nothing at all was said about it as part of the Church's ministry, or about the purpose of the film to stir us up to greater giving because the Church's work was so worthy of it. In other words, the pulpit message preceding the film should have prepared the people so that they would put that dramatic incident in its proper place.

We shall get the most out of a church film when we use it thoughtfully and skilfully as an experience in the lives of our people. That is an end devoutly to be desired, and to attain it, certain steps are deserving of serious consideration.

We should select every film carefully, to fit a particular need and to serve a particular purpose. Unfortunately, there are few opportunities whereby we can see a film before choosing it, for distributors do not have the facilities to render this service.* We can, however, get brief synopses of the contents as well as critical appraisals from such sources as the Resource Guide of the International Council of Religious Education, revised edition to be published in the fall of 1950; and the latest Catalogue of the Religious Film Association, 1950-51. But even these are limited, since obviously they cannot give, as promptly as we should like, detailed information and critical evaluations of the newest films. The most comprehensive listing of church films, but without critical appraisals, is the Master Guide to Religious Motion Pictures, published by Selected Films Release Service, Whittier, California.

It is not how often we use a film, but how well we use it, that is of first importance. It takes much skill to use a film so that it becomes an experience to the people. After years of experimentation, we are convinced of that in St. James Church. In the Sunday Church School we use films about once a month in the instruction of pupils from the fourth grade up. In Church we use films two or three times a year at Sunday morning services, and about half a dozen times at evening services.

A church film should always be considered as an aid in learning. We should avoid giving the impression that the film is the "feature" of a service or of a lesson. As a feature, the film is likely to be accepted as entertainment, for the

* To provide this service to the churches of Greater New York, the St. James Audio-Visual Workshop, of which the writer is director, has been established under the sponsorship of the Federation of Churches of Queens Borough. The Workshop will specialize in presenting the newest and best church films, and show by demonstration and discussion how to make the best use of them.

word is associated with the movie house. People come to church to worship and to learn, and we should guide them to look upon a church film as an aid to a clearer understanding of the Word of God or the work of His Church.

When announcing a church film, we should avoid the use of flyers and throw-aways such as a movie house would use. It would be well even to avoid the word movie; the word film is much better. The announcement should of course be set up as attractively as possible by the printer or in the mimeograph stencil. But its wording should harmonize with the dignity of the Church. Here is the wording of one that has been used:

Thanksgiving Eve Service with a Beautiful Film

Our United Lutheran Church has a new film titled "Fujita." It is the story of what really happened to an orphan boy in Japan when he came under the care of American Christian missionaries there. It will help us to be doubly grateful at this Thanksgiving season for the Gospel of Jesus and His glorious Church.

When people come to see a church film, we should be sure to have everything set up in a way that is worthy of the church. People can hardly feel inspired if they see a projector on a kitchen table in the center aisle, with wires running up the aisle to a speaker placed on a nondescript stand, and a screen standing conspicuously bare at the front.

The screen should be of sufficient size. If it is on a tripod, it should be set up beforehand. If used in the church sanctuary, it should be off center, so that it does not obscure the view of the altar or communion table. The screen will look better if it is covered with a curtain of a rich red or other harmonizing color.

The speaker should be placed about four feet above the floor, on a stand that harmonizes with the other furniture. Wires should be concealed as much as possible; they should be placed along the side instead of in the center aisle.

The projector should be kept out of sight as much as possible. If there is no balcony, the projector should be at the rear. If the present lens makes the image too large when projecting from the rear, a lens of the correct focal length should be secured.

As soon as the film arrives, we should preview it carefully. A good procedure is to see the film twice. The first time we should relax and see it as the people or pupils will see it. The second time we should look at it critically, and make notes on how we may get the most out of it.

A church film should be used in a churchly setting. The best is a worship service, though it be ever so brief; and there is no more churchly place than the church sanctuary itself. We have found at St. James Church that the value of a church film is enhanced immeasurably when used in the church sanctuary. Quiet music as the people or pupils assemble is also important.

The film should be projected quietly and reverently. Suggested as a good procedure is: Start the projector, with volume on low. Put out overhead lights—it is important to put the lights out *after* the projector has been started, to be sure the church is not in complete darkness at any time. Then turn the volume up slowly.

The film should have also a churchly closing. At the word "End," put on the overhead lights, turn the volume down slowly, then turn off the projector. As the film music fades out, some quiet organ or piano music should come on, for a moment or two, followed by a benediction.

The time we spend on careful planning for the best use of a church film will be amply rewarded when we see what it can mean to the people. Perhaps you would like to hear how it is done in St. James Church. We shall be happy to have you come with us to the principal service on the Sunday morning when we are using the film "The Difference," to see and hear for yourself.

Entering the church you observe that it is not large, and certainly not costly, but it is beautiful in the simplicity of its design and of its furnishings. Your attention is drawn irresistibly to the hand-carved altar and to the dossal hanging back of it and reaching up to the two stained-glass windows high above it. Later your attention is drawn to the aisle windows with their stained-glass medallions depicting scenes from the life of our Lord. The beauty you see starts you wondering whether a film would not be out of place in a church which so readily inspires devotion and reverence.

But since you know a film is to be used, your practical mind doubtless tries to figure out how, for there is nothing in the church that appears to be different from what is there on other Sundays. You see no projector, no screen, no speakers, no wires in the center aisle. Could it be—and you shudder at the thought—that the person responsible for projecting the film is late, and will at any moment now rush in and set up the apparatus in full view of those who have come to church to worship?

While you have been letting yourself get into this un-devotional mood, the organ has been playing the prelude softly. Suddenly it catches up with you, when you hear some familiar hymns played on the twenty-five note memorial organ chimes. The chimes always do something to people to lift their hearts up to God. In your case, we hope that they have at least helped you to forget about the missing apparatus.

Soon the service begins, as the organ swells to full in the processional hymn. The choir and pastor, in churchly vestments, come from the sacristy and proceed to the chancel in stately procession. The service is conducted as on other Sunday mornings. The only change you may notice is that the offering is received before, instead of after, the sermon.

After the offering is received, the pastor proceeds to the pulpit. There is always a brief word from the pulpit when a film is used, for the film is part of the sermon, and not a feature. The message today has to do with the concerted effort of the United Lutheran Church to provide greater opportunities for Christian higher education. To make the message more compelling, the Church has produced a film titled "The Difference." The film demonstrates with unusual force that the church related college has something for the youth which the purely secular institution does not have to give. The brief statement concluded, all heads are bowed for a prayer, then the whole congregation joins in the Lord's Prayer.

The organ then plays softly the tune "Aurelia," introducing the hymn "The Church's One Foundation." We use this hymn because the film opens with a stanza of the same hymn. Our organist had previously keyed her tune to that of the film.

As you join heartily in singing the hymn, the choir is

proceeding in orderly recession from the chancel to the balcony, and the deacons are quietly lowering the almost hidden shades over the aisle windows. You do not know it, but since some of the normal ventilation is cut off by lowering the shades, one of the choir members has by a switch in the chancel started a noiseless exhaust fan.

The choir is now in the balcony, and the hymn comes to a close. But instead of singing the "Amen," the organ chimes repeat a stanza, the overhead lights are dimmed out, and you see unfolding before you the beautiful image in color of Sallman's "Christ at the Door." You are so taken with the inspiring figure of the Christ that you may not even see the screen, electrically controlled from the balcony, slowly descending from above the chancel arch. The slide projector light had been turned on before the overhead lights had been dimmed out, and the unfolding image that you see is on the descending screen.

As the screen locks automatically into fixed position, the organ chimes are completing the stanza. The film, well designed to fit into a worship service, begins with a view of the chancel of a church, with only a fleeting moment given over to the title, while a choir in the background concludes the hymn sung by our own congregation. The choir voices come through speakers hidden in the chancel arch under the hymn boards; all you see are the carved oak grilles. The slide projector light, meanwhile, has been turned off.

As the hymn-on-film is completed, a pastor in churchly vestments steps into the pulpit, and begins reverently and earnestly: "I want to talk with you today about Christian higher education, about our church colleges. What is different about a church college?"

It is done so gracefully that you feel he is a guest preacher, invited into our pulpit for today.

The guest preacher's message is an absorbing one, and it is completed all too soon. When the message is over, you are still in church. The guest preacher stands in the pulpit, closing his message with the benediction, just as in our own church. The few necessary credit lines at the close of the film are so inconspicuous that you likely do not notice them.

As the film ends, you see once more the Christ image, and hear the full organ. The screen, meanwhile, has been started on its graceful way upward, but the Christ image continues in projection until the screen disappears above the chancel arch.

With the screen gone from view, your eyes are focused again upon the altar, before which stands the pastor, still in full vestments. The lights slowly come on, the organ stops, the congregation rises, and the pastor turns to the people and pronounces the benediction. There is a moment of prayerful silence, then the organ chimes peal out a stanza of the familiar hymn "Beautiful Saviour." After another moment of silence, the congregation leaves quietly and reverently.

As you leave the church, you know that you have witnessed no mere showing of a movie in church, but have participated in a religious experience that you will not soon forget.

Some may feel that this experience is possible only because of the unusual equipment we are fortunate enough to have. Let me assure you that it is not elaborate equipment, but careful planning and perfect timing, that are of first importance. The same experience was attained a summer ago in a series of services with films at a school for pastors and their families, where an old barn served as the chapel and all equipment had to be brought in.

It is always good to take time out afterward to evaluate the experience resulting from the use of a film. But how shall we evaluate that? Shall we expect better attendance at Church or Sunday School after a film, or better support for missionary or benevolence causes, or more God-like attitudes in the lives of the people?

Films are much like oral sermons or Sunday School lessons. Which of our sermons or lessons have had direct results? Even when we are in a parish long enough to see people's lives change Godward, which sermon or lesson started the change? Or did it take a lot of them before the change was perceptible? Or was it something we said personally that did it? Or was it the visible evidence of the Spirit of God in the pastor or teacher, aside from anything he may have said, that did it?

Doubtless it would be wise for us to evaluate film experiences in the same way we do our sermon experiences. No one film, any more than a single sermon, will likely accomplish much. So the writer's suggestion, based upon the experience of a quarter century in the Church's ministry, is that we evaluate critically just one item: Did I do the best I could to present the film in a way that made it possible for the Lord to use it for the greatest good? That seems to fit aptly with the Apostle's counsel of old, that while one man plants and another man waters, still it is "God that giveth the increase."

—*from* PULPIT DIGEST *for October, 1950*

Public Relations

and the Pastor

BY STEWART HARRAL

*Publicity Director, University
of Oklahoma*

HOW CAN I get more news of my church in the newspapers?" That question has come my way scores of
times—at pastors' schools, by mail, and from those who
drop by my office.

Most of the pleas are about the same. "I wrote a lot of
stories but the editor doesn't use all of them. He gives a
lot of space to other activities so why doesn't he run more
church news? What can I do?"

My answer is usually the same: "You can get a high percentage of your stories in the newspaper provided they are
written from the editor's point of view."

First of all you must understand what is known as "the
newspaper mind." Many factors are involved—a knowledge of news values, newspaper make-up, reader interest,
news patterns, and circulation. These things will not be such

65

a mystery when you understand some of the basic philosophies and problems of the press.

Always remember that newspaper space is limited. The editor has the task of trying to please hundreds of readers, each of whom has different interests and desires.

The editor's first duty is to his readers. If a newspaper has betrayed the confidence of its readers, it has lost everything. An editor must select the facts and then present those facts to his readers honestly and fairly.

If an editor likes your stories and has room for them you may be sure that some of them will appear in print. It never does any good to fume, rush to the newspaper office, and ask: "Why didn't you use all of the material which I brought last Tuesday? Why don't you run more church news instead of so much sensational material?"

Editors, like elephants, never forget. Once you have distorted a story, garbled a few facts, or missed the deadline, the editor is likely to remember you by one of those incidents.

What are some of the basic foundations in press relations? Are there certain pitfalls to avoid? What procedures have shown their worth through the years?

After some meditation we came up with sixteen "C's" which are neither unique nor complete. But even so, they can serve as some of the main guideposts to good will.

COPY: Your success in getting church news printed will depend most of all on your copy. Evaluate your news through the eyes of the editor. Ask yourself: "Is this significant, timely, unusual, accurate, and newsworthy?" Study the structure of well-written stories. Beware of thinly disguised propaganda and advertising. Beginning paragraphs should have punch and life. Respect deadlines. Always submit typed copy, doublespaced, with ample margins. Omit headlines. Compact writing is necessary today. Avoid stories with unimportant details. Watch your English. Avoid editorializing.

CAMPAIGN: Each step should be planned in advance. If you are planning a new church, for instance, outline a series of stories. Give each story a different twist and yet relate it to others in the series. Sit down with your editor and get his suggestions for a series of stories. Then follow his advice.

CORRECTNESS: Make sure that every item in every story is accurate. Create a reputation for accuracy. Avoid guessing, hearsay, rumors, faking. Even the smallest mistake hurts.

COVERAGE: Know what's going on in your church. Watch for news possibilities, not alone in meetings of the official board but in every phase of church life.

CIRCULATE: Get around, talk to people, attend as many meetings as possible. Some of your best stories will require digging, running after people, checking and double-checking, lots of leg work, drudgery. Remember that promotion is two-thirds motion.

COORDINATION: No matter what size church you are serving, it is best to let one person release the news. You can direct the publicity program or work with someone whom you have designated. Minor stories can be released by other persons but the big stories should be handled in the pastor's office.

COOPERATION: Develop the cooperation of the editor,

the reporter, and also of everyone in your church who sends you tips or items.

CONSEQUENCES: Be alert to follow-up possibilities in every story. If you had a short item in yesterday's paper about the board meeting last night, then write a story today on what happened—provided it is news.

CHUCKLES: With so much heavy material in newspapers, editors welcome bright little human interest and feature stories. Most saints have a sense of humor—get that into a story.

CARD INDEX FILES: Alert pastors watch newspapers published in other towns for ideas for stories. File the clippings regularly and soon you will have many excellent ideas for your own publicity program.

CHARACTERISTICS: To be effective, a publicity program must be desirable, timely, truthful, attainable, definite, understandable, and continuous.

CALLS: Use your telephone in gathering information for your news stories. Keep in close touch with your leaders —those who really know what's going on.

COURTESY: Be courteous both to news sources and to reporters and editors. Thank those who help you. Express your appreciation to those who bring or send you material for stories.

CALENDAR: Keep a regular date-book in which to jot down coming events. Often a date suggests a story. Watch for news possibilities in future programs.

CHANNELS: Use the newspaper to be sure, but do not overlook other channels such as church bulletin, letters, bulletin board, and other media.

CARBON COPIES: If time permits, make a carbon copy of each story and file it. Your editor always prefers the original copy—not the carbon. Even when you plan to give the same story to several newspapers it pays to give each one an original copy.

There is no royal road to effectiveness in a church leader's relationship with the press. Only experience, study, observation, and a critical evaluation of his own tactics can bring proficiency. Above all, he must seek to understand the functions and problems of editors, so that he will be able to judge church coverage from the standpoint of the press.

Proficiency in improving your relationships with the press may be acquired. Press relations are more than "ten easy—do them in your home—lessons." No hard and fast rules can be recommended, because each situation is dependent on so many variables. So give your publicity some time and thought, because you will be more than repaid in increased understanding and support.

—*from* PULPIT DIGEST *for October, 1946*

The Minister and the

Funeral Problem

BY EDWARD C. DAHL

Pastor of Centre Congregational Church,
Brattleboro, Vermont

THERE is a funeral problem. Every conscientious minister must admit to himself, if not to others, that time and
again he finds perplexing difficulties in many of the funerals
he is called upon to conduct. Fortunate is the clergyman
of one of the liturgical denominations whose service must
follow an unvaried pattern. Yet even he must make some
choice among his appointed materials, however limited.
Pastors of churches belonging to those fellowships which
are accustomed to the free ordering of public worship often
find themselves hard put to it when attempting to arrange
a funeral service that is fitting and personal, yet conducted
with a dignity and loftiness of tone worthy of the best in the
Christian tradition.

In the hope that what appears in these pages may prove
suggestive to the great number of ministers who feel dis-

satisfied, as does the writer, with what they have accomplished on numerous occasions, this department is begun and will be continued.

In recent years an increasing number of individuals from varied church backgrounds have remarked to the writer that, when they die, they do not wish anyone to arrange a funeral service for them. Often this desire is expressed in the form of a suggestion that there be "just a prayer at the grave." Such requests, revealing as they do a certain revulsion against traditional funeral procedure, indicate that all is not well with burial customs as they exist today.

When rightly conducted, a funeral should be something so helpful and uplifting that no one could doubt its value or, indeed, its necessity. If such is not the case, the reason lies in the abuse to which funeral occasions have often been put. Most people have memories of harrowing and unwholesomely morbid funerals, and it is no wonder at least a few conclude that nothing at all is an improvement over that with which they are familiar. But the abuses that have been connected with funerals are almost invariably non-Christian practices. There is still a place for the distinctly Christian funeral today.

Nevertheless, with many intelligent people it is necessary to prove the value of a funeral service. Why do we continue to conduct them year after year? If it is only because of a tradition that is now outworn, let us abandon the custom altogether. But as every pastor knows, there is much more to it than that—and it is his task to bring the layman to an appreciation of that fact.

In the first place, a funeral gives the bereaved family and the friends of the person who has died something definite to do. It is a concrete way of expressing the feelings that arise at a time of deep stress. Psychologically we need some way of using up the emotional energy stored within us at such a time. By doing something of a specific nature and by participating in some definite and recognized procedure men find release from the tension within. One often hears it remarked that so-and-so's friends are grateful for the chance to go somewhere and do something as an expression of their affection and loyalty to him and his family. If we did not have an already established funeral custom, we should need to invent it for this reason.

More than that, however, the Christian funeral, when rightly conceived and conducted, need not be a distressing and unpleasant ordeal. It can be something of infinite helpfulness to those who mourn.

Many a service, conducted in the Christian mood of victory and hopefulness, has taken away the sting of fear and doubt and bitterness. Surely the ideal that every minister should hold before him is that men and women will look forward to his services as the most helpful and healing thing that happens in a sad and darkened day.

By stressing the positive and Christian elements in his liturgy, a man can help create a new attitude toward the recent shock of bereavement, and give strength to those who have perhaps faced the future in bewilderment and fear. Grieving men and women have been lifted again and again into the joy and peace and confidence of the sensed presence of God.

If something like this is to happen, however, the clergyman in charge of a funeral must keep four fundamental principles in mind. They will guide his thinking and planning as he approaches an event that may seem routine to him but never to those whom he serves. (And woe unto the minister to whom *any* funeral becomes a routine matter! Each is unique, calling for his best effort and most searching prayer.)

1. A funeral is not the minister's to do with as he pleases. It belongs first to the people who are bereaved, and second to the church he serves. We must recognize a subtle temptation to pattern what we do in our church work after our own desires and prejudices, without much regard for the many other persons involved.

We wish, quite properly, to do a piece of work that satisfies us, and so we must if what we do is to mean anything to us or to anybody else. But a funeral is never the occasion for a minister's pet theories or his private liturgical experimentation. The funeral is, quite literally, a matter both of life and of death to the persons to whom bereavement has come. What the minister does must be meaningful, satisfying, and helpful to them, or else he had better not do it at all.

Sometimes one hears a poem read at a funeral that is either so emotional as to be uncomfortably heartbreaking, or so complicated and literary in style that anyone without extensive poetical knowledge never grasps what it means. This will not happen if the minister in charge remembers that the funeral "service" is quite simply *service* to specific individuals with their specific experiences, desires, and needs.

For this reason, then, a minister will read or do almost anything, when requested, in order to make his service conform as closely as possible to the desires of the people he seeks to assist. There may be occasions when some request made in connection with a funeral is in such poor taste that the minister will seek to dissuade the one who has asked. But he will suggest substituting something of a similar nature that is more fitting and helpful, rather than arbitrarily refusing the request. Perhaps someone close to the family has suggested that the daughter or an intimate friend sing a certain song. The minister may then offer to read the words instead, and save the person from what could easily become an excruciatingly painful ordeal.

2. To the sincere minister a funeral will never be just another ceremony or exercise. It is always an imperative call of the deepest human need. An infrequent occasion arises when a funeral seems to serve no one in particular. A pastor in a community adjoining a mental institution, for example, is from time to time asked to conduct a brief service over the remains of some lonely person without a relative or friend being at hand. But who is to say that even such a situation does not give the minister a chance to provide an answer to a real and unmet human need? Indeed, it is well for him to keep careful record of what he says and does at a funeral like this, though he and the mortician are perhaps the only persons present. Years later someone may appear to whom it matters greatly, after all, what was said and done that day.

Since a funeral is not to be considered a routine professional exercise, but rather an answer to a call of human need, the average minister will probably never refuse to conduct any such service for which his presence is solicited if he can possibly be there. The circumstances are sometimes strange and "questionable." But who is he to stand in judgment or to insist on prerogative when people have turned to the Christian Church and the God he represents for help in the hour of bewilderment and distress? What is said and done at one of these funerals of an unusual nature will be quite different from what the minister will plan under other circumstances, to be sure. But all who desire it have a claim on the Christian minister's services at such a time, and without any consideration of remuneration.

In this connection, it is well to remember that a minister will not conduct the funeral of a member of some other clergyman's parish without his consent and cooperation. To such a request made to him on behalf of another minister he will willingly accede.

3. The funeral service is a living organism. It should grow naturally. This is especially to be remembered by those who are not limited by a prescribed ritual. The minister will begin with the individual who has departed this life. He will then think of those most closely associated by ties of family or friendship. There will almost always be something—a scripture passage, hymn, poem, or classic prayer —that will appeal to him as peculiarly suitable for use at the service. He will commence his formal preparation there. Then the service will often complete itself almost inevitably by a strange law of inner growth. The final result will be a unity, with various lesser contrasts contained within.

Though the spirit and tone as well as the materials used at a funeral will vary under the circumstances, its progress will always follow a certain pathway. Beginning with what has happened and the need of persons present (about which little or nothing need usually be said) the service will move on to the answering love of the God and Father of our Lord Jesus Christ, who always "giveth us the victory."

While a service will have variety and a certain change of tempo, it must also be an organic whole and not a series of disconnected items fastened together as it were with scissors and paste.

4. A funeral is always to be understood, in its profoundest reaches, as an opportunity not so much for man as for God. A man plans. A man reads and prays. But if he is wise, he knows that his task is only that of an intermediary. He is appointed not to present some brilliant and "fitting" remarks, but rather to convey a message to hungry souls from the living God.

He has accomplished the purpose of his ministry only if he has made those who hear him aware not of himself and the materials he has used, but rather of the continuing presence of God. Let that be the most real thing about a funeral service! Let God speak His message through His Holy Word.

This conception of the minister's task is high. Perhaps we cannot ever finally attain unto it. But it is the chief reason for having a Christian funeral at all.

We seek not to do something of ourselves, but to provide an opportunity for the healing Spirit of God. The man who is complimented on this or that item—this poem, that tone of voice—suspects that he may somehow have failed. When someone expresses a fresh awareness of the overbrooding love and faithfulness of the Father who will not let us go, then he has succeeded, though no one remembers exactly what he has said and the way he has said it. The pastor had better not work at all unless he can truly become a co-worker with the God in whose service he is employed.

Something like this, then, will be the spirit underlying the minister's approach to the funeral problem. When he views his task in this light, he knows that, however difficult or unattractive it may seem, it is also a privilege of the highest sort. It is hard to think of any other time in his life when a man can be of such service to people as at the hour when death has come. Never does his ministry so greatly depend not on what he plans and does but upon his own awareness of the presence and guidance of the ever-working Comforter, his God.

In the months that follow, this department will be concerned with matters of a practical nature, such as orders of service, the minister's choice of Scripture passages, prose, and poetical selections, and the selection or composition of his prayers.

In the consideration of such details it is hoped that no reader will allow himself to forget the one fundamental purpose of the funeral. If there is, as we believe, a valid reason for a funeral, then let our funeral procedures live up to this reason. The service will then no longer seem an intolerable burden which some desire to dispense with. It will become, instead, a gracious benediction to the ending of an earthly life, in which all will wish to share.

Some Helpful Books

The Funeral, by A. W. Blackwood (Westminster Press)

A complete manual on all aspects of the funeral and its procedure. Omits very little. An excellent book for both the experienced and inexperienced minister.

A Living Hope, by Jesse Halsey (Abingdon-Cokesbury Press)

A comprehensive collection of funeral materials filed loose leaf style, so that each minister may assemble his own services as he pleases. An introductory booklet includes indexes and suggestions for specific types of services. This is the most useful collection the writer knows, though the possessor will add many materials of his own as time passes and there are some items included that he will never make his own.

A Service Book, published by The National Selected Morticians.

An excellent selection of first-class funeral materials. Lacking in suggestions for complete orders of service.

Devotional Services, by John Hunter (E. P. Dutton & Co.)

Includes a burial service and what are, to the writer, the most satisfying printed funeral prayers. They might well serve as models to the non-liturgical minister in the composition of his own prayers.

Prayers for Services, by M. P. Noyes (Scribner's)

In the section devoted to funerals will be found many of the best funeral prayers.

Minister's Service Book, by J. D. Morrison (Harper)

In addition to much suggested material for funeral services there will be found in this book some very helpful complete funeral services with committals.

The various denominational manuals and service books are helpful to ministers of many fellowships. *The Book of Common Prayer* (Episcopal), the *Book of Common Worship* (Presbyterian) and the services in *The Methodist Hymnal* are worthy of the attention of every Protestant minister. Let him "read, mark, learn, and inwardly digest" these services before attempting to plan his own.

—from PULPIT DIGEST *for October, 1948*

Putting Our Brains to Work
in the Service of Religion

BY ROBERT J. McCRACKEN

Pastor of The Riverside Church, New York City

TEXT: *Thou shalt love the Lord thy God with all . . . thy mind.*—MARK 12:30

WHAT Jesus is saying is that there is a place in religion for the exercise of the intelligence. God wants our heads as well as our hearts. We gather here for worship and our aesthetic sense is quickened by the beauty of line and stone which is all around us, our emotions are stirred as accompanied by choir and organ we sing in unison the great hymns of the Church, but our minds should be kindled too.

When Schleiermacher in the classroom at the University of Berlin kept reiterating that feeling was the basic, constitutive element in religion, Hegel, through the wall from him, would expostulate, *"Aber, meine Herren, das Denken ist auch Gottesdienst."* To think, and to think hard, is a

79

religious duty. For Hegel, devoting one's mind to the service of God was every bit as necessary as private prayer or public worship. Wasn't he right? When God claims a man, He claims the whole man, his brains included.

Look into the story of the Church. What would have become of Christianity had it not been for the thinkers— in the first century men like Paul and John and the unknown author of the Epistle to the Hebrews, in the second and third centuries men like the great Alexandrian Fathers, Clement and Origen? They never made a virtue of ignorance or credulity. They labored to commend the Christian faith to the intelligence of their contemporaries. They honored the mind as the instrument that apprehends and appropriates truth. They were abreast of the best thinking of their age. Soon they were more than abreast of it; they were the intellectual leaders of their day. Dr. John Knox is no more than stating the facts when he writes:

> Christianity began magnificently. It stepped from the soil of Palestine on its westward march with the tread of a conqueror. . . . . It did not sit at philosophy's feet; philosophy was soon sitting at its feet. For all its humble origin among Galilean peasants and working men—poor and unschooled—it became the teacher of Greece as it became the ruler of Rome.

So it has been in every creative period of the Church's life. When men put their brains to work in the service of God, things begin to happen. First you have the Revival of Learning and then, as inevitably as day follows night, you have the Reformation. First you have a stirring in the minds of John and Charles Wesley, both of them university men, and then you have the Revival which goes by their name, sweeping through England like a flame of fire and cleansing the life of England at every level, personal, political, social, and ecclesiastical. First you have a youth in Buffalo intellectually coming of age, finding many of the traditional views of the Bible untenable, distressed by the discovery, and obliged because of it to go out in search of a personal faith, a faith that would scorn to tamper with truth and that would do no violence to his intelligence. Then for over forty years you have the ministry of Harry Emerson Fosdick, a ministry unparalleled in this generation, reaching out through the spoken and written word literally to millions of people, clarifying their thinking about the things that matter most, resolving their intellectual difficulties, building them up in a faith that knows no fear of truth because its innermost conviction is that God is Truth.

Yes, great things begin to happen when men put their brains to work in the service of religion. Who have been the commanding figures in the history of the Church? Call the roll and what do you find? They have been men of intellectual strength—Paul, Athanasius, Augustine, Aquinas, Calvin, Temple, men who regarded the mind not only as a useful instrument, but as a sacred instrument to be devoted to the glory of God and in the furtherance of His purposes.

If only that were the whole story! Unfortunately there is another side to it. Far from regarding the mind as a sacred instrument, there are some who distrust it.

A man went into a church and heard the preacher say in the course of the sermon: "Few things, my friends, have done more harm in this world than thought." He then proceeded, though it was surely quite unnecessary: "Don't, my dear friends, put me down as a thinker; put me down as a believer."

But that is a false antithesis. What is the value of belief without thought? Belief without thought is superstition. It is the acceptance of opinions at second-hand and on hearsay. In religion the second-hand is intolerable, yet how much religious life is the echo of an echo. Thousands stay away from church on Sundays because going to church means listening to a sermon in which thought is divorced from feeling, a sermon that is an affront to their intelligence.

This distrust of reason has all along been widespread. Plutarch tells us that when he went to his father with questions about religion, all that he could get from him was: "The ancient faith is enough; if you begin to criticize, there is no knowing where you will stop."

The words were spoken hundreds of years ago but they have a familiar ring. "Ask no questions about religion. What was good enough for your forebears ought to be good enough for you. Questions are dangerous."

Plutarch was not put off by such an evasive reply. No person of independent mind would be. One thing he should refuse to do; he should refuse to cheat about his religion. He is not going to be asked to put up with old-fashioned science or old-fashioned business methods. Why should he be asked to make a fetish of old-fashioned religion?

When Robertson Smith was on trial for heresy and making a spirited defense of his position at the bar of the General Assembly of the Church of Scotland, an elder of the Church, a good, devout man who by profession was a lawyer expressed himself thus: "Granted that Robertson Smith is right, if it is truth, it is dangerous truth, and he has no right as a professor of the Church to upset the Church by declaring it." He was overheard by a lad who was in his freshman year at Edinburgh University, a lad who thought the pursuit of truth, the whole truth and nothing but the truth, a religious duty. He said that had he been then intending the ministry he would probably have been put off it by the elder's attitude, but that instead it served as a call to his life's work—the search for truth which would shine in its own light in the face of all inquiry. The lad was John Oman, who was later to write one of the best books about the Christian religion—*Vision and Authority*—to appear in fifty years.

Notice what the effects are of this distrust of reason. A schism is set up between the heart and the head. There is an attempt to fetter free inquiry and to keep belief fixed and static. Can you imagine a scientist clinging tenaciously to traditional expressions of belief?

The scientist is like Socrates ready to follow truth wherever it leads and to give up the most venerable of ideas once it is demonstrated that the truth is not in them. Christians who believe that God is a God of truth should be no less open-minded. If people have fantastically fuzzy ideas about God, as Henry Luce complains they do, if they are bewildered and puzzled as to what they should believe and why, if the attitude of nine persons out of ten to Christianity is a sort of inert agnosticism, the reason is not far to seek. They have not brought the same intellectual interest to religion that they have to the other concerns of life. Enterprising in most fields of endeavor, they are indolent in this. They have not learned to love God with all their mind.

A remark made by a church member years ago has

stayed with me. "I am," he said, "a Free Mason high up in my order, and what I know of Masonry today is quite a different thing from what I knew ten years ago. But I cannot say that there is much about my faith which I did not know twenty years ago." Progressive Masonry, static churchmanship. And why? Because in the one case you have keen interest, deep attachment, while in the other you have a relationship which somehow has done nothing to alert or engage the mind. Of how many of us is that the story? The apprehension of God has not kept abreast of our other apprehensions. We pride ourselves on being informed about most things, yet we let our spiritual life stand still. Mature in all else, in religion we remain at the childish stage.

How, for example, do we think about God? Have we done anything to purge our minds of crude and childish conceptions of Him? A student in answer to a questionnaire wrote: "I think of God as real, actual skin and blood and bones, something we shall see with our eyes some day, no matter what lives we lead on earth." For a child to think of God in such fashion is natural, but no adult should be content to entertain notions as immature or unworthy.

What about our prayers? There are men and women who have carried over from childhood a form of words which they use still, with little thought for its meaning and relevance, and sometimes with little genuine belief that it has a Hearer. They pray partly in conformity to long established habit, partly as an emotional need, and also because they believe there may be some kind of telepathic influence, but their minds are not brought into any kind of vigorous action. They resemble Mundanus as William Law describes him:

Mundanus is a man of excellent parts and clear apprehension. He is well advanced in age and has made a great figure in business. Every part of trade that has fallen in his way has had some improvement from him, and he is always contriving to carry any method of doing anything well to its greatest height. . . . The only thing which has not fallen under his improvement, nor received any benefit from his judicious mind is his devotion. This is in just the same poor state as it was when he was only six years of age, and the old man prays now in that little form of words which his mother used to hear him repeat night and morning.

About such a state of affairs there is only one thing to say. When a man keeps his secular interest always on the move and lets his religious life stand still, it is not to be wondered at that it shrinks from a major concern to a minor detail and that the practice of it ceases to be a joy and becomes solely a duty, if even that.

Many men today are dissatisfied with their religion. They have good reason to be dissatisfied with it. It is substantially the religion of their boyhood. Much of it consists of vague memories of what they were taught at Sunday School. They are competent at business, wide awake as to what is happening in the world, conscientious and forward-looking in their citizenship. They have moved on in their knowledge of other subjects—politics, history, science, music— but in their knowledge of Christianity they have stood still.

Sometimes, ironically enough, they complain that the Church is failing to keep abreast of modern knowledge. What is happening is that they are failing to keep abreast of religious knowledge. They read magazines and books in plenty but none, or next to none, that have to do specifically with Christianity. They do not give themselves a chance to know what it is about or what it has to offer.

Frequently in their dissatisfaction they turn from Christianity altogether. The Christianity, alas, from which they turn is often enough an infantile brand which any informed and mature Christian would repudiate with even greater finality.

A man with whom I recently had a discussion about Christianity credited it with conceptions many of which may have been current years ago but which no literate Christian entertains today. Since he was a student of physics I could not refrain from asking what he would think of me if I went for my ideas of science to textbooks put out in the middle of the nineteenth century, or if in what I had to say about science I betrayed that I knew nothing of its recent or current developments. The look that came over his face was more expressive than the answer I got.

If I am describing the position of anybody here, why not do something about it? Read a book like *Christian Behavior* by C. S. Lewis or *The Meaning of Faith* by Dr. Fosdick or *The Alternative to Futility* by Dr. Trueblood or *The School of Prayer* by Olive Wyon. At any rate, give Christianity a chance before you criticize it or reject it. Be sure you understand what it is and what it offers.

So I come back to the first and great commandment. "Thou shalt love the Lord thy God with all thy heart, and with all thy soul, and with all thy strength, *and with all thy mind.*"

There is a place in religion for the exercise of the intelligence. God wants our heads as well as our hearts. To think, and to think hard, is a religious duty.

How one wishes that more men and women would give their brains to the service of religion and do it with something like the diligence and devotion that fill their days from Monday until Friday. How one wishes that more of the daring and enterprise, the grasp of essentials, the power of initiative, the directness of decision, that mark the world of business could find their way into the life and work of the Church.

In this congregation there are people who are able and gifted, their minds disciplined and effective instruments. To them I say now: Are you putting your brain to work in the service of religion? You recognize it to be an indispensable tool. Do you recognize it as something else: as sacred, as an instrument to be consecrated, to be given back to God who gave it to you?

The person for whom that is a discovery has a double offering to make to God.

> Oh God, I offer Thee my heart—
> In many a mystic mood, by beauty led,
> I give my heart to Thee. But now impart
> That sterner grace—to offer Thee my head.

—from PULPIT DIGEST *for April, 1950*

Christ and This Crisis

BY SAMUEL M. SHOEMAKER

Rector of Calvary Episcopal Church, New York

THE BLOW has fallen, and America is at war. For a long time we staved off the possibility of it from our minds, and hoped against hope that we might not be engulfed in the catastrophe that has now become practically planetary. There was not only a great deal of softness and selfishness, but also much stupidity, in thinking that we could live in the world that has been in existence for more than two years, and still not quite be a part of that world. The horror of anticipation now becomes the horror of fact; and while we here in the east still seem a little remote from personal danger, events have already involved someone we know, and may move nearer to us at any time.

What has Christian religion—our traditional American faith—to say to us in the crucial hour?

We look back to the eternal Figure of Christ Himself. He still towers above the ages, above the wrecks men have made of this world. We know that, in spite of the shortness

88

of His life, and the shame of His Cross, He is the one Success of all history, the one Success in a history of almost universal failure. He had the secret of living; by it He lived Himself, and by it He enabled others to catch something of His spirit. We still look to Him for personal strength and help. John the Baptist spoke of Him as "one mightier than I." All of us—civilians at home, or men risking their all on land or sea or in the air—all of us in time of danger look for "One mightier than I," and find that He is there, and that He does not fail us. He is the real heart of all real national defense, for He alone can give men faith and courage, free from hate and bitterness. As we look back to Him, we realize that we are also looking forward. Christ is not back of us. He is ahead of us—far ahead of us. War does not point to the failure of Christianity, but only to the desperate need of it. When we look to that "One mightier than I," we shall find that the peace which is in His heart can come into our hearts and so into our world. He still is the Prince of Peace, and there is no other.

Christ is telling us, all the while we find and fulfil our obligations to the world that is, that we must keep preparing for the world that is to be when the war is finished. Whatever else may be true about it, that world must be a world *community*. I believe that, all down these nineteen Christian centuries, God meant us to learn the art of community on smaller and compassable scales, so that when finally the world should be drawn together by science and commerce and education, we should be ready for community between the nations. We did not learn that art, and therefore we signally failed to have patterns of experience on which we could draw for international community. It

seems to me clear that we must go back and pick up that
stitch where we dropped it. England has almost totally gone
off the individualistic standard, and on to the community
standard. A friend just back from there tells me that everyone thinks and lives in community. This, as I see it, is not
only a war-exigency, but also a preparation for the world
that is to be. The Church was, from the time of Pentecost
onward, an experiment in community. It must become today a more realistic, effective, and pattern-forming experiment in community. Christ, with His hands out-stretched
to all, caring for all, is the world's great Leader in the art
of association, in the practice of community.

Christ is telling us, also, that while we work for that
world that must be, we need to be realistic and practical
in the world that is, and to carry each of us a man's share
in this crisis. Most of our young men will enlist in some
branch of service for the defense of our country. Many of
these have the belief that this is God's call to them, to stand
for right against wrong, and to sacrifice themselves, if need
be, for the sake of their country's ideals and safety. There
will be some who feel that God's call to them is to stand
against the process of war itself, and to be conscientious
objectors. However strong your convictions that this war
must be fought, I beg you to keep, and use your influence
so that the country will keep, genuine toleration of those
who believe that all war is wrong for them. None of us,
whatever our scruples, however, has any right to avoid or
evade personal sacrifice or danger, right up to the point of
the loss of our lives. No Christian can ask the exemption
from the danger of death, when His Lord asked no such
exemption. All of us will find some service which we can do

for our nation, either in our regular routines, or in some special fields where we are needed. 'New occasions teach new duties,' and with them always comes new strength, so that we shall be able to accomplish all that we ought to do. Through these services we shall find ourselves caring more for our fellow-citizens and more for our country, as we serve them better in a crucial hour.

Christ is offering to us all the most important element in national defense; and that is faith. The heart of morale is faith—faith in God, faith in democracy, faith in our government and in our people. It is the supreme task of the Church to send out into the nation today powerful rays of faith. The other day an officer in the United States Army, and a member of this parish, came to say good-bye to me on his way to Washington. He told me what this Church had come to mean to him and how happy had been his associations here, and how much he hoped the time would be short until he could resume them. Then he said, "This Church has taught me how to be free of fear and hate. When I came here, I had lots of both; but they are gone."

It is easy to see how fear is an enemy of morale and national strength. But hate is also an enemy of the nation's best interests. Last Sunday evening, after we had heard the news of the attacks by Japan on our island territories, some of us gathered in a meeting; we began by reading a story just printed about a Japanese Christian boy, a friend of some of us here, in which he tells this incident about himself.

A year before the present war with Japan began, I went to China. A young Chinese told me how detestable Japan was. I didn't try to dispute. I told him I knew how my country had been in her attitude toward China, and how wrong I myself had been. Because *I* was honest it made *him* want to be honest, too, and he told me where he and his country had been wrong. So we became friends and, before we parted, we pledged ourselves to be spiritual bridges between the two nations.

I know that boy, and I love him as a brother in Christ. There are hundreds in the enemy countries today who deplore this war as much as we do, and in exactly the same way. Hate the wrong in Japan, Germany and Italy if you will, remembering also how much wrong there is in ourselves: *but never hate Japanese, Germans or Italians.* One of the first things I did last week was to seek to get in touch with a Japanese friend of mine, to re-establish a long bond with him, and to tell him that I knew what he was suffering. I did the same thing with a German friend. Let us always remember that the true divisions between men never run *vertically*, between classes, races, groups, nations; but horizontally, between levels of life. In all the countries with which we are at war, let us remember those who are Christians before they are anything else. The whole hope of the future lies in those who live upon a level higher than national interest alone.

During the last world war there were some ministers of the Gospel who allowed themselves to become past-masters in the art of hating, and thought that they did God service when they spread that hate abroad. I hope they all repented of their ways, but they could not undo the harm that was done by what they had said. When one talks with men who have fought in actual war, they seem strangely free from hate; but one finds many 'fireside haters,' people who stay at home, and take out their enthusiasm in bitter feelings and bitter words. Those never won a war. They deplete the spirit of our citizens and our armed forces. Let us help our men to get on with the grim business of war, but let us do all we can to see to it that the Church reduces hate and fear to a minimum in this nation. She can render America no better service in this critical hour.

The Christian has always a difficult task in the world. He must hate sin, and he must love sinners—always and under all circumstances. Christ did that, and we must do it. Christ's way is to change men's hearts, which is the practical way of both loving them and helping them to stop their sins. The New Testament makes it quite clear that He often rebuked men for their sins, and that He would at times use force to carry the point of right. Christianity never lies down in the presence of wrong, and lets wrong have its way; and a vast deal of harm has been done by those who think that Christianity is nothing but unchallenging kindness. But we know that Christ never used force except as part of a redemptive process. War seems to have been thrust upon us, and the nation's response is self-defense. Let us always remember how many people in the enemy army and citizenry are not responsible for it, hate it as we do, and long for the end of it; and let us pray for the Japanese, Germans and Italians, their leaders and their people, that they and we may learn something from this war that will show us how to go about producing a just and lasting peace when it is over. While we hate the sin, let us love the sinner. Then we can go on praying, without hypocrisy, "Forgive us our trespasses, as we forgive those who trespass against us."

I should like to suggest a few concrete ways in which it seems to me we Christians can be helpful at this time.

1. *The people who have God are the people who have*

the answer. He can keep us from the common fear, the common hate, and the instinctive selfishness which are the temptation of all, and into which it is very easy for all of us to slip, unless we have the control of God upon us. God can keep these things out of our hearts, and therefore out of our words and actions. This is not only a privilege and personal consolation; this is also a high responsibility. We must conduct ourselves as those that believe in God, remembering that others will look to us, not only to live up to our faith and principles, but to give them help and a lead. *The people who have God are the people who have the answer.*

2. *Let us listen to God more than we listen to the radio.* Millions have been glued to the radio this past week, eager not to miss a bit of news. This is very natural, and some of it very necessary. But this is purely passive. It may become purely selfish. Listening to God quiets our own spirits, restores our inner poise, and shows us what to do next. *There is no security in a crisis like the security of knowing what to do next.* That comes when you listen to God. Last Tuesday three women were lunching in a club. Tongues flew, fear was rife, and some were not far from the 'jitters.' The three women got up, went into a side-room and prayed and listened to God. In prayer, it came to them what to do next, and they did it calmly. Another woman joined them, interested in what they were doing; it gave one of them the chance she had long wanted of witnessing about Christ to her. That is more than finding personal direction; that is true national service.

3. *Let us stop rumors and gossip—positive or negative.* Negative gossip can instill fear in others, and positive gossip can instill false confidence in them. Let us keep our minds

much more on what we and others should be doing than upon the truth or falsehood of a rumor. We have all heard fantastic stories during the past week. I hope we have done to them what rubber does to electricity—be a non-conductor that puts an end to them.

4. *Let us faithfully and cheerfully obey the government and city orders that come to us.* Let us go where we are told, and do it when we are told. Let us pocket our individualistic ideas, and remember that those in authority have considered more problems and questions than we have. In a democracy our ideas are as good as anybody else's, and we can speak our minds at the proper time; but in a crisis, let us be ready to take orders from those responsible. Let us all begin saving now where we can. The city water supply is low. The government needs many kinds of metal. This crisis can teach us Americans some lessons that we have never been willing to learn before.

5. *Let us remember that confidence is as contagious as panic.* Last week I listened to several people tell of what they were doing to establish confidence amongst the people they were working with every day. One was a teacher, who spoke openly about her own faith in God to parents and pupils. One works in an office, and was quietly laying the dust of rumor and the spread of hate and fear. One was a red-cap in one of our great terminals, and he told us how he was "calming people down," as they passed hurriedly through the station, speaking to them freely of his own faith, giving himself to them for those few moments, and living out his own morale, so that at the end they would thank him and tell him how wonderful he had been to them. A woman in this congregation went home one day

this week, and found the chamber-maid in her house full of fear. She stopped and talked with her. The woman quieted down, caught something of her God-given confidence, and said, "Well, now I can go and do my work." Confidence is as contagious as panic. And God gives confidence.

6. *Let us remember the value of small groups—six to fifteen—whom we might gather weekly for spiritual fellowship and active cooperation.* Faith, confidence and cooperation are nowhere so easily seen and so readily caught as from a small group that possesses and practices them. Honest talk, about our problems, fears or opportunities; prayer together for ourselves, for our fighting forces, for our President and all in authority; and the acceptance of some steady responsibility, in which we seek help from one another— these might be the soul and heart-beat of commercial firms, schools, hospitals and churches, of villages and towns and countrysides. The Church ought to take the lead in the formation of such groups for prayer, fellowship, and action.

In the end, we come back to the "One mightier than I." Last Tuesday, when we had an air-raid scare in New York, I went to school and brought back my child. As we walked home, we talked of some pretty unpleasant possibilities, and we faced them together. "Gee, Daddy, I'm a little bit scared," she said. But we talked about how much people like ourselves, with faith in Christ, have bolstered the courage of those who have not the blessing of faith. After a few steps during which we were silent, she said, "Well, we always have Jesus. No bombs can touch Him."

"We always have Jesus." She knows the "One mightier than I."

Would God that all our American children, and all their

parents, knew Him and trusted Him, in the days of our prosperity, and in the days of our tribulation! And may God bless and hallow to us all the pain and sacrifice and loss that probably lie before us, to bring us back to the one thing which this nation needs most, faith and obedience towards "One that is mightier than I."

—*from* PULPIT DIGEST *for February, 1942*

Too Proud to Receive

BY RALPH W. SOCKMAN

Pastor of Christ Church Methodist, New York City

BENJAMIN FRANKLIN has told us the exercise by which he once tried to attain moral perfection. He drew up a list of the twelve virtues which he thought embodied the essential traits of a good life. He kept a little book in which a page was allotted to each virtue. Then he ruled each page with seven lines, one for each day of the week. His program was to focus his mind on one virtue a week at a time, keeping track of each daily violation. Thus he went through the list, thinking that since his conscience told him what was right and what was wrong, he could attain the good and avoid the bad.

Showing his list to an old Quaker friend, he was gently informed that he had omitted the virtue of humility. Franklin added it at once. His list then read as follows: Temperance, Silence, Order, Resolution, Frugality, Industry, Sincerity, Justice, Moderation, Cleanliness, Tranquility, Chastity, Humility.

98

Ben Franklin's homely wisdom and practical counsel have made him an oft-quoted guide in our search for successful living. But when we ponder his precepts, we see that while they make for adjustment and advancement in our relations with men, they differ in spiritual depth and emphasis from those given by the great Hebrew prophets and Jesus of Nazareth.

Take this matter of humility. Franklin put it last in his list of virtues, but Jesus put it first in his Beatitudes: "Blessed are the poor in spirit, for theirs is the kingdom of Heaven." And Christian theology has pretty consistently put pride as the first and most basic of the deadly sins. Saint Augustine, sixteen centuries ago, asked: "What could begin this evil will, but pride, that it is the beginning of all sin?" C. S. Lewis of Oxford in our day declares: "Pride leads to every other vice; it is the complete anti-God state of mind."

Humility, then, is not just an added grace which adorns man's other virtues to make them more presentable and likable. It is the foundation of all other virtues. Pride is not just a flaw on the surface of life, which mars the appearance of man's virtues; it is the basic sin at the bottom of all our wrong-doing.

Perhaps the reason that pride is the primary sin is suggested in these words: "God resisteth the proud and giveth grace to the humble." That is a statement which I take from the First Epistle of Peter, the fifth chapter, but which I could take in substance from several places in the Bible. The principle here revealed is this: Pride is the basic sin because it begets a resistance that stops growth; humility is the primary virtue because it possesses a grace of receptivity which makes for growth.

Let us look at some situations where we become too proud to receive what God has to give us.

First, when pride shutters the mind. Pride is so basic because it is related to the original roots of man's nature. Human beings, like all living creatures, have a vitality which pushes them out to preserve themselves. The little child takes its first step, and then looks around with pride for the applause of its elders. Later the boy brings home from school his report card, and both he and his parents take a justifiable pride in his progress. Such pride seems a legitimate part of our native motive power. Where then is the point at which pride develops divine resistance?

We sometimes say about a certain person that his learning has "gone to his head." Of course, that is where learning is supposed to go; but in this case, it seems to have gotten there in the wrong way. The person has become intoxicated with his own achievement. When success "goes to the head" it inflates the ego with such self-importance that the man fails to see the import of things around him. He becomes so proud of his own opinions that he argues to show how right he is rather than discusses to find out what is right. He talks when he should be listening. He is arrogant in his judgments and uncharitable toward those who differ with him. He closes the shutters of his mind against the light of new truth which might reveal the dust that has settled on his cherished convictions.

Reinhold Niebuhr says that all human knowledge has an ideological taint, that is, it tends to form a pattern of ideas and then the pattern tends to stop the growth of truth. That was the situation Jesus faced in the scholars of His day. The scribes and Pharisees had built up a system of doctrine which Jesus of Nazareth did not fit. They scornfully asked: "Whence came this carpenter's knowledge?"

Certainly we in our time have been made familiar with these idea-patterns. We call them ideologies. We talked about the conflict of ideologies in World War II between the Nazi totalitarianism and our free societies. Now we speak of another clash of ideologies between Communism and our democratic institutions. But if we are true to the spirit of Christ, we do not try to pit one pattern of ideas against another set of patterns, but rather to turn on the light of truth which will show up falsity wherever found. Christ came to impart the Spirit of Truth of whom He said: "He will guide you into all truth." Christ is our eternal guide, the same yesterday, today, and forever, for the very reason that He did not give patterns of truth, but paths to truth. Christ did not give definitions, but directions. Directions are never outgrown.

The proud man closes his mind with patterns, with preconceptions, with prejudices. Thus God resisteth him because he is too proud to receive the truth.

But God "giveth grace to the humble." Just as the head of wheat which is filled with the best grain bends on its stalk, so the mind which is best filled bows humbly, realizing how much more there is to know. Charles Kettering, whose name has become a household word because of his contributions to science and industry, attributes his progress to what he calls "intelligent ignorance." The hope of advance lies in those who are intelligent enough to be aware of their ignorance. Thomas Huxley once wrote to Charles Kingsley: "Sit down before the facts as a little child, be prepared to give up every preconceived notion, follow humbly wherever Nature leads, or you shall learn nothing. I have only begun to learn content and peace of mind since I have resolved at all risks to do this."

Would we be humble enough to receive the grace of God in this matter of truth? Then we must modestly admit that the truth as it is in God is too vast for us to claim a monopoly for ourselves or our group. Whether we be Protestants or Roman Catholics, Presbyterians or Methodists, we must humbly hear Our Lord as He says: "Other sheep I have which are not of this fold." We must face facts with the open mind of a child, willing to follow where the truth leads, cost what it may. We must turn off the inner light of pride as the motorist turns off the inside light of his car so that he can see the lights and objects outside his car.

Pride cannot be cured by one dose of humility. Humility is a medicine to be taken daily, drop by drop. Each day we must study to be open to new ideas, to be patient with opposition, to be ready to listen to reproof, even when we are not convinced that it is deserved; and to be willing to confess our error when it is shown to us. As each morning we raise the blinds of our windows to let in the light of day, so we should also open the shutters of our minds to let in the light of truth.

A second situation in which we are too proud to receive is when pride locks the heart. I once knew two brothers who lived for about twenty years near together and yet without speaking to each other. When they grew to manhood, they jointly managed their father's farm. Property was held in common. But gradually they grew apart. The younger brother prided himself that he was smarter than his older brother and could make more money sitting on the fence than the other could plowing the fields. Consequently he spent considerable time on the fence. The other felt aggrieved at having to divide up after having done so much of the work. Finally they separated their holdings. Then for all the ensuing years until death they did not speak, although living only a few rods apart. Thus they forfeited that fellowship which can be so fruitful between brothers. And whenever anyone tried to effect a reconciliation between them, the attitude of each was: "I'll not be the first to forgive."

How often we are too proud to receive the love and life that are waiting for us! Take it between generations. Grown-ups can become so proud of their opinions and attainments that they fail to welcome the contributions which youth can make to their lives. And young people on their side often show what the Archbishop of Canterbury, last summer, called "that courteous contempt which youth has for age." The smart young fellow sometimes takes a patronizing attitude toward his father as a nice old dodo who means well but lives in a past age. The late John Buchan, Governor General of Canada, recalled the inspiration he received as a young lawyer in London from associations with older members of the bar, and deplored the modern tendency to segregate professional and social groups along age lines. Nothing is more important than the religious training of our youth; but in our programs toward that end let us cultivate the areas in which the different ages can learn from one another, thus overcoming the pride of age consciousness.

Think, too, how the pride of race locks the heart. When a person has nothing else of which to be proud, he can always fall back on his race, provided he is a white Aryan. So much of our race prejudice is fomented by persons who have so little else than race to distinguish them.

Or consider the form of pride which we call vanity. Vanity is shallow pride, manifest in small ways and on slight grounds. The vain person preens himself before every show-window that he passes. By turning windows into mirrors he keeps seeing himself when he ought to be seeing the things around him. Thus pride makes him a prisoner of himself. The person who gets stuck on himself is stuck with himself. He has himself on his hands for nobody else wants him.

Or take the pride of achievement which separates a person from God. The record of King Uzziah illustrates it. Listen: "His name spread far abroad; for he was marvelously helped, till he was strong. But when he was strong, his heart was lifted up to his own destruction." Similar statements occur again and again in Old Testament biography. Success breeds a sense of self-sufficiency. Men no longer feel the need of God. Then they fall. In that way it can be said: "God resisteth the proud."

But God "giveth grace to the humble" in heart. Richard Boxter was wont to say: "Know thyself and thou canst not be proud." But if we are to know ourselves, we must not do as the ancient Corinthians who "measuring themselves by themselves and comparing themselves with themselves, were not wise." We must see our lives in the light of God. When I go to buy a piece of cloth for a suit, if I am wise, I ask to see it not in the artificial light of the store but in the natural sunlight. So with the life that goes into the suit, I should see it in the light of God's love and wisdom and holiness. And when I do look at what I have done alongside of what God has done for me, when I think how indebted I am to others for what little I have accomplished, I feel with George Matheson:

> O love, that wilt not let me go,
> I rest my weary soul in thee;
> I give thee back the life I owe,
> That in thine ocean depths its flow
> May richer, fuller be.

Let us go on. Not only does pride shutter the mind and lock the heart but it also corrupts the conscience. This is the third way in which we become too proud to receive. Pride is so basic a sin because it spoils even our virtues.

When a person becomes proud of his purity, he becomes a prude. When he prides himself on his correct behavior, he becomes a prig. When he becomes proud of his righteousness, he is like the Pharisee who thanked God that he was not as other men are, unjust, extortioners, adulterers. And we all remember how Jesus praised by contrast the publican who prayed: "God be merciful to me, a sinner." But you know, even the publican's humility can be carried to the point of being spoiled by pride. Recently in a New Jersey town a questionnaire was put out among the children in an elementary school. The teachers were apparently trying to discover which pupils needed special attention to develop their social attitudes. One question was "Which student in the class brags the least about herself?" One little twelve year old girl put down her own name. Well, I suppose it was something like that which Saint Jerome had in mind when he said: "Beware of the pride of humility."

There are some persons who make no religious profession. They do not join the church. And they take a kind of pride in this fact, for they say: "At least we do not pretend to be what we are not." They are, no doubt, sincere, and the virtue of sincerity is one of the noblest. But do not take pride in sincerity when secured by simply taking low aim. Christian humility is attained by aiming at the highest we know with the utmost we have and then feeling how far short we come of the ideal. The Christian, if he is a Christian, goes to church not because he pretends to be better than those who do not go, but because he humbly knows he would be worse if he did not go.

The other day a New York minister was telling a little group of his colleagues about his call to the ministry. When he informed his mother of his intentions to be a minister, she told him of an experience of hers aboard a ship bound for Europe. A program had been arranged for the ship's passengers. A noted actor was aboard and he was asked to participate. He did so by reciting the Twenty-third Psalm. He did it with artistic beauty of manner and diction. An elderly and rather unknown preacher was asked to close the program. He did so by repeating the Twenty-third Psalm. At the end, the actor went over with bowed head, shook the hand of the old minister. The contrast was deep. In the first case, the hearers thought of the actor. In the second case, they thought of the Good Shepherd.

In that simple illustration, we are getting at the secret of handling pride. There is a justifiable pride which, as we said at the beginning, is a part of life's motive power. We should take pride in our work. But we should not take pride to ourselves from our work. We should have push, advancing good causes. But we should not be "pushers," elbowing our-

selves into the limelight. Jesus made this distinction clear
when he said: "Let your light so shine before men that they
may see your good works and glorify your Father which is
in heaven."

What is our main ambition in life, to make something of
ourselves or to make something with ourselves? Well, all I
shall say is that those who forget themselves are the ones
whom the world holds in longest remembrance. True it is
"God resisteth the proud and giveth grace to the humble."
Are we then willing to say with Isaac Watts:

> When I survey the wondrous cross,
> On which the Prince of Glory died,
> My richest gain I count but loss,
> And pour contempt on all my pride.

Prayer: O God, our great Companion, by whom the meek
are guided in judgment, grant us humble hearts to seek
Thy will, and honest minds to follow Thy truth. Grateful
that we have entered into the labors of other men, help us
so to labor that we may leave a worthy heritage to those
who come after us. Make us manly enough to bear our own
burdens and godly enough to help bear the burdens of
others. Keep us from foolish fears and worldly anxieties,
that with singleness of mind and purity of heart we may
seek first Thy Kingdom. Minister to those who are ill, give
cheer to those who are lonely, comfort those who mourn.

And, O God, give us such a passion for peace that we
may find the path to brotherhood: we ask through Jesus
Christ Our Lord.

—from PULPIT DIGEST *for September, 1950*

The Cool of the Day

BY WILLARD L. SPERRY

Dean of the Harvard Divinity School, Cambridge, Massachusetts

TEXT: *And they heard the voice of the Lord God walking in the garden in the cool of the day.*—GENESIS 3:8

THE OPENING CHAPTERS of the Book of Genesis have had varying fortunes at the hands of their readers. Formerly they were accepted as a literal statement of fact because they were included in the verbally inspired Bible.

As our modern interpretation of the Bible became the manner of the day, these first chapters of Genesis were dismissed from mind and forgotten. The biblical account of creation was superseded by the sciences of astronomy and geology and biology. And no one troubled to pay a mental visit to the Garden of Eden.

In more recent years, however, these ancient records have been given a more sympathetic reading. The first chapter has, by some strange accident, a curious parallelism to the stages of the evolution of life on this planet. It progresses from a first nebulous chaos to the appearance of man, and on the whole it marches with our modern knowledge.

More particularly, the story of the Garden of Eden is little short of a gold mine to those who are concerned to get behind and beneath the surface aspects of human life to its elemental, primitive, unconscious thrusts.

Anthropologists differ among themselves as to some date which should mark the arrival of authentic man on the scene. This event would be for them the equivalent of what used to be called the creation of man. I have sometimes thought that moment might be correctly timed if we could ever discover when a creature, previously conscious of the world around him, became conscious of himself. Self-consciousness is a great mystery. How and why and when did the mind of man become aware of itself and turn in upon itself, with those searching and insoluble questions which ever since it has asked of itself?

More especially the story of the fall of man raises another and still more difficult problem; how and when and why did man arrive at the distinction between good and evil? What made him do that? It is at this point, above all others, that he differs from the long evolving stages of animal life which brought him into being. What is called "the dawn of conscience" is a great miracle and a great mystery.

The story of the temptation and the fall cannot, alas, be explained on the modern and rather obvious theories that morality is merely a matter of the mean high level of the usage of a society, or definition of the greatest good of the greatest number. For, in the third chapter of Genesis, there is no society and there are no great numbers; there are only Adam and Eve. But there is one other person also: God.

Any religious account of the dawn of conscience will have to reckon with the theory, proposed in the record, that the dictates of conscience cannot be dissociated from man's relation to God. Good and evil, right and wrong, are not the whole of religion, but they are a very necessary part of it.

Professor Whitehead once said that a maturing religion passes through three stages. It is a transition from God the void to God the enemy, and from God the enemy to God the friend.

One can suppose that Adam and Eve were originally happy and content and quite self-sufficient in their garden. They were naked and unashamed. The first time they became aware of the presence of God was after they had eaten the fruit of the tree, knew that they were naked, and sewed the fig leaves together to hide their shame. Psychologically the Book of Genesis is quite right. Of all forms of shame, the awareness of that nakedness is the most primitive and elemental.

Then, at this point, the story says: "They heard the voice of the Lord God walking in the garden in the cool of the day."

There is something almost unearthly, and strangely arresting, in those words. Yet there is something very familiar, something close to our common human experience.

With their fall our first parents—if you take the story as it stands—had made the first transition in their religious life, the transition from God the void to God the enemy. They had become aware of something critical of themselves, hostile to themselves. On the whole, this was a gain rather than a loss.

It is not hard to translate the tale into more modern

terms. Their awareness of the Lord God walking in the garden in the cool of the day is a pictorial account of our own sober second thoughts upon the choices we have made and the life we have lived. It stands for all our reflective regrets and self-criticisms addressed to our own past. Thus, one thinks for instance of Carlyle, going over his wife's intimate papers after her death, and realizing to the full and for the first time how unhappy he had so often made her. In that moment, he cried out: "If I had only known; if I had only known." He had, as it were, been faced with the Lord God walking in the cool of the day in the garden of his home in Chelsea.

No one of us can avoid the Lord God walking in the garden in the cool of the day. We cannot avoid that meeting simply because we are self-conscious, and have a conscience. It is said that man is the animal that can wait. But he is more than a waiting animal. He is a being who can and ought to envisage to himself in advance the consequences of his own action. When the time comes for a moral decision to be made—and it is by no means always easy to make such a decision—it is the part of being fully human to be ready to accept the results of our choice, to see what they will be and to stand by them.

Adam and Eve hadn't thought ahead. Perhaps in the state of innocence they could not think ahead. Perhaps they had to eat of the fruit of the tree in order to learn to think ahead thereafter. That, at any rate, is what we have learned from them.

In some ways the most human and the most disappointing part of the story was their unwillingness, once they had come to the cool of the day, to accept the responsibility for what they had done. Adam blamed Eve and Eve blamed the serpent. That is what most of us instinctively do at first. Such evasion is the coward's last resort. My heredity was bad, my environment started me wrong, society is responsible for my mistakes, the times were against me. But no man is either fully self-conscious or fully moral who has not the candor to say when he meets the Lord God in his own reflective conscience: *"Mea culpa, mea culpa, mea maxima culpa.* It is my fault, my most grievous fault."

Let me turn to the other and the final transition in one's religious life—the transition from God the enemy to God the friend. The parable of the wise and the foolish virgins has passed into our speech as a rather commonplace cliché. The foolish virgins need no explanation; they explain themselves. Most of us recognize ourselves in them only too well. Their fault was this, that they could not or at least did not think ahead. Life with its great occasion found them unprepared for the event.

The persons who are hard to understand are the wise virgins, who, when the time came, had oil in their lamps. One could wish that Jesus had taken a little more time to explain them. Where and how did they get their wisdom?

Few of us get through life without sooner or later being aware that we need religion. Crises in personal life come to us, times of proving and often of great opportunity for which we know ourselves to be unprepared. Our cause is in peril and it finds us sleeping, as in the garden of Gethsemane. Our instinctive appeal to all that is meant by religion at such a time is a commonplace in the record. Lincoln, as the story goes, went down on his knees at the time of Gettysburg, because he, as he said, could not stand an-

other Chancellorsville or Fredericksburg, and he had nowhere else to go.

The most arresting statement of this situation of which I
know is that by the psychiatrist Jung. You probably know
it, but let me remind you of it in this connection.

> Among all my patients in the second half of life—that is to
> say, over thirty-five—there has not been one whose problem
> in the last resort was not that of finding a religious outlook on
> life.

The difficulty is that what is meant by religion, tried and
proven and fit for the emergency, cannot be come at on
short notice. A man who has consistently neglected his
health for fifty years cannot expect to have it restored to
him by a single visit to the doctor and a prescription to be
filled at the drug store. So with a life that has been lived in
consistent neglect of the major constant ideas which we
associate with religion.

In the hour of proving our opportunity, these considerations and resources have to be a matter of our whole mental
habit. As an honest chaplain, writing from the battlefield,
put it: "A religion come at in emergency is not the Christian
religion. The religion of Jesus bore the severest test, namely,
the quiet of normal and uneventful day. We are bidden by
Christ not to be anxious for the morrow. But this does not
mean that we are forbidden to think ahead to tomorrow,
otherwise the parable of the wise virgins is meaningless.
One has to realize to the full in advance of the fact, that oil
for the lamps of life is a matter of long views rather than
short views, and to live accordingly. Here is the reason and
warrant for the religious observances of every day, which
so often seem unnecessary and perhaps even irrelevant.

We all of us know what it is to hear, in our hours of sober second thought and self-criticism, the voice of the Lord God walking in the garden in the cool of the day. This is the voice of conscience passing its reflective judgments upon us. That experience is only a half-way house. Christianity is the record of the transition not merely from God the void to God the enemy, but from God the enemy to God the friend. There is, thank God, such a thing as meeting God the friend walking in the garden in the cool of life's reflective hours. To hear that voice is our greatest reward for living. Fame and money and power are relatively trivial things beside it.

It is said that beside and beyond the Bible the greatest book in our tradition is the *Imitation of Christ*. Listen, then, to the voice of God, speaking from the cool of those quiet pages. God the friend has seldom spoken more clearly.

The glory of a good man is the testimony of a good conscience. Have a good conscience and thou shalt have every joy. Thou shalt rest sweetly if thy heart do not accuse thee.

—*from* PULPIT DIGEST *for December, 1949*

The Family of God

BY A. GORDON NASBY

Pastor of Edison Park Lutheran Church, Chicago, Illinois

RELIGION is a subject on which all men feel qualified to speak. Opinions of God, regardless of who holds them, are thought to be the last word. No study, experience, or discipline seems to be necessary before a man is qualified to speak on God. This is strange, for of all possible subjects for thought and speculation, God is the most staggering in scope.

The many denominations in the Church today witness to the right man feels he has to assert his ideas about God. The Church has felt the effect of this natural independence of judgment and sovereignty of mind in man. But it would be a regrettable error to conclude that the Church's history can be explained simply on the basis of the human element.

To dismiss Christianity with a futile gesture because of its splits into denominations is childish. If we see nothing but the divisions in the Church we are reading her very superficially. From the outside the differences of the Church

115

are magnified. A closer reading of the Church's history reveals why we have different denominations. As the Reformation came in various countries of Europe, leadership influenced the emphasis. The church spoke different languages. In America the language problem created separate bodies.

It must be frankly faced that men have sometimes put personal considerations above the welfare of the Church. Hugh Price Hughes was once asked why the Church did not unite. "There would have to be a few leading funerals first," he said.

The Church today can be found in a wide variety of forms and types. There is a fellowship and worship for everyone. One rigid communion could not possibly serve individual emotion and spiritual needs as effectively as the Church in its present form is able to do. We have discovered also that loyalty to a smaller communion evokes a greater support and response to needs. The work of reconstruction the churches have been doing through their group loyalties might not have been possible in a larger, more impersonal set-up.

A unity of the Church in the world, made possible only by conformity, would not be desirable. It would be a tragic thing if the churches all got together as one simply because they were tired of their differences. The differences in the churches (far fewer than is usually imagined) often serve, it has been said, as elements in an organic tension like the string which transforms a length of stick into a violin bow.

The truths which are emphasized in separate denomina-

tions are often truths we all covet. Controversy is not always
to be deprecated. It is often a sign of life.

Now let us consider what is far more important, the *unity*
that prevails in the Church. Rabbi Isserman has related an
experience of a visit to a cathedral in France. As he entered
the sanctuary in a religious mood he was disappointed that
the mood of mysticism quickly left him. His attention, however, was soon arrested by the crouched form of a crippled
lad kneeling in prayer. The rabbi drew near, and as he did
he saw tears trickling down the face of the boy, who sought
to confront the handicaps of life with dignity and heroism.
At this the devout rabbi said tears came to his own eyes
and he prayed with the lad. "Surely," he said, "God was in
this place and I knew it not."

Men from any church whatever would understand this,
for the Church everywhere is aware of the needs of man.
It seriously studies his frustrations and longings. It earnestly
endeavors to probe into the causes of man's unhappiness.
And it concludes with Augustine that man is restless until
he finds his rest in God. All churches endeavor to lead men
to peace with God.

I like the description of the Church given by Charles
Clayton Morrison:

> The Church is not a society of integrated personalities, nor of
> philosophers, nor of mystics, nor even of good people. It is a
> society of broken personalities, of men and women with
> troubled minds, of people who know they are not good. The
> Christian Church is a society of sinners. It is the only society
> in the world, membership in which is based upon the single
> qualification that the candidate shall be unworthy of member-
> ship.

The teachings of the different denominations are surprisingly uniform. The Bible is universally honored, loved, and accepted as a guide book. A denominational ring cannot be put about the Sacraments, Christian morality, the ideal of Christian character, or the creative factors within the Church. All churches unashamedly point to Christ as our ideal and declare that if He is ignored the consequences will be tragic.

Christianity declares God is a God of love. It would be strange to find a Church that had no interest in fallen man. I know of no Church that would look complacently on a man lying in the gutter. Can you imagine any Church saying to such a one: "Now take your own medicine, you asked for it?" Hardly! Instead the Church keeps passionately before men the loving God who in Jesus Christ has brought forgiveness to the world. The mission of the Church in the world is everywhere admitted to be the redemption of the world through Christ.

An Indian leader declared that India will accept Christ. But, declared the leader, India will become Christian at the fountainhead—in Christ Himself. It will not go downstream to find Him in some denomination. Men from all churches will support this idea, for we know well that Christ is the cornerstone of our faith. Few churchmen would think of putting the Church before Christ.

More than any time in history we now realize the universality of Christ. The Church has ever declared that Christ is universal, and in every communion this conviction has brought about missionary efforts. All churches seek to bring about the Kingdom of God on earth.

Anyone with a peeve on the subject of religion is likely

to ridicule the creeds of the Church. Now here is an amazing consideration—practically all the churches in the world accept the major creed of Christendom—the Apostles' Creed. Every week millions of men join in their churches spread over the world to declare their faith in God as outlined in this Creed. Statements here cover faith in God as the Creator, Jesus Christ as His Son and our Lord, the Spirit of God, the family of God, the forgiveness of sins, and the life hereafter. Many people would be astonished if they looked into this matter. They would then understand that the fundamental teachings of the Church are universally held.

When, of course, we talk about the Church we should define what we mean by it. There is a visible church which seems to us to be divided. The concern of man, unfortunately, seems almost exclusively devoted to this visible Church with its buildings, personalities, resolutions, charities, and quotas. There is, however, another Church, the invisible or true Church.

Rufus Jones tells of a priest with whom he became friendly. To the priest Jones put this question: "I should like to know what you would say if you met a person who obviously and plainly possessed divine grace in his life and who yet never used what your Church calls the Means of Grace."

Without a moment's hesitation the priest declared: "I should say that that person belonged to the 'Invisible Church,' and I should admit to you that it is more important to belong to the invisible church than it is to belong to the visible one."

During the first World War three American soldiers escaped from a German prison camp. As the three were making their escape one of the men was struck by a bullet. The wounded man was hid by day and carried by night until it became imperative that refuge be found. The wounded soldier grew weaker and was nearing death. The fleeing men stopped at a tiny parish church and knocked at the door. An aged priest answered, discovered the soldiers were Americans, and led them to a place where they would be safe from enemy searching parties.

During the night the wounded soldier grew weaker, and died. Before continuing their flight, however, the two men made arrangements for the burial of their comrade. They asked if a plot could not be had in the cemetery near the church. "Was the soldier a Catholic?" asked the white-haired holy man.

"No," they answered, "he was a Protestant."

A look of sadness spread over the priest's face. "Ah," he said, "that is unfortunate, for only Catholics can be laid to rest in this cemetery." Then his face brightened. "But we can put him yonder just outside the fence."

The soldiers watched from a window in their underground hiding place as their comrade was laid to rest. The service over, the priest pleaded with the men to remain a time, and they stayed for another night.

A strange sight met them as they looked in the morning to where their comrade lay buried. The fence had been moved to take in the soldier. The priest smiled. "A Protestant," he said, "may not be buried in the cemetery, but there is no rule which says we cannot move the cemetery to include a Protestant." Such a spirit, we know, is pleasing to

Christ, and would be approved by the vast majority of folk in any church.

In almost any church you will find hymns sung which are the heritage of the whole Church, despite the fact that they came out of a particular denomination. The experience of Christian faith is universal. Christianity's language of the heart is everywhere understood.

Never before in history have the forces of materialism been so well organized and powerful. When the churches become fully aware of the mobilization of these anti-Christian forces, an outward union will become more apparent. When Christianity itself is imperiled, the churches may astonish the world with their unity. This hour may even now be about to strike.

An ancient story tells of two knights who disagreed as to the color of a shield. Their disagreement led to a duel to prove which was right. After some fighting, however, the two lost heart and agreed on a truce. "Let's look at the shield," one suggested. To their astonishment both had been right. One side was gold and the other silver. If we confine ourselves to actual experience of God, we discover how much we have in common. Hasty consideration, on the other hand, makes us intolerant.

Christ Himself prayed at one of the most sacred points of His life that His followers might be one. It is therefore the duty of Christians to strive for a more perfect union in the Church. Our test of conduct should be: "What would Jesus do?"

Phillip of Spain, it is said, was a devout churchman. In the hour of his death he asked if some of the reverses which accompanied the end of his life were not due to the fact that he had not burned enough heretics. We know instinctively what would have followed if Jesus had been consulted.

Christ warned of the peril of judging others. The critical spirit is fatal to the cultivation of humility; and humility, according to Christ, is indispensable to the man bound for the Kingdom of God. A mother whose son had lately joined the army went down to view the regiment as it passed in parade. "See," she proudly exclaimed, as the soldiers passed "they're all out of step but my Johnny!"

Baxter once declared that he expected three surprises in heaven. First, he figured he would be surprised to find some people there he had never expected. Second, he would be surprised to find some missing. And lastly, he would upon arrival be surprised at being there himself. This, it seems to me, is more properly the Christian approach of humility.

All Christians should remember that any form of Christianity is better than none. In the family of God we should not expect the children of God to follow one pattern any more than we expect all children in the human family to be identical in all respects. To force all Christians into the same mould would be tantamount to confining or limiting the influence of the Spirit of God.

Dwight Moody once invited Henry Drummond to the Northfield Conference which he headed. Drummond's views were not accepted by all participants in the program, and Moody, in consequence, was taken to task for inviting the famous English speaker. Moody declared: "I cannot say I believe in all his notions, but he is more like Jesus Christ than any man I know. That is why I want him at Northfield."

When the Salvation Army was finally well launched in

England, most so-called respectable people deplored it. A high Church official was asked his opinion of the Salvation Army. "I don't like it at all; but I am afraid Almighty God does." This has been said to be the remark of a man who has begun to grow up.

At Dachau concentration camp, on Christmas of 1944, Martin Niemoeller was granted permission by the Nazis to hold a religious service in his cell. This was the first one he had conducted in seven and one-half years in prison. In that cell there crowded seven men—a Dutch cabinet minister, two Norwegian shippers, a British major from the Indian Army, a Yugoslavian diplomat, and a Macedonian journalist, together with Martin Niemoeller, the heroic pastor. All the men spoke tolerably good German and sang the hymns together with zest. There these men put into practice the One Holy Church, gathered around God's Word, and celebrated the Lord's Supper together. Among these men were Presbyterians, Lutherans, Anglicans, and a member of the Greek Orthodox Church.

Had you or I been there we would have rejoiced as these men did in being united as disciples of the same Teacher and Saviour. Where men truly follow the Lord Christ, this union of heart is already a fact. The invisible or true Church is not divided, but is in fact the family of God. If we turn from the Church because she is outwardly divided, we allow a petty consideration to rob us of the only permanently interesting thing in life—God.

—*from* PULPIT DIGEST *for July, 1950*

Eternity in the Heart

BY A. D. BELDEN

*General Director, Pax Christi League,
London, England*

TEXT: *He hath set eternity in their heart.*
ECCLESIASTES 3:11

THE BOOK OF ECCLESIASTES contains, like all the wisdom books of the Scripture, many cryptic utterances which require careful meditation to penetrate their meaning. An excellent illustration of this is the sentence in the third chapter, "He hath set eternity in their heart."

What the author means is that the inner life of man reflects in a marvelously adequate manner the universe outside him. The word "heart" in Scripture has a wider meaning than it has in our modern speech, where we tend to reserve it almost entirely for the emotional aspect of the soul. It corresponds very much better to the use we make of the word "mind," to indicate the whole interior life of man. Possibly the still better translation of this pregnant little sentence would be, "He hath set infinity in the soul."

The sentence lights up the majesty and glory of human

124

personality and as such it introduces us to one of the most important assumptions of the Christian outlook. There is a strong tendency in these days, especially on the part of the scientifically minded, to regard the ascription of personality to God as something so limiting to Him as to be both inadequate and irreverent. Yet unless God is at least personal, the *soul* goes out, not only of Christianity, but of the universe, and it is important to grasp the fact that this difficulty arises fundamentally from a poor and insufficient estimate of human personality.

The German philosopher, Lotze, long ago argued at length that there is no need to assume that in calling God personal we in any way limit Him to personality as we know it in the human situation, for such personality is essentially a growing and developing thing and there is a vast difference between its lowest and its highest forms. Hence in its perfection in God, personality may easily be possessed of dignities and powers far beyond our present conceiving and yet not be inconsistent with intelligence, feeling, and will.

It is urgently necessary, therefore, that modern thought should revive its sense of the sublime in man, since only upon such a conviction can there be built up that consistent respect for "all sorts and conditions of men" which recognizes even in the lowest of them something of the image of Deity.

We recall how fierce Jesus was against the sin of human contempt. How He warned us that no man should call his brother "fool" lest he be in danger of judgment, and how He identified Himself with the criminal in prison and the poor perishing with hunger. Let us then draw aside the veil and look into the soul of man.

Every human in some degree can think. The mental characteristic of humanity is essentially the capacity to think of oneself. It is possible to think quite definitely about oneself, and then to think of oneself in the act of thinking about oneself, and then to think again of this self in the act of thinking about oneself thinking about oneself. It is possible, moreover, to keep that process up until the number of selves runs towards infinity. The human mind is like an endless series of looking-glasses that reflect themselves. This is but one indication of the illimitable depth of the thought process in man, but there are many others.

Take, for example, the marvel of memory; consider all that is packed within it without any sense of burden—the innumerable faces of one's total acquaintance, the names of one's relatives and friends, and even their addresses, the substance of one's education over many years, the capacity to revive sense of color at will, and even to imagine sounds, in the absence of sound, quite accurately.

Modern science has revealed to us the vast "forgettory," which is a subtler form of memory, where innumerable occurrences, indeed all the experiences of the self, lie folded in convenient oblivion until required. Moreover, there is reason to believe that below the level is a deeper stratum still where are stored memories reaching far back into our ancestral and even racial history, and all this vast treasure the mind carries without burden or distress.

That great thinker, St. Augustine, has in his "Confessions" a remarkable passage in which he pays tribute to the marvel of human memory. He writes:

I come to the fields and spacious palaces of my memory where are treasures of innumerable images. Yet the things themselves do not enter in, but only the images of things are held there in readiness for thought to receive. Even while I dwell in darkness and silence in my memory I can produce colors if I will. Nor will different sounds break in and disturb the image I am reviewing, though they are there lying dormant. Then these, too, I call forth and forthwith they appear. Out of the same vast store do I myself with the past continually combine fresh and fresh likeness of things which I have experienced. So speak I to myself out of this treasure of the mind. Here also is all learned of the liberal sciences—removed as it were to some inner place (which is yet no place)—nor are these now images, but the things themselves, reasons and laws innumerable of numbers and dimensions, none of which has any bodily sense impressed. Great is the power of my memory, a fearful thing.

Indeed it is true, "He hath set eternity in their heart." We turn next to the majesty of love within the soul of every human. How long can you love? When the soul knows a true affection, is it able to tolerate any time limit? On the contrary, does it not know that even death itself cannot diminish love? Elizabeth Barrett Browning's tender appeal in her famous XIV Sonnet finds an echo in the heart of every true lover:

Love me for love's sake, that evermore Thou mayst love on, through love's eternity.

The circle of love to the poorly educated heart may be small and mean; many have love only for their domestic circle and are on their guard against the rest of the world; but when we begin to think of the great humanists and philanthropists of history, St. Francis of Assisi, Wilberforce, Shaftesbury, Elizabeth Fry, David Livingstone, and William Booth, we find that these great hearts of humanity possess the genius of their Divine Lord, whose love streamed forth with a noble equality to every member of the race. The development of the heart in each personality is to be measured by its approximation to this achievement.

It is a useful illustration of the difference between the finite soul and the infinite to think of the mother with her sweet brood of children; she divides between them a loaf of bread, each child receives a piece, and presently no loaf is left. That is finitude, exhaustion at last. But she divides between her children her love, and each child has its share, and each child has it all, and still her love remains for her husband and even for humanity. Surely here, as we peer into the depth of such a heart, our souls are touched with awe, we are in the presence of the Infinite. "He hath placed eternity in the heart."

Few facts can stir the soul with greater awe than the mystery of the will. This curious operation which proceeds from some seat of power deep within the human constitution decides the course of life and the flow of energy now to this limit and now to that, presently to north and again to south, and yet again to east and west, hurling the body through space, arousing or arresting it sharply, yielding it up to sleep, doing any of the thousand maneuvers required for a day's life, and all, as we say, "at will."

It is particularly in the soul's pursuit of its ideals and purposes that we see the will stretching out to infinitude. The further progress it makes the more it discovers the ideal to be enlarging; like some brave mountaineer scaling the utmost peaks, who sees range succeeding range in ever-increasing height, so the soul must be forever generating fresh energies of will for fresh conquests. In lifting its will to God the soul pursues a flying goal. It is ever achieving yet ever aspiring. The hero-souls of the past have discovered an inexhaustible capacity for the renewal of their resolution, and not even death itself nor indescribable torture have been able to corrupt or end the pure passion of their striving. This is the infinitude of the will.

"He hath set eternity in their heart."

All this that we have described is true not merely of the heroes of our human story, but of the humblest and lowliest of humans. We can recognize something of this in every specimen of humanity, however depraved. The potentiality lies there, though often, like a pearl of great price, it is sunk deep in mire. Of certain vast numbers of what we call average humanity, of myself and yourself, shall we say, it is plainly true by what we know of the stirring and depth of our own being.

Man lies, in spite of his limitations, cradled in the arms of Deity. The growing finite is encircled by the Infinite. Hence let no man despise his brother, nor even himself, nor think it strange that Christ, in revealing to us the Eternal Father, should do so in terms of personality.

—from PULPIT DIGEST *for January, 1950*

Eyeless in Gaza

BY IVAN H. HAGEDORN

*Bethel Evangelical Lutheran Church,
Philadelphia, Pennsylvania*

JOHN MILTON packed a whole book in a few words, when he wrote "Eyeless, in Gaza, at the mill, with slaves," for each word drops like slow tears. Surely, the picture of the blind and fettered giant grinding in the prison of his foes is a pathetic sight, made all the more so when one realizes that he was grinding for the Philistines, when he might have mastered them. But Samson's blindness revealed itself long before the Philistines gouged out his eyes. He had lost his vision before he became eyeless in Gaza.

Samson was blind when he forgot his mother's wonder and his father's prayer. He must have listened often to the detailed description of the supernatural circumstances of his birth, from the lips of his parents. Though fitted by nature and training for a great task, he dissipated his fine talents. Surely, that is blindness. On the day in 1874 that David Livingstone was buried in Westminster Abbey, the

130

streets of London were lined with thousands seeking to pay respect to the memory of the pioneer missionary. In the crowd was noticed a poor old man, unkempt, poorly clad, weeping bitterly. Someone went up and asked him why he was weeping when all were seeking to honor the illustrious dead. "I'll tell you why," the sad old man replied. "Davie (Livingstone) and I were born in the same village, brought up in the day school and Sunday School, worked together at the same loom. But Davie went that way and I went this; now he is honored by the nation, and I am neglected, unknown, and dishonored. I have nothing to look forward to but a drunkard's grave."

Sometimes our vision fades slowly through neglect. At the beginning of his married life, Samuel Clemens made an effort to follow the religious leanings of his wife. But he soon fell back. And she, through love for him, sacrificed all its comforts too. As age came on, Clemens bade his wife to fall back upon her faith. Sorrowfully, she said, "I can't, Youth, I haven't any."

> For sadder sight than eye can know,
> Than proud bark lost or seaman's woe;
> Than battle fire or tempest cloud,
> Or prey birds' shriek or ocean shroud,
> The shipwreck of a soul.

Samson was blind because he was unwilling to subject himself to discipline. He wasted his manhood, indulging the whims of his unworthy self. And self-indulgence is bound to spell defeat. The Emperor Valentinian, of Rome, was so devoted to the sports of the amphitheater that his Prime Minister remonstrated with him, saying: "You are neglecting the affairs of the state. The empire suffers for

your amusements." The Emperor immediately registered a
solemn vow that he would never again cross the threshold
of an arena. He kept that vow. Not so Samson, and as a
result he became

"Eyeless, in Gaza, at the mill, with slaves."

E. Stanley Jones once said, "What Americans need most
is discipline." Who knows but what God, through the throes
of these tumultuous days, is building America's manhood
once more! The call to youth is no longer "Play the game,"
but "Stop playing the game and get down to living." The
Spartans had a famous dish of black broth at their public
meals, which all were compelled to eat. The broth was part
of the Spartans' discipline, which forbade all luxury and
indulgence. Having heard of the famous dish, a certain
king sent for a Spartan cook, that he might dine as these
famous warriors dined. He found the broth, however,
utterly disagreeable and unpalatable. "The broth" explained
the cook, "was nothing without the seasoning of fatigue and
hunger." Without the Spartan discipline, the Spartan menu
had no relish.

No word is so likely to be misunderstood today as the
word "freedom." I'm afraid for most people it simply means
"to be free to think as they please, speak as they please,
write as they please, worship as they please," and so they
suppose that they can get freedom by merely striking out
violently against opposition or restraint. But freedom, if it
means anything, means to be free of hatreds and prejudices
and bigotries. It means to be free to decide justly, fairly,
without heat and without being unduly influenced by others.
Jesus expressed it, "Ye shall know the truth, and the truth

shall make you free." And again, "If the Son shall make you free, ye shall be free indeed."

3) Samson was blind, when he was unwilling to cut away from his unsavory companionships. Samson went among the enemies of God for his outings and pleasures. What a regrettable course that is, when men and women making pretensions to godliness desert the paths of righteousness and neglect their posts as Christian leaders to pander after the world. What blindness is here revealed. A young minister was leaving a North Country town, and was bidding an old lady good-by. "Well, sir," she said, "you'll be busy packing up your belongings, I expect?" "Yes," he replied, "I have only a few things to get into boxes now." "There's one thing you won't be able to pack up, sir," said the old lady. "You'll have to leave that behind." "I don't know— whatever is that?" questioned the minister. "You can't pack up your influence, sir," she answered quietly. That is true, whether influence is good or bad. What kind of influence will you leave behind when God's call comes?

Samson's capture is ever Dagon's glory. The worst consequence of a fall of a saint is that it gives occasion for God's enemies to blaspheme, and so bring discredit upon God and His people. The faults and weaknesses of professing Christians are the bulwarks of unbelief. Claiming to be devoted to Him, and yet running to the world to satisfy their desires. Surely, that is blindness.

"Eyeless, in Gaza, at the mill, with slaves."

4) Samson was blind in his presumption. Our gifts and our talents are not given to us for display, but for use. Therefore, when their high purposes are prostituted to base ends, the last chapter is bound to be dire. Selfish misuse of divine

gifts is blindness. Samson was fond of the sensational. He loved to do things in a spectacular way. His very strength and his very charm became his snare. With braggadoccio, he said, "I will go out, as at other times, and shake myself." The big show-off!

The whole world for a time played up to him. He got the idea he could never lose. In this, he is not unlike many young folk I know. They have fine bodies, fine manners, and likeable personalities. Then, they get the idea the world will fall down and worship them. They are more anxious to get on in life, than to master life; more eager to shine in society than to serve it; more desirous to find thrills than to give attention to God. It is little wonder then that like Samson they find themselves

"Eyeless, in Gaza, at the mill, with slaves."

Samson was blind when he grew careless about his tresses. They were symbols of his power. Delilah asked, "Tell me where the secret of thy great strength lieth." We need to guard well those lines of communication between our inner life and the life of God. When these lines are broken down, faith grows weak, zeal ebbs, and one grows daily less able to meet successfully the temptations which constantly confront him. There was a day, when men had a feeling that they could be ready for plagues, ready for devastation, ready to meet the zero hour with courage and strength. God was real to them. But today, we have so shifted our standards and sense of values that we find it difficult to be in the clear of what is good and bad, what is light or dark. There is a woeful lack of conviction in these matters. We have let God go and so like Samson we are

"Eyeless, in Gaza, at the mill, with slaves."

Robert Ingersoll was famous for the library of infidel books which he possessed. One day, a reporter called on Mr. Ingersoll for an interview, and among other questions, asked: "Would you mind telling me how much your library cost you, Mr. Ingersoll?" Looking over at the shelves, he answered: "Well, my boy, these books cost me, anyhow, the governorship of Illinois, and perhaps the Presidency of the United States!" It is ever thus. When we let God go out of life, we are bound to miss life's highest goals.

Samson was blind when he got tired of being good. For twenty years, he had been judge in Israel, and then he yielded to the desire for a fling. We are reminded of the Scriptural admonition, "Be not weary in well-doing, for in due season we shall reap if we faint not." Far too many of our professing Christians have grown weary in their well-doing. If only all who name the Name of Christ would take the good counsel of George Muller, of Bristol, who when he was asked, "Would you not advise young Christians to do something for the Lord?" replied, "No, I should advise them to do EVERYTHING for the Lord."

It must be glorious to be able to go down to old age like Samuel. Remember his words, spoken in farewell to the people he had served so long and so faithfully. He asked, "Of whose hand have I received any bribe, to blind my eyes therewith?" A public utilities company, seeking a franchise in a large city, sent an unscrupulous representative to interview a city official whose vote was sorely needed. When the official intimated that his vote was not for sale, the representative exclaimed: "Think of the money, man! It's the bargain of a lifetime. You'll never have another chance to make that much money so easily." "So easily!" replied the official. "Listen, friend! No one ever yet got a bargain in sin. It's the highest priced thing in the market. You tell me that all I have to do is to vote 'right.' Well, it isn't. That's only the beginning of what I'll have to do. I'll have to carry the consciousness of my dishonesty to the grave. I'll have to live with a remorseful conscience. I'll have to pose before my wife and children as someone I know I am not. Don't tell me it's a bargain."

Samson was blind when he laid his head in Delilah's lap. He became bewitched with a fair face. How many are like him, willing to sell out their manhood for a dimple? I suppose she called him, "My big hero." Flattery is a splendid cure for a stiff neck. There are few heads it won't turn. That is one of the saddest forms of blindness, when a youth is willing to squander his very manhood. Tennyson hit a great truth, when he said of his true knight, "His strength was as the strength of ten, because his heart was pure." Surely, we should find a strong sermon on personal purity by beholding Samson

"Eyeless, in Gaza, at the mill, with slaves."

When the Church sees fine youth, like that of Samson, hitting the slimy trail, it should grow red hot in its attack on those dens where gambling, intoxication, and moral looseness are fostered. Many a youth is today grinding away because of alcohol and vice. Oh, why will youth surrender the sunshine of life, choosing to be drenched and drowned in the cess-pools of iniquity?

Dr. W. Leon Tucker was leaving his hotel to catch a three o'clock in the morning train. The orchestra in the dining-room was playing "Three O'Clock in the Morning." He stopped to pay his check at the desk. The night-clerk had evidently had too many drinks himself. He said to Dr. Tucker, "That's my type of music. I belong to the 'Three O'clock in the Morning' crowd. Don't you, mister?" Dr. Tucker replied, "No, I belong to the 'Three O'clock in the Afternoon' crowd." The night-clerk didn't seem to understand, so Dr. Tucker explained that it was three o'clock in the afternoon that Jesus Christ died for him and for all who would believe, on Calvary's cross.

Let us avoid those paths which land us at last *"Eyeless, in Gaza, at the mill, with slaves."*

—*from* PULPIT DIGEST *for September, 1941*

It's Good to Be Hated

BY LOUIS H. VALBRACHT

Pastor of St. John's Lutheran Church, Zanesville, Ohio

TEXT: *Marvel not, my brethren, if the world hate you.*
I JOHN 3:13

RECENTLY I read a story about the early American frontier. The incident concerned a missionary preacher who had come to a certain section of the frontier to convert the Indians to Christianity. The old frontiersmen in the area discouraged him. The Indians were on the warpath, and they felt that for the time being no white man could deal with them. There was going to be a bitter fight before long. They would all be in it.

The missionary protested: "But I don't want to get into any fight. I love the Indians and I want them to love me." He had scarcely said the words when a shot rang out and a bullet ripped through the walls of the cabin in which he was standing. "I hate to disappoint you," said one grizzled old frontiersman, "but it seems you are in this fight whether you want to be or not." He handed the missionary a rifle.

138

"You go on lovin' 'em, but we'd better lick 'em or they'll never have a chance to love you."

Somehow this simple story is a rather precise illustration of where Christians must stand today. It is, indeed, an expression of what a Christian's attitude toward the world has had to be throughout the history of the church, and what it must be in this epochal day. At the outset we must recognize these undeniable facts: We are in a fight whether we want to be or not; we will have to fight most bitterly against some that we love most, and who we would like best to love us; that we will have to defeat our enemies if we are ever going to bring them to Christ.

We must in addition explode forever a few ridiculous, naive misconceptions concerning the church: that the church is a benign little organization which flits through the world like a maypole dancer on the green, waving an olive branch wherever it goes; that the church is at peace with the world; that since it requires no strength and courage to be a Christian, the church is an institution to be made up largely of feeble, aged persons and little children; that if you are a good Christian everyone will love you dearly; that the church should be a "popular institution."

If these things are characteristic of our attitude concerning the church, then we are making the fatal mistake which was made by the heroine in one of Ibsen's plays. At the beginning of the drama we see this woman come into the room filled with people and she gushes upon them: "I love you all, and you are all my very dearest friends." But events of the play reveal that which she never suspected—that everyone seated there in one way or another was her bitter enemy.

For a few decades now we have been laboring under the very foolish notion that the world has opened wide its arms to Christianity, that wherever the church goes it is met by instant approval and help and friendship. The time is now at hand when we need to be blasted from our comfortable complacency and open our eyes to recognize that, whether we like it or not, we are in for a fight, and that the world, strangely enough, does not love us, but hates us bitterly.

So here it is, a strange paradox; and yet it could not be more clear. John is writing concerning our love for our brethren in the world. He is spending nearly an entire chapter of his epistle showing how our love for the children of the world is the true measure of our Christian faith. But in the very midst of the chapter he makes this shattering statement: "Marvel not, my brethren, if the world hate you."

He has just referred to an incident which shows that the situation has been in existence since the beginning of time.

"You remember," John tells us, "how Cain hated his brother Abel, and how he murdered him." Why did he hate him? Why did he murder him? Because his own works were evil and his brother's were righteous. So, says John, "Don't be surprised if the world hates you." The unrighteous of the world will always hate the righteous for their righteousness.

It would seem that ever since the birth of the church men have been making a mistake about it. The disciples of Our Lord made it. They had wonderful illusions about His kingdom. It was to be established on earth with invincible power and great glory. The world would inevitably share a common allegiance to Christ and, since he would rule invincibly, there would be complete peace, concord, and justice throughout the world.

Our Lord did his utmost to disillusion them. Again and again he assured them of the hatred of the world: "Think you that I came to bring peace to the world? I tell you verily not peace, but a sword."

But they were happy, complacent. They didn't believe that anyone could really hate them. And so it all came as a horrible shock. They saw the mutilated body of their Messiah, dripping its blood from the cross on Golgotha. Someone actually hated them! So, bewildered, frightened, they ran and hid until driven into battle by the power of the Holy Spirit, each of them in turn to give his own life in the conflict.

Saint Paul constantly warned the members of the early church: "Put on the whole armor of God, that ye may be able to stand in the evil day." Yet today we are endeavoring to make a young ladies' finishing school out of the church of Jesus Christ. Some men put it quite bluntly that they feel that the task of the church is a job for women. Well, maybe it is. Maybe men don't have enough strength and stomach for the job any more.

When Christ chose his disciples he chose twelve men, men of rugged strength and endurance. What of today? In every church group there is a larger percentage of women in the membership. The percentages run from 85 men to every 100 women down to the shocking figure in one denomination of 3 men to every 100 women. We may sing lustily "Onward Christian Soldiers," but it begins to look like a petticoat army.

If the church has no enemies, as some believe, then we had better make some.

If we have no enemies, then we have probably gone over to the enemy's side.

If we have no battle, then we have probably already surrendered.

If men do not hate us for what we preach, then we are not preaching the truth.

If men do not despise us for what we do, then we are not doing the right things.

Our Lord has told us that we should love our enemies. How can we do that if we don't have any? He took it for granted that we would acquire some. Many of us would like to live our lives in the sloppy sentiment of Edgar Guest: "I want to sit in the house by the side of the road and be a friend to man." The only way we can be a real friend to man is by fighting to bring him the saving gospel of Jesus Christ, and unfortunately we can't do that sitting in a house by the side of the road. Our Lord said, "Go! Into all the world."

May I suggest, however, that if we open our eyes to face the reality of things today we will not have to look far to find some fairly good enemies available. Only four years ago the people of the western world had locked in a lover's embrace the Soviet Union. Gaily we were knitting daisy chains, and twining them in each other's hair. A short time later, to our horror, our lover had turned out to be an unfaithful harlot. But still we were naive enough to believe that she still loved us.

So, desperately in this interim we have been trying to

reconcile two fundamental philosophies. We have been trying to find a compromise between two absolutes. The one said: "I am the Lord, thy God. Thou shalt have no other Gods before me." The other said, in the words of Stalin, its leader: "Lenin is God." The one said, "Thou shalt not take the name of the Lord thy God in vain." The other said, in the words of Beboshnic, "The very first and vilest moonshiner was named Jesus Christ." The one said: "Remember the Sabbath Day to keep it holy." The other said, in the words of Soviet law: "The Sabbath and Sunday are to be suppressed."

The one said: "Honor thy father and thy mother." The other said, in the words of Lenin: "Children must be taught to hate their parents." The one said: "Thou shalt not kill." The other said, in the words of Stalin: "The dictatorship must be a government resting directly upon violence." The one said: "Thou shalt not steal." The other said, in the words of Stalin: "All means are justified." The one said: "Thou shalt not bear false witness." The other said, in the words of Lenin: "Adopt all tricks, dodges, and illegal methods of concealing the truth."

Need I go on? This, then, was our great, friendly ally with whom we were going to be wed in the bonds of inseparable peace. We were going somehow to smooth out the difficulties and differences between these two violently antagonistic philosophies.

A former Chief Justice of our Supreme Court used to say: "There is only one sin worse than being hardhearted, and that is being soft-headed." It would well seem that we have been guilty of the greater sin.

Our forefathers in the church of the Reformation fought,

bled, and died through the Thirty Years' War, the longest war in history. They endured the terror of the Inquisition and the loss of every earthly thing that they might salvage the truth of evangelical Christianity from the corruption under which it had been buried by the vile hierarchy of the Roman Church. Yet today we are willing to hand all that our fathers fought for back to Rome.

We say: Catholics are such fine, earnest people, so faithful to their dogma, so conscientious in their worship, that certainly they could mean no harm, and we should do everything to assist them in that which they are endeavoring to do—take over the government of the world, political, economic, and ecclesiastical, and put it directly into the hands of the Holy Papa in Rome; take the treasure of the world and pour it into the plush-lined pockets of the Roman Court; take the truth of the gospel of Jesus Christ and water it down with the sewage of ignorance, suspicion, and fear!

At least some are awakening. The Presbyterians, belonging to the World Alliance of Reformed Churches, meeting at Buck Hill, Pennsylvania, expressed alarm at the growing political and ecclesiastical despotism evident in the United States. The points recognized as outlined by "The New York Times" were: 1) The effort of the Roman Church through its partisan legislators to get $300,000,000 diverted from the United States Treasury for the expansion of the Roman parochial school system; 2) the situation in New Mexico where the Roman Church was running the public schools, the classes were taught by garbed priests and nuns, and attendance at mass by all students, Roman or otherwise, was obligatory; 3) the banning of certain reputable national periodicals from the public school libraries because they had in one issue contained some unpleasant truth concerning the Roman Church; 4) the systematic persecution of Protestant Christians in Spain, Mexico, and South America; 5) the efforts of Roman statesmen to get recognition diplomatically for Fascist Spain.

Yet they mean us no harm. They are our dear friends and our fellow Christians. When will we be shaken from our Pollyannaism long enough to realize that we are dealing not with a group of well-meaning, conscientious people whom we meet from day to day in our neighborhood, but with a world conspiracy conceived and conducted by a powerful international hierarchy of despots!

Oh, we may have others in the world who should hate us. The materialists, those who would make the people of the church believe that their life and happiness rest upon their bed and their belly and their body.

The secularist who infringes more and more upon any hold that Christ might have on the life of his people. Apparent to all is the constant desecration of the Lord's Day.

We might find fairly good enemies in the administration and faculties of some of our educational institutions. Many of them are teaching a life philosophy which, they say, can be learned through the microscope, telescope, or in the bubbling test tubes of the chemical laboratory. For them the problems of life can be solved through the simple expedient of an interview with a psychiatrist.

A pretty good array, isn't it? Are they hating us? They had better be! We had better be doing something to hurt and destroy their causes so that they do hate and despise us, and find in us a dangerous adversary. If we are the army of the Lord, it is time we went into active duty. Too long our weapons have been stored in moth balls. Let us use them—the girdle of truth, the sword of the Holy Spirit, the helmet of salvation. Let's get into the fight.

What is our defense against all of these enemies? There is an old axiom from the military field and on the athletic field that seems to be applicable, that "the best defense is a good offense."

We have the program. Our greatest need is a consecrated devotion to that program. The evangelical gospel must be preached with uncompromising vigor. We must pursue our efforts in evangelism with a fanatical (are we afraid of that word?) zeal. We must use every means at our hands to hurt and destroy the causes of those who are pitted against us. And all this must be done in the dominant spirit of love, a love so great toward God and fellow man that it will not shrink before any foe.

And so, on with the battle! And then, "Marvel not, my brethren, if the world hate you."

—from PULPIT DIGEST *for September, 1950*

New Lives for Old

BY JOHN OLIVER NELSON

Director of Religious Field Work and Associate Professor of Christian Vocation, The Divinity School, Yale University

TEXT: *If any man be in Christ, he is a new creature.*
II COR. 5:17

THIS WEEK we take down the old calendar and put up the new. We cancel the old lease and draw up another. We start off with new officers and committees, new budgets, new laws—and new hopes. And millions of people profoundly wish this week that they were starting off the year with new lives—new attitudes, new abilities, new friends, new relationships of every kind.

When we hail each other with "Happy New Year," often we mean to wish each other at least a *new* New Year— something fresh and exciting, unprecedented, creative.

Yet the fact is, of course, that for the vast majority of human beings this new year promises little they have not experienced before. In the gloomy words of Ecclesiastes they shrug that "There is nothing new under the sun." Or

147

in the characteristic cynicism of our own time they repeat the wry proverb: "Blessed is he that expecteth nothing, for he shall not be disappointed."

I recall vividly watching an earnest woman evangelist speaking to a group of lounging park-bench hearers in a downtown square, telling them of the remarkable experience of God which had revolutionized her life. As my eye traveled from face to face each man was saying as plainly as though he had shouted it: "New life? What you say really never happened to you; it's impossible. We know. Things like that don't go on in a world like this. You're mistaken . . ."

So in spite of the hilarity and abandon which has become typical of America's welcoming of the New Year, few really believe that it is new, that there is any actual change of situation. Life, they know, will go on as usual—the same old buildings, the same old amusements and neighbors and weather and taxes, and the same old lives.

Historically, it was in just such an atmosphere that the movement of Christianity began. Greek philosophy had long been saying that there is really nothing new: all comes and goes in cycles, time and reality and history slowly turning again and again the identical facets as the years and ages pass. That stern Roman god of the new year, Janus (from whose name January comes) was able to look both ways at once as he stood on the threshold of time, but he obviously did not expect to see anything new, nor was he able to help the Roman civilization produce anything essentially new. The idea of creativeness in history, of progress upward, was something of which the ancient world was stoically, stolidly unaware.

One Hebrew national leader who shared that general view, despite the noble tradition of his people, was Nicodemus, a man who was astounded when Jesus of Nazareth talked of a person's being *"born again."* A tax collector named Zacchaeus, a dwarfish little man who probably had long ago decided that not much change could be made in him, was remade one day when Jesus came to dinner with him. A tough-minded, many-times-divorced lady whom the Master met at a well one day discovered that she could yet start right living all over again with the new power he gave her. Many hundreds, who sincerely believed that Jesus Christ could make them over, were cured—of blindness, of leprosy, of paralysis, of self-defeating distrust and anxiety.

It remained for one of the ablest whom Christ remade in that generation, the Apostle Paul, to declare from his own experience: "If any man be in Christ, he is a new creature" —or, as a good variant translation has it, "a new creation." Here, Paul said, God began all over again with a person, creating a brand-new life in Christ.

What took place, as this process was again and again realized in actual lives, was that there appeared an actually new force in world history.

First there were colonials and slaves, merchants and tentmakers and sailors and guardsmen. Then there were houses packed with listeners as the claims of Christ were preached. Then the Christian movement rose from the catacombs and the Roman martyrs' arena to claim all Western culture.

Here were people who never took it for granted that "nothing really changes": they declared that everything changes, once God gets hold of it. With them the typical Western idea of progress began to spread, an optimistic, living demand that Almighty God is working out a purpose in the world, through ordinary Christians who have been reborn in His divine intention.

Thus where ancient civilization had looked at the barbarians, and decided that although they might be militarized they could surely never be taught and transformed, Christianity proclaimed that these hordes might yet be reclaimed as people.

The fresh, devoted life of the monasteries worked along through centuries of slow rebirth. Even in epochs when few so-called Christians were actually made new by the Gospel, that leaven was at work. But, gathering its strength, the Christian movement in the Reformation and counter-Reformation showed dramatically that it could rekindle vast creative forces in an old civilization. Again in a later century, nation-wide revival in Great Britain sprang from one man's heart-warming experience of being reborn spiritually, to sway the destiny of the world.

Then began the renewal of other people around the globe, as the world-wide missionary movement reached out with this same Gospel. Individual lives, whole towns and nations, were recast into new molds of custom and attitude and freedom.

You may remember, for instance, that in 1833 the great scientist Charles Darwin visited Tierra del Fuego and found its people bestial and crude almost beyond description. Thirty-six years later he revisited the island to discover these same people with an entirely new culture, gentle, literate, and hospitable. Darwin in some amazement sent off twenty-five pounds to the London Missionary Society, and asked that he might be enrolled as an honorary member. Here were people on this remote savage island who had not been just educated: they had been made over into new beings by Christianity.

A great many people who are familiar with that age-old story of Christian rebirth among persons and nations, however, wonder whether such renewal is possible today.

Like the philosophies of the ancient world, or the skeptical hearers of an evangelical story of conversion, millions of Americans do not see that sort of Christian history being made today. Is it happening at revival services? Or just in faraway lands? Or in rescue missions for down-and-outs? Wherever such rebirth is to be found, we seem to see it seldom if ever among our own friends. Can Almighty God take this new year and within it make *us* new persons? It seems unlikely to most people.

Yet, there is a man who last year found the power of God to give up drinking and promised to give God the four dollars a day his alcoholism had been costing him: he is a new man right now, acting differently, feeling differently, thinking differently because he has found Christ.

There is a woman in Chicago who had suffered many things of many psychiatrists without a cure, whose tragic neurotic troubles have within the past six months actually disappeared as she has progressively learned to pray: that is rebirth.

There is a youth in college who thought communism held the whole promise of a brighter day for humanity until someone last year showed him the nobility and message of Our Lord: today he is relaxed, radiant, powerful, planning to be a foreign missionary.

More, there is a church which two years ago was dejected,

discouraged, lifeless—until two people in it began to pray for the Spirit of God: their little group has taken new life, leading to phenomenal growth of the congregation, calling of a pastor, and great new power in that community.

What is the secret of such rebirth, in our own day as in the past centuries of the Church? It is that persons—and thus the Church itself—be "in Christ."

That means for one thing being "in his frame of mind," seeing people and problems and possibilities as Our Lord sees them. We shall have to steep ourselves in the Old and New Testaments this year if we are indeed to share Jesus' viewpoint and to that extent be "in Christ." We shall have to discipline ourselves with obedience to his requirements, seek deeper insight by prayer, discover within the Christian community itself what is involved in living the Christian life today.

But again, being "in Christ" means living "in his grace" —trusting him, believing in him, accepting him, finding security and power in him, being released from guilt and morbidness and fear through his power.

An old woman's definition of faith was this: "It's taking God at His word."

To be "in Christ" is to be deciding, day by day, that his promises and his power for our lives are genuine and constantly available. The renewal which comes about when we are "in Christ" by his grace is the same revolutionary activity within the human personality that it has always been in Christian experience.

Now of course I am not saying that such rebirth of persons and churches and civilizations takes place all at once. There is nothing Cinderella-like about it, suddenly transforming life at the stroke of midnight—or even here and now at the threshold of a new year. So I am not asking you here today to seek renewal for your lives all in this first week of the new calendar.

Rather, I am declaring again Paul's great word: "If any man be in Christ, he is a new creature"—and assuring you earnestly that God does and can make new from old in this year ahead. I am saying that we may well walk into the new year expecting great things of God, reassured that He does still deal in revolutionary ways with life which is yielded to Him.

Possibly God will speak or act *suddenly* in your life or mine this year to freshen and rekindle our spiritual selves. He is as able to work swiftly as He has been in the experience of the apostles and saints and reformers. As we may be swept by a great Christian impulse in these days and months ahead, let us not say: "This cannot be God reaching out to me: God doesn't deal with people thus nowadays!" Rather, be assured that God may have some great new intention for you this year, and expect His power in your life.

Or it may be that your being recreated into a new person in Christ is a *gradual* process, each part of you being quietly and successively remade through his indwelling Spirit. Just as the human body is gradually renewed all the time, until within a few years it is entirely replaced, so our becoming new creatures by his working may be a gradual development in grace—what the Reformation called Sanctification. That too is rebirth.

Whatever the process of renewal of any life, one fact remains unchanged: we do not achieve new lives without handing over our old ones. Paul says: "he is a new creature"

—the same person in whom the process is begun becomes new. God does not make a new life out of just some part of our old life: we must hand over the whole of it if the renewal is to be complete. If we are to receive new lives for old, the old must be fully presented.

This means, at the year's end and year's beginning, that God wants you and me to hand over *all* that we are and have been, so that He may remake it all for His purposes. We are to hand over all the memories of what we have been, or failed to be. We are to hand over all our powers as we now have them—not just some of our abilities and time, but *all*. We are to hand over the plans which we ourselves have thought up for this new year, asking that He remold and shape them according to His will. If you and I are to have new lives in this coming year, we must yield to God all that we are, of sin and pride and indifference and selfishness, so that in the power of Christ these may be transmuted into that which He would have us be.

Is the claim of renewal in the Gospel out of date or ineffective today, as we look forward, as through a glass darkly, into the year ahead? The fact is still this: "If any man be in Christ, he is a new creature"—making a new family, a new community, and a new world in the power of God. To give over our old lives and the old year, in out-and-out dedication to Christ, can make this year the first year of the Kingdom of God in our lives.

—*from* PULPIT DIGEST *for December, 1948*

The Christian's

Marching Orders

BY R. P. MARSHALL

*Pastor of St. John's Methodist Church,
Sunbury, Pennsylvania*

AN OPPONENT of foreign missions once asked the
Duke of Wellington his opinion of the need of missionaries. The gruff old soldier replied by a question: "Sir," said
he, "what are your marching orders?"

That is the question every Christian must face. Behind
it, all considerations of convenience and expediency fade
away into insignificance. Are we discouraged when war
sweeps away the work of a hundred years of missionary
endeavor? Do we ask "What's the use?" when a nation
such as Germany turns her back upon Christianity and
worships the gods of war and blood; when we look upon
the destruction wrought by so-called Christian nations,
and the seeming failure of our long years of missionary
endeavor?

The answer comes again: "What are your marching
orders?"

155

Well, what are they? Listen to the words of the risen Lord as he speaks to his disciples in the Upper Room. "Go," he said, "and make disciples of all nations, baptizing them in the name of the Father, Son, and Holy Ghost, teaching them whatsoever I have commanded you."

He did not say that the task would be easy, or that it would be soon accomplished. He did not set any time limit to their activity. Their task was to obey orders; their privilege to know that they were doing so; their reward, the constant presence of their Leader.

It is significant that Jesus prefaced his command with the statement: "All power is given unto me in heaven and in earth; *therefore, go ye . . .*" It is because of the fact that our Leader possesses all power that he gives us orders. It would be possible for him to bring the world to his feet without our help, but he does not intend to do so. We have a part in the redemption of the world; we are messengers, his priests, and his teachers.

A friend of mine was traveling through the wilds of Alaska. Cold and weary, he came at last upon a little settlement where a mission school and church ministered to the natives. "What are you doing in this out-of-the-way spot?" he asked the missionary, as he noted his evident culture and education. What a pity, he thought, that such a man should be wasted in a place like this!

But the missionary said with a smile, "Here I was sent, and here I shall remain until I die, or until I am given further orders."

"But it's so hopeless here. You haven't made many converts in all these years, and the results seem small."

"Results are not my business," answered the missionary. "I leave results to God. My job is to do my best at the task he has set me. It may take fifty years; it may take five hundred. Who knows? But the Church has plenty of time. Some day the results will come."

That is the spirit of consecrated missions. It is far removed from our clamor for statistics and our worship of numbers, but it is according to the teaching of Jesus. All power is his; the task is ours.

Despite the slowness, results do come. That incident happened many years ago. Today a flourishing mission station stands in the midst of a growing settlement. The boys and girls educated in that school are now teaching other children; the Church is winning in its long fight against sin.

The missionaries who went out into the wilds of Borneo fifty years ago may have wondered if their sacrifice was in vain, but not long ago I read a letter from a native preacher whose grandfather was a cannibal. Our soldiers in the Pacific paid tribute to the missionaries who had gone before and who left a Christian people where once were only savages.

"Make disciples," said the Master. What did he mean? Only this: that they should gather around them those men and women who would follow him. They might not be strong in the faith—neither was Peter. They might not always exercise good judgment—neither did James and John. They might turn out to be traitors—like Judas. But they would, at least, begin the journey.

It is not our task to convert people; that is God's work. We cannot undertake to remake their lives completely; that is the task of the Holy Spirit. Sometimes the Church has undertaken to bar the door to those who do not measure up to certain standards of doctrine, but Jesus did not set us as doorkeepers. He is the Door. The Church is not a group of wholly sanctified saints: it is, as Wesley said, a company of men among whom the pure word of God is preached and the Sacraments duly administered. It is composed of those who are seeking to be saints.

Jesus' second injunction is followed by the provision for the first act of ritual, the introductory sacrament of baptism. "Baptize them," he directs, "in the name of the Father, the Son, and the Holy Ghost." Baptism is an outward sign of an inward process. By baptism we are signed on in God's army, and thus it is a sacrament which cannot be neglected without serious consequences.

Baptism is the sign of a good conscience toward God, said Paul. Because of this, the act of baptism calls for a twofold interpretation. The candidate expresses, by his submission to the rite, his faith in Christ as his Saviour. This is man's part. But there is also the supernatural element by which grace is given to the baptized soul, grace which can only be received by faith.

Not only were the disciples enjoined to baptize, but they were ordered to teach. In this task all of the functions of the Church are compressed, for teaching includes preaching, administration, and instruction. Even the Sacraments are means of teaching as well as of grace.

It has been the fashion to decry doctrinal preaching. As a result many preachers have attempted to warm the heart and stir the emotions of the congregation, without sufficient basis of sound doctrine. There is, of course, an element of enjoyment in listening to a good sermon, as there is in listening to fine music or in looking at a work of art. But interesting and enjoyable preaching is not always intelligent preaching, and the sermon which pleases the crowd does not always edify it. Ignorance of sound doctrine has led thousands of Church people astray. The wildest teaching of self-styled prophets finds acceptance by good people who have no idea that much of such teaching is contrary to the Word of God.

We ministers should not blame our people for running off after wildfire if we fail to feed them on the word of God. Look at the advertisements of the cults and you will see that they are proposing to answer questions which come to all earnest Christians. If we will not give answers, our people will go to those who do.

Someone has said that the reason Easter services are so popular is that only on Easter morning do the preachers grapple with the problem of all problems: "After death, what?"

"How can a man be born again?" asked Nicodemus. Jesus did not put him off with a learned discourse on how to solve the problems of the world; he told him in specific terms what to do. But Nicodemus was not the first, nor yet the last, to ask that question. Our churches are full of men and women who want to know how to live the Christian life. They may not have the opportunity to grapple with the problem of international affairs, but they must face each day the problem of how to live.

The task of teaching is a never-ending one, and the man who feels called to it can never relax in the comfortable feeling that his job is done. It is no wonder that, of all so-called professional men, the minister is often the least willing to stop work. Why should it not be so? Can he ever say to himself: "There are no more souls to save, no more children to instruct, no more sorrowing ones to console?"

In a certain city there stands a once-beautiful church building on a corner of a downtown street. Windowless and desolate, it now does duty as a garage, and no one who passes can fail to feel the sacrilege. Better perhaps that it should fall into decay or be torn down than that it should stand dishonored before the world. So it is with the minister who once vowed to carry the gospel message, but who ends his days as a seller of insurance or a so-called "business man." What greater business has a man than that of proclaiming the gospel?

"Lo, I am with you always," said Jesus, "even unto the end of the age." And by those words he made persecution light, and death a sacrament. A new translation gives fresh meaning to those words: "Lo, I am with you *all the days*." We can see what that means. "All the days" includes the Blue Mondays, the discouraging Sundays when the "faithful" are unfaithful, the dark days and the bright, the hours of suffering and the moments of glory. He has not merely promised to come to our aid when we are in trouble; he has said that he will stay by our side as long as life shall last. In the words of Andrew Blackwood: "The promise is as up-to-date as the morning newspaper."

But this promise was not given only to the ministers. It is yours, as well as ours, for all are commissioned to carry the Gospel to every creature. *You* are his messengers, his priests, his evangelists.

When we consider these words we see that our marching orders come, not only from the Christ of history, or the

Christ of prophecy, but from the Christ of every day. It is a present call for a present service. The task is hard, the way is long, but the reward is sure; and, by our side, in the midst of danger, blood, sweat, and tears, walks Jesus— the Risen Lord, the Triumphant King, the Christ of every road.

—from PULPIT DIGEST *for January, 1948*

Bread and Brotherhood

BY JOHN G. CLARK

Pastor of First Baptist Church, Pulaski, Virginia

TEXT: *If I have eaten my morsel alone.*—JOB 31:17

THE AUTHOR of the Book of Job attempted to deal with the problem of evil. Until then the usual way of explaining suffering and evil was that they befell a man who had sinned, that they were the just consequences of wrong behavior. Job's comforters—who turned out not to be very comforting—tried to get Job to admit that he had sinned. This would have explained the loss of all his property, the death of his family, and the disease that afflicted him. Job stubbornly denied sinning. In the thirty-first chapter he answers his so-called comforters by saying that if he had done the things of which he was accused, then he could be justly punished.

Strangely enough, one of the sins that he lists is that of eating alone.

For us in the western world today, where eating has neither the ceremony nor significance it had in Job's day,

162

we are puzzled when Job seemed so concerned about eating alone. The dining table for us is another filling station. Eating is a matter of stuffing our stomachs, and we do it as dispassionately as a man has his gas tank refilled.

But to the oriental mind in the day of Job, *bread was sacramental.* I do not mean in the sense of any religious dogma, but in the sense that bread was more than just bread.

In the first place, bread was sacramental because man did not get it by himself. It was grown. Growing grain was a cooperative venture between man and God, the Lord of creation. In our day, especially those of us who live in towns or cities, we are likely to think that everything, including food, is made by machines. But it isn't. It never was.

> Back of the loaf is the snowy flour,
> And back of the flour the mill,
> And back of the mill is the wheat and the shower
> And the sun and the Father's will.

Bread is sacramental, too, because it is a social product. If Job had been a peasant, which he was not, he still would have been dependent on others. What was it that protected his fields, his vineyards, and his herds from marauders, from the pillaging of thieves? The community. Who was it that planted and harvested the grain? Who was it that prepared and served his bread? Others, on whom he was as dependent as we are. Food is a social product even more in our own day. When you buy a bag of flour or a loaf of bread, ten thousand hands and more have had something to do with it, from a grain of wheat to the flour or bread.

This reminds me of an incident that happened to a missionary to Africa shortly after his arrival on the field. He was on an expedition through the country with an old native who had been associated with the mission for some years. They stopped for rest at noon, after a long morning on the trail. Mr. McDowell, full of American vim and vigor, ate his lunch in a hurry and began chafing over his companion's delay. Meanwhile, the old African continued blandly eating his meal with full deliberation. "Have patience," he pleaded. Do not ask me to hurry. Don't you see I am eating my wife?"

To the young man fresh on the field that remark had an ominous sound. He looked apprehensively at the old man, wondering if perhaps his religion was only skin deep, after all. An explanation was soon forthcoming. "My wife fixed this lunch for me. She spent her time and her strength upon it. Part of her love and her life went into it. Do you want me to gulp it down with no thought or respect for her?"

You remember David at the cave of Abdullam. Word came to him that the enemy had taken possession of Bethlehem. Bethlehem! There swept over him a surge of homesickness at the very word. He could close his eyes and see the city of his youth. He could hear voices long since forgotten. He could see the crowd gathered at sunset about the curb of the well by the city gate. Hardly knowing that he spoke aloud, he sighed: "Oh that I might have a drink of the water of the well that is by that gate of Bethlehem!"

Next day three of his devoted followers brought to him a cup filled with the water. It was, they explained, water from the well of which he had spoken. Over the hills they had gone the night before, weary and dangerous miles. Through the lines of the enemy they had crept, where capture would have meant instant death; and then back. Three lives risked gladly, and without a murmur, for the joy of satisfying the whim of a leader they loved.

When the truth dawned on him, he was almost speechless with humility. Tears must have filled his eyes as he looked down into the cup. He shook his head. "I cannot drink it!" he exclaimed. "It is the blood of three men. It is too sacred just to drink." And he poured it out on the sand as an offering of gratitude to Almighty God.

Every day you and I eat the bodies and drink the blood of men and women who have spent their strength that we might have the means of life. The words of Our Lord come to my mind: "This is my body broken for you." In this sense bread is a sacrament.

Job also felt guilty if he had eaten alone because he recognized that brotherhood is not just an idea. Brotherhood is an experience that is real, and *it has an economic basis*. Food is a symbol of all the material things that a man needs to live, including clothing and shelter. That's why Job said in the verses immediately following the text: "If I have seen any perish for want of clothing, or any poor without covering; if his loins have not blessed me, and if he were not warmed with the fleece of my sheep . . . then let mine arm fall from my shoulder blade, and mine arm be broken from the bone." It was incongruous to Job that he should enjoy the blessings of life while others were destitute.

Food is the basic requirement in living. It is not surprising to read that out in Texas where men have used up the reservoir of water underground for crop irrigation, a barrel of water brings more than a barrel of oil. Before man needs oil he needs water and food. The first request for material things in the Lord's prayer is for bread: "Give us this day our daily bread." "Whenever we pray, 'give us this day our daily bread,' " says Dr. E. M. Poteat, "we give assent to one of the major premises on which social life must rest . . . Sharing the physical goods of the earth is as mandatory upon the Christian as preaching the gospel. It is, indeed, properly understood as a part of it."

Jesus so identified himself with the needs of men that he could say: "Inasmuch as you did it unto one of the least of these, you did it unto me." In fact, as presented in the closing chapters of Matthew, this was the test of whether men were his disciples.

There are those today who hastily condemn the Russian experiment in communal living. It hasn't succeeded, and it is wrong. But it is not wrong because it says that there must be an economic basis for life, that all men must have the necessities of living. It is wrong because they think that man can live by bread alone. However, they are no more in error than those who think that you can have brotherhood without any attention or concern about the elemental needs of man. The Kingdom of God is more than a concept. It is not just a Sunday fellowship. Brotherhood is that which men are able to create and achieve in daily intercourse with one another. If it is true that man does not live by bread alone, it is equally true that he must have bread.

One other thing troubled Job about eating alone, that is, *that eating together is the highest expression of fellowship.* So much was this true in Job's day that the host was obligated to protect the guest for twenty-four hours after he had eaten a meal. Eating together today is the highest expression of fellowship. Whenever we wish to honor our friends we invite them to a meal.

Yet just as it is the finest gesture of friendship, it is likewise the surest social stigma to eat with the wrong people. Every generation of people everywhere, I suppose, has its social outcasts.

They had them in Jesus' day, and one of the social sins that he committed was to eat with them. Poor Jesus! He was blacklisted as readily as you or I would be if we ate with the wrong people. Thus they said of Jesus: "He eats with publicans and sinners." He not only disgraced himself, but he in turn became an outcast.

The test of brotherhood is eating together. Thus on the last night of Jesus' earthly life when he had finished the meal of the annual Passover Feast, whether by forethought or the inspiration of the moment, he took some of the unleavened bread and the wine and gave it to the disciples saying: "as oft as you eat the bread and drink the cup, do it in remembrance of me." It is not accidental that one of the first occasions when Jesus was recognized after the resurrection was when two men invited a stranger to supper only to discover "in the breaking of bread" that the stranger was the risen Christ.

The early followers of Jesus understood it to mean that when they ate together they were to remember him, and they did. For a long while the Lord's supper was a regular meal, as Paul tells us in his letter to the Corinthians. Not until churches outgrew the households in which they first met, and the size of the group made it impractical, did they substitute the symbolic for the actual meal.

One of the ironic commentaries on the history of the

Christian Church is that the observance which Jesus in-
stituted to keep men together should become such a source
of division among us, so that today there are four or five of
the largest bodies of Christians who refuse to eat together
at the Lord's table, and who, in the name of Christ, exclude
all others. This is neither the time nor the place to discuss
the doctrinal differences that account for this division among
us. My point, however, is that Jesus said that the one place
above all places men should remember him was in the
breaking of bread. For it is here, as we all know, in the matter of eating bread, that men are either united or divided
with all the miserable consequences that result from such
division.

Jesus came into the world to create in men a sense of
community, and to redeem them from all the evil that pre-
vents their realizing it. Salvation is not just a vertical relationship, an affair between man and God. It is this. But it is
also a horizontal relationship, an affair between man and
the other men about him. The Kingdom of God is not a
man making his pilgrimage to the Holy City alone. It is a
social concept. The church is not a boarding house nor a
bus where men are accidentally brought together without
obligations to the other. The church is a community of men
and women who know themselves bound to God and to
each other, like-minded and mutually dedicated.

Whenever we pray the Lord's prayer, as we did this
morning, we are likely to think that Jesus gave this to his
disciples as a public prayer. On the contrary, Jesus told
them to pray the prayer in private. This makes it all the
more significant. Nowhere in the prayer is the personal pro-
noun used in the singular, but always in the plural: "Our

Father . . . our daily bread . . . our debts." When we pray
the Lord's prayer we stretch out our hands to others about
us as we make, not our individual, but our common supplication. To drop hands is to break faith. Nothing would
seem more pitiful than someone praying: "Give *me* this
day *my* daily bread," as if others about him had not the
same need for bread.

In olden times a Scottish village in the highlands always
kept a sentinel on watch lest an enemy take the people by
surprise. High up on the mountainside he kept watch. If
ever he saw the enemy, he would come to the hillside overlooking the village, and cupping his hands to his mouth,
cry: "Shoulders together!" At this signal all the men would
come together and stand as one man against a common
enemy. Would God that in our day we could discover the
sense of community that makes men brothers, that we could
feel the incongruity and sinfulness of eating alone, as Job
did. Then, and only then, may we expect him to be known
of us in the "breaking of bread."

—from Pulpit Digest for February, 1950

Patrons or Partners

BY FREDERICK M. MEEK

Pastor of Old South Church, Boston, Massachusetts

TEXTS: . . . *to disclose now through the Church the varied wisdom of God according to the eternal purpose which He has accomplished by Christ Jesus our Lord.*—EPHESIANS 3:9-11

Neither will I offer unto the Lord my God of that which costeth me nothing.—II SAMUEL 24:24

IN ONE of the annual reports of the Rockefeller Foundation the director suggested that the Foundation's supporters were either patrons or partners. And the hope was expressed that the patron attitude might become the partner experience.

Look with me this morning at this same choice, because during the week ahead we will be thinking of ourselves and the ongoing work of our Church. Are we patrons of Christ's Church or are we partners?

A patron is usually a person esteemed in the community, and known for his breadth of interests. He is sure that the institution or the cause of which he is a patron is a "good

170

thing." He makes his subscription or he buys his tickets, and the assumption is that he will permit the organization to profit by using his name publicly as a person who is interested. The patron usually is present at some one or more of the institution's meetings, or he attends "a performance" with his friends. It all makes a pleasant relationship between the patron and the cause, without complicating commitments, and with the patron determining the measure of his support. Meanwhile the hours of work and at times of sacrificial toil, which are part of the ongoing life of the institution, or which are involved in any preparation for "the performance," are little or none of the patron's concern or experience.

Here is our comparison. The increasing number of liberal Protestant people who assume that their relation to Christ's Church is akin to that of a patron is American Protestantism's greatest single weakness. Patrons are sure that the Church is "a good thing." They are willing to support the Church on the same basis and for the same "sensible" reasons that they and other people support other desirable institutions and performances. For the act of buying tickets, they substitute patronizing the collection plate or the subscription list. They imagine that they can even "lend their names" to the Church: "Oh yes, I belong to such and such a Church." The admission is made almost as if they thereby conferred distinction upon Christ and His Church, and upon the Creator God.

The patrons attend what is for them the public "performance," the public worship of God—if the music be inspiring, the sermon passable, and the seats cushioned! Ah!

but the meeting with God face to face in public worship with all its moving glory, with its particular perspective on right and wrong, on success and failure, with its disturbing realization that there is so much more than we have yet done, still waiting to be done for God's cause, all pass the patron by.

For his relationship is external, and he judges the public worship of God as if it were a meeting of men with men, concerned with matters wholly human, in an institution guided and directed by the same human patterns and values used in operating any other institution on Main Street. The attitude of mind and heart that makes a man act as if he were a patron of God and His Church keeps that man from ever understanding the meaning of God's purpose for him.

Let any man who has imagined that his casual self-directed support in time or by substance fulfills his obligation to God's cause heed these words spoken to Job:

"Where wast thou when I laid the foundations of the earth?

"Canst thou command the morning? Canst thou number the months?

"Canst thou bind the influence of the stars?

"Have the gates of death been opened unto thee?"

Is it possible to imagine that we can be the patrons of One Who speaks thus to men and nations? Do we imagine that even a generous gesture of personal attention, of time, of substance, fulfills our obligation to One upon Whom both we and our world depend for every breath we draw?

The Church is the fellowship of people who have determined to follow God's way—"the varied wisdom of God."

Thus the Church is God's human agent in Boston and in our civilization. You and I who are part of the fellowship are asked in the New Testament word "to disclose *now* through the Church, the varied wisdom of God, according to the eternal purpose which He has accomplished by Christ Jesus our Lord." In "disclosing the varied wisdom of God," we are asked to be partners with Him—not patrons of Him. And that is an amazing almost incredible relationship!

⚹ A partner brings himself and his resources—completely, and he commits his present and his future to the cause in which the partners share. The effort and work which the cause demands, sometimes requiring profound personal sacrifice, are literally his life. The achievement of the purpose of the cause depends upon him as a responsible partner in the work.

But see what this partnership of the Church is! Here is a partnership, a sharing with God in His concern for people (all the people), what they are and what they do, that there may be a better than human quality in it all. To share in God's caring for people, and in making known His wisdom for their lives and the life of a world, is both privilege and pain. The planned partnership is well called: "God & Sons, Inc."—God and ourselves, together doing His work.

The partnership's concern is building the Kingdom of God on earth with human material—an incredible undertaking. The work is accurately described as "human engineering," done under God's direction. Inasmuch as His is the blueprint and the plan, and His the raw material, earth, air, water, sea, minerals, why do men hesitate to follow His purpose and design? The more nearly we approximate His plan, the more satisfying and creative life is. When we attempt to create our own structure of life and of society by evading His purpose and turning our backs on the partnership, only disaster—and for us it will be extinction—can come.

The question then for each of us is this: Do we believe and understand that we must so live by His purpose? Do we feel that God's way really makes any difference to us men and our destiny? Have we found God's answer for our own life's living? Have we brought our lives under His scrutiny, honestly and without equivocation? Do we know in our own lives the moving tides of God's power and affection and forgiveness? If this is our firsthand experience or our desire, then we will want beyond anything else in the world to be His partners as He seeks to bring that experience at firsthand to others.

So there is work to do. There is work to be done by this Church in a partnership. The question is: How can the work be done? It requires two things. It requires life—the time and effort of people like you and me. And because we live in our kind of world, it requires money—yours and mine—and that too is life. For a dollar bill is simply minted life and effort put into an exchangeable form. The partners bring both themselves and their substance to the work of the Church—the making known "now of the varied wisdom of God."

But the people of the Church, living as they do in the midst of the pressures and mores of a secular society, almost inevitably have a secular-minded approach toward the support of the Church as it seeks to do its work. Here the patron attitude predominates. Within the week I have learned of one university that looks forward to raising ninety million dollars for its program, another university seeks twenty million dollars, a woman's college expects gifts of seven and a half million dollars, one of our academies anticipates raising three and a half million dollars. We do not regard those as exorbitant claims upon the generosity and the interest of our society.

Meanwhile the Church has every right to ask if the partners envision any comparable necessary generous support for the Church, the primary institution of society. For without that wisdom of God, the economics of society brings civil strife, the politics of society brings a deadly struggle for power, and the education of society can so easily bring self-destruction. But in general the man-envisioned and the man-directed plans for society receive the most generous support of life and substance, while the attempt to make known "the varied wisdom of God" and the Creator's purpose, is treated by the practical men of our society as worthy only of the residues of their support.

How could it be otherwise, when these same people have never scrutinized what they do from the point of view of God's all-empowering and commanding purpose? Consequently we Americans spend $1000 for national protection through the medium of war-making powers and devices for every $1.00 that we spend in supporting all the peace machinery in the world. Man's way in this present is violence. God's way is peace for a world family. But we do so little to strengthen the human agencies which labor to make God's way a possibility. Thus we become patrons of peace and partners of violence.

And the Christian Church in its broader effort to make "God's wisdom known" fares little better!

The President of "Editor and Publisher" recently compared two consecutive thirteen-year periods in American history—1920 to 1932 and 1933 to 1945, from the point of view of philanthropic contributions. Between these two thirteen-year periods we increased our spending for luxuries by fifty-eight billion dollars; beyond that we increased our tax outlays by fifty-one billion dollars; beyond that we increased our savings by one hundred and eighteen billion dollars, all in a time when we increased our national income by three hundred and eighteen billion dollars.

While this increase was building up, we *decreased* our gifts to the Churches and to Christian benevolences. In the 1940's, gifts to Church benevolences were 73% below the 1932 depression level. "The varied wisdom of God," presented to men on a world scale, finds us patrons, not partners. Last year we spent $2.00 on tobacco for each $1.00 given to our Churches and character building institutions; and approximately $8.00 on alcoholic beverages for each Church dollar; and in the last year for which figures are available, Americans spent $90,000,000 more on their pedigreed dogs than they give directly to the Christian Churches. Here I would refrain from commenting on the patron-partner relationships.

But look at this matter of partnership from the point of view of Church members. 618 members of the Second Baptist Church in Houston, Texas, last year gave $310,000 to their Church for its budget, of which some $85,000 went for the missionary enterprise. There is a Congregational Church in Greater Boston that gives well in excess of $100,-000 to the work of Christian Missions in each current year, apart from its current expenses.

I have an uneasy conscience because we Congregational-
ists rank seventeenth, below most of the major denominations, in our giving to the world work of Christianity—and
yet ours is the oldest mission board in the world. Our Episcopalian friends give double per capita what we do. United
Presbyterians give three times per capita what we do. In
the end it is all a matter of expressing our Christian concern for the Christian cause. It is a matter of what counts
most in the life scheme of liberal Christian people.

The fact is that you and I *will have to give* in this generation, in one way or another, of both life and money.

Governments ask and take billions of dollars and our
lives and the lives of our children that we may insure the
protection of our country. Governments ask and take billions of dollars for crime prevention and for the care of
delinquents and criminals. Our choice is between making
expenditures of money and of life under fear and compulsion in these areas, *or* of making comparable expenditures
for character building, Christian benevolence, and the work
of the Church. Support freely given for making the varied
wisdom of God known among the nations would provide
us with at least the chance to make unnecessary the giving
of limitless sums for the possible destruction of war, and
as the power of Christ's word reached out in society, because we empowered it by our money, it would alter the
character of many a man's life, even as it has made new
people of some of us. We have a choice. We can give in
one way or another—for the one cause or the other. But
give we will have to.

⋆ Is our giving an expression of a life that itself has been
given in partnership to God's cause and purpose?

Here in Old South Church we are working to fulfill our responsibility for God's cause in this community and far beyond. We minister to one thousand students and working young people, the largest active group of its kind in any Congregational Church in America. Here children and young people gather for Christian education, and the instruction given equals the standard of the best of the private schools in Greater Boston. Here men and women gather for Christian fellowship and service. Here men and women come from all over Boston that they may counsel with members of the staff. Some come seeking guidance for new life, some to be saved from despair, some have stories of bludgeoning by the circumstances of life that are incredible in their horror, some come seeking to know what God has to say to them in their circumstances.

Inevitably the question comes to us personally: what is my share? So often we say to ourselves: "I do not have enough to give this or to give that." Canon Peter Green once said that "enough is always a little more than you now have." Thus none of us ever really has "enough"! A "large" or a "small" gift has nothing to do with the size of the contribution that is given to support the work of our Church.

A "large" gift, and that alone represents a partnership, is always and only that gift into which some sacrificial strain enters. It may be 10¢ a week—it may be $100.00 a week! There are people in our Protestant Churches who give $5.00 to God's cause who should give $25.00 in the light of their responsibility. There are people who are congratulated as handsomely supporting the Church by a gift of $100.00 who in actuality should be giving $500.00.

Some give $500.00 who should assume the responsibility of the support of a member of the staff, or the support of a missionary, or the support of a hospital abroad as it ministers in Christ's name in our behalf. That is partnership.

A partnership differs from a patronship in that the patron gives as little or as much as he pleases, while in a partnership the need and the demands of the cause determine what the partner does.

There was a time when our forefathers (in a line going back to the Old Testament) observed the tithe—the act of partnership of giving ten percent of their income to God (the Giver of every good and perfect gift) and His cause. There are some who still follow the practice. But there are many who regard such a practice with wonderment and a sense of defeat, for they say: "We could not possibly afford any such giving of our substance to the cause of the Church and the benevolent enterprises of the community." And yet it is not an impossibility, because when any man says "I will pay my obligation to my God first," he introduces an entirely new standard of values and of discrimination into his life, so that the rest of his life's expenditures are made in the light of his partnership with God. And such a man finds that the unnecessary and the debatable and the wasteful expenditures are winnowed out, and almost automatically excluded, because the active partnership of working with his God gives him a different standard of what is important and necessary. It has been aptly said: "When part of one's income is consecrated, the rest is less likely to be spent for unconsecrated ends."

You and I are entrusted with varying amounts of money with which to meet the needs of our days. Each one of us determines by his choices how that substance is to be handled, and also the deeds that he believes to be *most* important. It is at this point that a story told of a light keeper on the mainland coast has relevance for us.

The light keeper had been given enough fuel to tend the light for a month.

Days passed, and there was a knock at his door. It was a woman pleading for fuel for her stove that her child might be warm. A father, living nearby, came asking for fuel for a lamp—enough for only a few hours that his boy might study. In such seemingly reasonable philanthropies, the light keeper from time to time parcelled out small fractions of his fuel.

Came a night when the light in the tower flickered and died. The fuel tank was empty. That night three ships missed the course of safety and one hundred lives were lost in the fury of the sea.

On the morrow the government agent came to inquire. The light keeper, grieved and distraught, told of parcelling out his fuel for pressing needs, all worthy in themselves.

But the answer was: "You were given one task above all others—to keep this light burning. Other demands were secondary to this. Your light went out, three ships went down, and more than a hundred persons were lost."

No amount of righteous philanthropy or spending, let alone the chronic money waste in our American society, excuses us from our neglect of making it possible that the Light of the World, God's wisdom, be seen. If we let that light go out, nations will go down, people will be lost.

This Church and what it can do in our generation are both in our keeping. This Church asks its people to share in its work as partners. As we do that, we become God's partners and fellow workers. And on this Sunday it asks that you and I sustain its growing work by empowering it with our lives and our money. The people of this Church in partnership should be matching by their gifts in this generation, the resources which this Church uses that come from gifts made by other generations.

If we believe that without God's way life ends in futility, if we believe that beyond all else God's way is our salvation, then, when during this week our chance comes to fulfill our partnership in this Church by our gifts, we will say: "I will not offer unto the Lord my God of that which costeth me nothing."

—*from* PULPIT DIGEST *for March, 1950*

Now Is the Time for Greatness

BY EDWARD HUGHES PRUDEN

Pastor of First Baptist Church, Washington, D.C.

TEXT: *Now is my soul troubled; and what shall I say? Father, save me from this hour? But for this cause came I to this hour. Father, glorify thy name.*—JOHN 12:27

AS WE VIEW the world scene around us today, we are reminded of the words of the poet, Arthur C. Coxe,

> "We are living, we are dwelling,
> In a grand and awful time."

But the poet was a man of faith, and refusing to be alarmed at what he saw, he continued his lines in a spirit of courage and confidence, when he added:

> "In an age on ages telling
> To be living is sublime."

Someone tells of an old Scottish highlander who went to church one night and heard a sermon on the greatness and expansiveness of the universe. The preacher had a great deal to say about the tremendous distances between the

182

various stars and planets and the general immensity of space. The old man was momentarily depressed by all he had heard, and as soon as the service was over he went out into the darkness and stood alone for quite a while looking up at the stars. A little later, as someone passed near him he heard the old man saying to himself, "I refuse to be astronomically intimidated."

And so in like manner the poet refused to be intimidated by the awe-inspiring nature of the time in which he lived. Instead of trying to run away from it all, he chose rather to believe that: "To be living is sublime."

Some of our present-day prophets have reached the same conclusion concerning the era in which *we* live. Herbert Agar gave to his popular book the title: "A Time for Greatness," and Dr. Harry Emerson Fosdick's recent book is entitled: "A Great Time to Be Alive." It is altogether possible that the era in which we live will go down in history as the era in which more gigantic events took place than any other single period in all the history of mankind. Among these things are the following: (1) The conquest of Italy; (2) the overthrow of Nazi Germany; (3) the utter defeat of Japan; (4) the emergence of Russia as a world power; (5) the discovery of the means by which atomic power can be harnessed and used; and the formation of the United Nations organization. Some months ago the papers were full of discussions as to what should be done with this new power which is now at our disposal, and one noted scientist, testifying before a Congressional Committee, declared that a raid during one night could destroy forty million people in the United States by the use of atomic bombs.

"We *are* living, and we *are* dwelling
In a grand and awful time."

And how shall we react to it? For guidance concerning this we turn instinctively to Him whose name we bear, for He too lived in "a grand and awful time." When only thirty-three years of age, He felt the pressure of growing opposition, and knew that His cruel death could not be far away. It was in that hour that He said, "Now is my soul troubled; and what shall I say? Father, save me from this hour? But for this cause came I to this hour. Father, glorify thy name."

Here is every evidence of a great struggle. On the one hand was the normal impulse to run away from it all; and on the other hand was a sense of destiny which He could not ignore. We know the outcome of that gigantic struggle. What then shall be the Christian's response to the challenge of grand and awful days? "Father, save us from this hour?" No, for it was for this very hour that we were created. Therefore, we say, "Father, glorify Thy name." Great days call for the same qualities of character which characterized the life of Jesus; faith, courage, sympathy and understanding, consecration and sacrifice.

Great days call for great faith. This statement may sound trite upon first hearing it, but it will seem far more profound if we pause to consider what faith really means. Too often we confuse faith with credulity, or a servile acceptance of ancient dogmas; or even a rather forced espousal of time-honored institutions. But faith means none of these things. Faith, in its New Testament sense, means that quality by which a man is sufficiently confident to act upon any idea. True faith is the result of experience.

Peter on the day of Pentecost could preach with great power, not because he was born into a Christian family, nor because he accepted without question ancient doctrines; Peter preached with power because he had had a vital experience with One whose friendship had transformed his whole life and which friendship he sincerely desired to share with others. Paul, going about on his missionary journeys, could stand up under terrific persecution, not because he had received the ordinances of the church, or had given merely mental assent to the doctrinal views of the early church, but because he too had had a tremendous experience with a great personality. When faith is the outgrowth of such experience it provides an inexhaustible supply of confidence and assurance.

It was this kind of faith which the old Negro Christian had who maintained such a calm and serene attitude toward all of life's annoying experiences that he was finally approached by one of his white friends and asked why he could be so confident when many others all around him were visibly disturbed. He replied: "I formed the habit several years ago of saying to myself every morning when I get out of bed, 'Ain't nothing going to come up today what me and the Lawd can't handle.' "

Great faith will compel us to do that spiritual pioneering today which is so seriously needed. The stupendous problems of our time require much more than a mere perpetuation of spiritual gains already made, even if such a static arrangement could be guaranteed. The confused multitudes of earth have a right to expect of the disciples of Christ to call to spiritual advance which alone holds any promise of a better day. For too long a restless, weary world has assumed that the adventurous spirits are invariably iconoclasts and the anti-religious. It is high time that we remind men by our actions that we represent one who was adventurous to an almost unique degree, and who pushed back spiritual frontiers in the face of terrific opposition and relentless ridicule. Faith forces us to follow in his train.

Great days not only require great faith, but great courage. We read in the New Testament that when the contemporaries of Peter and John noticed their boldness they "took knowledge of them that they had been with Jesus." This boldness which they possessed was not something which they had been *taught* but something which they had *caught*, for the courage of Jesus was utterly contagious.

Hanging over the mantel in my study is Hofmann's picture of the lad Jesus at twelve years of age in the temple at Jerusalem, talking to the doctors of the law, answering and asking questions. I have frequently been intrigued by the picture because it tells me not only a great deal about Christ but about those who were standing around Him there in the temple. There is on the faces of these elderly authorities in Israel a rather benign expression which seems to indicate that they were thinking of Christ in terms of what He might become as He would grow into manhood. I can imagine that they were thinking within themselves: "What a fine young Rabbi this boy is going to make. He has such a vivid imagination; such a scintillating personality; such a persuasive manner. We must see to it that he is called to one of our finest synagogues, for there he will fascinate large congregations with his brilliant messages. He will be highly honored in the community and live to a ripe old age to receive the esteem of all his fellow townsmen."

But surely these elderly Hebrews did not know the type of person with whom they were dealing, for already Jesus was beginning to demonstrate that courage which characterized His whole life. He refused to fit into the mold which they had prepared for Him. He was not at all inclined to drop to the level of the thinking of those all around Him; He rejected altogether the prejudices with which so many of His fellow countrymen were afflicted; and that was why He could say while standing in the very shadow of the cross, "For this cause came I into the world. Father, glorify thy name."

How much more effective Christians we would be if we possessed sufficient courage to put into operation the principles and ideals of Christ! There are explosive social situations all around us today and we are afraid to take even the *simple* Christian steps which might relieve these tensions. We demonstrated our courage during the years of global war; now we must demonstrate an equal courage in solving the multitudinous problems which must be solved if we are to maintain peace. We recall the scriptural observation to the effect that "He who ruleth his own tongue is greater than he who taketh a city"; which is just another way of saying that more strength is required to effect moral and spiritual changes than is required to overcome one's enemies on the field of battle.

Great days also require great sympathy and understanding. You recall the experience of the inspired writer in the Old Testament who said, "I went to those of the captivity and I sat where they sat." As we face the problems of international relationships, we must have this Christian quality of sympathetic understanding or we shall utterly lose the confidence of those who look to us for leadership in creating a peaceful atmosphere throughout the world.

Recently there was a Town Hall radio discussion of the problems connected with our relationship to Russia. The first speaker was entirely suspicious of all Russia has done and is doing, and refused to accept in good faith anything that was being said by present-day Russian leaders. He was so persuasive in his presentation of his particular slant upon the subject that one was almost convinced by his arguments. The next speaker, however, had lived in Russia for several years and he gave quite a different interpretation of recent developments in that country. He had sat where they sit, and his viewpoint was one of sympathetic understanding and appreciation. His approach to the difficulties involved will be far more productive of a cooperative approach to peace in Europe than a suspicious approach could ever be.

A magazine writer points out that we are hardly fair in making a blanket charge against all Germans who cooperated in any way with the Nazi party, for he reminds us that we too have an expression which indicates that we cooperate with certain individuals and groups when we are not altogether enthusiastic about doing so. He tells us that not infrequently we Americans say, "I preferred not having any part in the thing which has just been done but I had to *play ball* with the party to which I belong, or the group to which I am indebted." Suspicion and ill-will will never bring peace and security, but sympathy and *good*will may do much to preserve that peace for which our fellow countrymen laid down their lives.

Great days, too, call for great consecration. We know

that the future can never belong to those who approach
their task with a divided allegiance. Lukewarm, half-hearted
Christians will not be able to influence the world. We have
seen with what power our enemies attacked us while committed to evil ideologies and desires. The world is waiting
to see what will happen when Christians confront humanity
with equal consecration to the cause of Christ and His
church. We would be the last to admit that the philosophy
of the Nazis or the Japanese militarists can produce more
determination and perseverance than the philosophy upon
which our Christian faith is established; yet, we shall remain
on the defensive until we have offered a more convincing
proof of the Christian's willingness to endure all things for
the ultimate triumph of his ideals.

Someone tells of the first impressions made by Kagawa
on a tour of the United States several years ago. Two college students were walking across their campus after hearing the renowned Japanese Christian speak, and one of
them confessed that he was disappointed in the visitor's
message. After some reflection, the other student replied:
"I suppose it really doesn't matter very much what a man
says when he has lived as Kagawa has lived." A consecrated
life is more eloquent and convincing than any array of
arguments or any attempts at oratory. The world will not
accept the way of Christ because we can out talk our spiritual opponents, but only because we can out live them. Such
a demonstration of the superior quality of our faith will
verify our professions more readily than any other effort
in which we can engage.

And, finally, great days call for great sacrifice. Jesus knew
this and was prepared for it. In the Garden of Gethsemane

He uttered words which give us some insight into the vast amount of spiritual preparation which had gone into His conscious approach to the agonies of Calvary. His submission to the will of God and His willingness to sacrifice Himself for others was no isolated incident in His life but characteristic of His whole existence. We shall never make our supreme contribution to the world as a nation until we learn the art of sacrifice. We must learn to sacrifice our pride and prejudices; our sense of superiority over other people; our narrow nationalism and individualism; our self-centeredness and our preoccupation with merely local interests. The world will never be on the road to permanent peace until we are willing to sacrifice for peace as much as we have been willing to sacrifice for war.

We need to remember that Jesus became the world's Saviour not by conquering the world, nor subduing the world, nor by coercing the world, but by dying for the world. "Now is my soul troubled; and what shall I say? Father, save me from this hour? But for this cause came I to this hour. *Father, glorify thy name.*"

—*from* PULPIT DIGEST *for March, 1949*

Were You There When
They Crucified My Lord?

BY LOUIS J. KOVAR

*Pastor of Central Presbyterian Church,
Saint Paul, Minnesota*

THERE is an old Negro spiritual which has been running through my mind. It asks a very pointed question: "Were *you* there when they crucified my Lord?"

The thoughtless answer is *no*! How could anyone living today take part in something that happened at the Cross nineteen centuries ago? But there is a host of familiar faces about the Cross, and the old spiritual is insistent in its query, "*were* you there when they crucified my Lord?"

I behold Nicodemus. He was there in all his judicial pride. It is true that Nicodemus looked upon Jesus with divine respect: "Rabbi, we know that thou art a teacher come from God." Nicodemus neither raised his voice against Jesus nor did he oppose the Master, but he did not openly associate himself with the "Teacher come from God." Nicodemus was not ready to face the bitter winds of persecution and sacrifice that such an association might demand. Nicodemus had too much to lose: social status, political

191

position, economic privileges and academic respect. Consequently, Nicodemus stood by as Jesus was led forth to die. His was a passive part, but a real part. Yes, Nicodemus was there because of his pride when they crucified my Lord.

Do you ever allow pride to rule any part of your life? Pride often destroys the very thing which in our souls we cherish most. Pride crushes the humility which makes souls radiant with faith and love. Pride of possessions! Pride of social standing, pride of learning! Pride is a deadly sin that makes us think of ourselves more highly than we ought to think. If you are a victim of this sin, you were there when they crucified my Lord.

I see Judas Iscariot. He was there when they crucified my Lord. Greed led him to the Cross. The grasping sin of greed caused Judas to sell Jesus for 30 pieces of silver. Greed caused Judas to cry out against the woman who anointed Jesus. Yes, Judas was there! He betrayed the Master with a kiss; he sold Him for 30 pieces of silver.

Do you ever find yourself a victim of greed? Greed is the basic cause of most wars. Greed is the sin that motivates men to sell liquor, dope, and narcotics which destroy millions of lives in every generation. Greed drives a man to rob his fellow man. Greed is the sin that makes a man stingy and selfish. Greed causes people to rob God in their giving. Greed is the evil spirit that makes thankless souls. Greed had much to do with the crucifixion of the Saviour; and if you are a victim of selfishness in any form, you were represented at the Cross.

I recognize Peter, the Coward. He was there. Peter denied his Lord thrice before the cock crowed. Where was

Peter when the crosses were raised on Golgotha? Nobody knew. Peter was not in sight. But Peter was there. Fear represented him at the Cross.

In our own day, Jesus is not hurt so much by skeptics, infidels, and atheists, for they do not speak with spiritual authority. The cause of Christ is hurt most by professing, unregenerated Christians who claim to be the sons of God, but spiritually they are the sons of Satan!—members who neglect their spiritual responsibilities, who do not put God first; members who will not humble themselves in the sight of the Lord and conform to His Commandments.

Ah, yes, we have spiritual cowards in every church and community, because it is often easier to face gunfire, bombs, and the sword than it is to stand by our spiritual convictions. Peter has many friends today because most people are spiritual cowards in some degree. Were you ever guilty of spiritual cowardice? If so, you were there when they crucified my Lord.

See Herod Antipas? He too was at the Cross. Herod was a powerful man. He ruled a fourth part of the Roman Empire. In the eyes of the world he was a great man because of his position. Herod was a specialist. Oh, no! Not in any virtue, but in the great sin of sensuality. He had no regard for the moral and spiritual decencies of life. He was superstitious, cunning, and one of the most immoral men in ancient history. He cared only for the satisfaction of his personal lust; he sent his own wife away and seduced his brother's wife to live with him in adultery, in open disregard of law and convention. Yes, Herod was there when John the Baptist spoke openly of Herod's awful sin with Herodias, the adulterous woman with whom he lived, and Herod was there when Herodias asked for the head of John the Baptist to be brought in on a platter. Yet Jesus had to be tried before a filthy scoundrel like that. Herod was there when he sent Jesus away to be crucified; but the paramount question is, were *you* there when they crucified my Lord?

Sensuality is not only an ancient sin, but it is found deeply embedded in the heart of modern life. Behold how long it took to close the night clubs at midnight during the war! Little does the average church member realize the extent of sensuality in America. The alcoholic must drink more and more to submerge his guilt and defeat; the pleasure seeker must stay longer and later, to satisfy his craving for excitement; the dope fiend must constantly increase his dosage to get relief; and the promiscuous adulterer must seek new fields of sin to satisfy the lust of the flesh. What are these four cravings? They are the demands of a sin-sick soul, a soul sick with the sin of sensuality. Are you guilty of any of these? If so, you were there when they crucified my Lord.

I see not only the people thus identified, but a seething crowd of people—a violent mob about the cross. On Palm Sunday they that went before and they that followed cried: "Hosanna! Blessed is He that cometh in the name of the Lord." Now, four days later, they cry: "Crucify Him! Crucify Him!"

What a contrast! The central figure is the same. Jesus is unchanged. Does it mean that the people were indifferent to Jesus on both days? Did they act without thinking? Did they weigh the evidence? Ah, yes, the indifferent crowd was there when they crucified my Lord.

Nor is it an ancient tragedy. Even today most people are

indifferent to Jesus Christ and His Church. Take a walk about any American city during the hour of worship and you will come back with a heavy heart. You can see what happened in the heart of G. A. Studdert-Kennedy after he took a walk about his city:

When Jesus came to Golgotha they hanged him on a tree,
They drave great nails through hands and feet, and made a
    Calvary;
They crowned him with a crown of thorns, red were his
    wounds and deep,
For those were crude and cruel days and human flesh was
    cheap.

When Jesus came to Birmingham, they simply passed him by,
They never hurt a hair of him, they only let him die;
For men had grown more tender, and they would not give
    him pain,
They only just passed down the street, and left him in the rain.

In a religious survey which was conducted by a nationally known woman's magazine some time ago, it was found that 91% of our American women believe in God, 75% believe that children should have definite religious instruction, but it was also discovered that only 47% of these women make any effort to attend church. What a graphic picture of American indifference!

How pointedly the Master said: "Not everyone that saith unto me, Lord, Lord, shall enter into the Kingdom of Heaven; but he that doeth the will of my Father who is in Heaven." Do you ever find yourself guilty of indifference? Rare is the soul that can escape. If you are guilty, you were there with the crowd when they crucified my Lord!

Listen! I want to make a confession. *I* was there when

they crucified my Lord. I was there when they nailed him to the tree. I was there when they pierced him in the side. I was there when they laid him in the tomb. O sometimes it causes me to tremble, tremble! But I was there, and I am glad that I was there.

There at the cross I first saw the light. There upon the cross I recognized the hope of salvation. There at the cross I realized that "God so loved the world, that He gave His only begotten Son, that whosoever believeth on Him should not perish, but have eternal life."

Yes, I was there; the mob was there; Herod and Herodias were there; Peter was there; Judas was there; Nicodemus was there; in fact, the whole human race was there.

We all had a part in it. "All we like sheep have gone astray." And as we all gathered at the cross to crucify the Lord with our sin, so we must all gather at the cross to be delivered from our sin.

—from PULPIT DIGEST *for April, 1949*

The Promise He Promised

BY ROY A. BURKHART

Pastor of First Community Church, Columbus, Ohio

TEXTS: *This is the promise he promised, which is life eternal.*—I JOHN 2:25

These are written, that ye might believe that Jesus is the Christ, the Son of God: and that, believing, ye might have life through his name.—JOHN 20:31

IT IS GOOD that we have Easter. We Americans are concerned about everything but the secret of life, the purpose of our creation, a mighty faith to live by, and the only real thing that matters, which is great character. Let this be an hour when we resolve not to be a zero in history, a block to the plan of the Eternal.

Let this be an hour when we pledge our lives to the spirit and way of Christ, who made a day called Easter and who revealed the human spirit so great that we know we are our bodies no more than a shadow is a tree.

The trouble with the world is that every one cries: "Me! Me!" That accounts for the broken promises, the broken

197

homes, the broken hearts, the broken minds, the bruised and broken nations.

It was so when Christ was crucified. The men around him were crying: "Me! Me!" The priests resented his attack on their collusion with the traders in the temple, and they feared that an uprising of the people on his behalf might shatter their whole system of comfort and pride. The traders in temple coinage and in animals for sacrifice had a good business, and were resolved to keep it. Pilate feared that an uprising of the people might lose him his office. Judas and the people, in fierce nationalistic hate, would rather kill him than give up hating. Peter and his disciples would rather desert him than accept his kind of death. They were all crying: "Me! Me!" But he was crying: "Father!"

We know this morning that in him, his words, his faith, and his spirit, we find the way, the truth, and the life. When he said: "I am the resurrection and the life; he that believeth in me, though he were dead, yet shall he live, and whosoever liveth and believeth in me shall never die," we believe him, for he is the proof of his own words. We know the promise he promised is true.

Jesus devised no statecraft, led no army, framed no set philosophy or ethic, sang no song—except the song in the soul of humanity. His cradle was a borrowed manger, his deathbed a felon's cross, and the tomb, the gift of a frightened friend. His disciples said that he rose from the dead, and they believed it. The faith of which in his lifetime they had been dull scholars, became in his death their overmastering passion. They turned the world upside down with the message that God is truly made known in Jesus. Nothing could be more amazing—except, perhaps, the fact that millions have taken them at their word. Rome, thinking to trample on him and finding in him no resistance, stumbled over him to its doom. He is the unspeakable human astonishment in our human history.

As Dr. Buttrick has said in *The Christian Faith and Modern Doubt* (Scribner):

> What manner of man was this, of whom within a generation it was said: "Cruel kings woke in fear when he was born. Stars were swung from their orbits. Sages came from far with royal gifts and knelt in homage. Shepherds in their gentle toil beheld through rifted midnight sky 'the hid battlements of eternity' and heard in awestruck wonder the seraph song and knew that God had come to earth"?
>
> He was not a fanatic—he played with children. Nor was he too indulgent: the ethic of the Sermon on the Mount pierces the marrow of our conscience. He did not lack artistic insight: he looked at the crimson oleander and said: "Solomon in all his glory was not arrayed as one of these." Nor was he a dreamer; his realism leaves no shuffling in our insincerities. He did not trample on human love: only a blind man could miss his homesickness when he said: "The son of man hath nowhere to lay his head." Nor was he a sentimentalist: he chose to die on a cross.

On this anniversary of the first Easter, may we ask: "Is Jesus authoritative today?"

Some say: "Times are different from what they were in the time of Jesus. We have this amazing machine age."

Yes, we do. But has the automobile changed the basis of right and wrong? Or of love and hate—though it may have placed more power in the hands of every motive. To misrepresent a second-hand automobile is as bad as to lie about an old horse. Human nature is still human nature, despite the radio. Perhaps it is all the more human—for once we had music; now we have advertising with incidental music.

Where do we stand with Christ this morning? What is our response to him? Will we respond in faith, in prayer, and in conduct to live his Golden Rule? If we will, then we will find life eternal so fully now that we will never die. If we live by truth, by love, by compassion, by faith, by justice, we will soon know great companionship.

For those who follow the way of Christ, faith in immortality persists despite all the logic of time or men. It is a hope that will not down. Sometimes it rises to the majesty of luminous conviction; sometimes it fails to a flickering spark, but it never dies; relentless rationalism does not smother it, because it hides itself in the heart of the rationalist; cynical despair cannot kill it, for in the midnight the cynic sees a far faint star and "listening love hears the rustle of a wing." Whether we doubt or affirm, whether we tread the valleys of gloom or climb the sunlit hills of faith, life keeps burning before our vagrant feet this kindly light of hope.

In the heart of every man is a voiceless question: "If a man die, shall he live again?" In the heart of everyone is an answer, sometimes the feeble whisper of a forgotten faith, sometimes the song of the soul's assurance: "This is not the end; man was not made to be lost in the abyss of nothingness."

Victor Hugo, in words that will be eternal, said it so well:

> I feel in myself the future life. I am like a forest cut down; the new shoots are stronger and livelier than ever. I am rising,

I know, toward the sky. The sunshine is on my head. The earth gives me its generous sap, but heaven lights me with the reflection of unknown worlds. For half a century I have been writing my thoughts in prose and in verse; history, philosophy, drama, romance, tradition, satire, ode and song; I have tried all. But I feel that I have not said the thousandth part of what is in me. When I go down to the grave I can say like many others 'I have finished my day's work.' Life is a thoroughfare. It closes on the twilight, it opens on the dawn.

And so do we all feel when we get beneath a superficial sophistication and listen to the elemental language of these human spirits, when we wholeheartedly choose the way of Christ. Whence springs this indestructible hope? Whence rise these deathless desires? Where lie the fountains of eternal hope? Where are the evidences of Christ's promise of immortality?

Well, I think they come in part from the very nature of man and his place in the universe, as Christ made it plain.

This universe conserves all energies. They may know transmutations from form to form—light becomes heat, heat becomes motion—but in all these changes of form there is no annihilation. Today scientists tell us that what we call matter is made up of whirling centers of energy; nothing is static; all is bewildering motion. Will a universe that so carefully husbands all its lesser energies destroy man with his power to think and love and will? When the evolutionary process reaches its apex does it suddenly reverse itself and begin to destroy energy? If the universe conserves energy; does it not also conserve spirit?

As human beings we must stop cowering before the vastness of nature, cringing before bigness and being the slaves of size. The soul has the right to assert its importance.

So far as we can tell in all the realm of nature, of which man is a part, he is the only being aware of himself. He alone can contemplate the nature from which he comes, rejoice in its beauty, be awed before its majesty and shrink from its terrors. In man, nature becomes aware of itself, and how it does it is the mystery of the ages. Perhaps that day of self-awareness in man is a day both of triumph and tragedy. The mountain does not recognize itself as a mountain and signal to the river that winds about its base upon its determined trailing to the sea. The Rockies are high but they never break into song; the sea is wide but it knows not the joy and grief of the lover nor the lonely loyalty of the martyr. The star-strewn sky is vast and bewildering but it needs man to feel its mystery and majesty.

"Though the universe encompass me," exclaimed Pascal, "by thought I encompass the universe." He meant that the vast realm of nature is not aware of itself, but you and I, so insignificant in size and strength, are aware of ourselves and the universe. And ponder this—all meanings are read into nature by man; the universe does not endow itself with value. A poem is but ink blotches upon paper until man touches it into immortality; a political event, a scientific concept, have no meaning until man gives it to them. Men enrich life with meanings that endure long after they are gone. We still think Socrates' thoughts after him; Shakespeare has long slept in his Avon tomb, but the world yet widens under his vision.

Frederick Myers has an essay on Virgil (quoted by Dixon in that remarkable book, *The Human Situation*) in which he shows how so many individual lines of the poem have gone out into the world and made history. Enumerating each, its story is told:

> On this line, the poet's own face faltered as he read; here is the verse which Augustine quotes as typical of all the pathos and glory of pagan art from which Christians must flee; this is the couplet which saintly Fenelon could never read without admiring tears; this is the line Filippo Strazzi scrawled upon his prison wall before he took his life to avoid worse ill. These are the lines like a trumpet call which roused Savonarola to seek the things above, and this is the line Dante heard in the 'Paradise of God.'

But does the universe preserve the works and destroy the worker? Can it be that the song is greater than the singer and the thought more enduring than the thinker? This strange being, man—so frail, so mighty, a part of nature but alone aware of himself and nature; he who alone finds meanings and creates them—in a universe that conserves its energies, shall he alone be destroyed?

Nay, rather in whatever altered garments, the mind shall survive "while castles fade and empires fall asleep."

Quality of faith lives on, as does a poem. When Harold Bosley was here, he told how when he was a boy they lost a corn crop because of a hail storm. He went to his father, who quietly said: "We needed that corn crop, but we will try again next year." Then almost in the next breath, he told about his own son who had been killed accidentally. He spoke of it in quiet courage, and how he and his wife tried again, recently having another child. Then he told about another one of his sons, seeking an answer about his brother's death. His father tried to explain, and the boy said: "Daddy, it's like this—I lend my pencil to a boy. It's mine, but he uses it, then finally he gives it back." The grandfather, the father, his son—all of them with a great faith!

Not only in the nature of man, but in his needs and aspirations, are the sources of Christ's promise of life eternal. Man's highest human experience is love. The divine in man is that which loves faithfully and purely. He that loveth is born of God. But love does not find its fulfillment in life. When lives have been intertwined in a sacrament of life-long affection, as the years go by love does not grow feeble and frail. Nay, rather, as the sensual threads are withdrawn, love becomes an understanding comradeship too deep for words. "These twain are one flesh." And whenever love kisses the lips of death, the heart rises in protest and says: "This cannot be the end, or at least it ought not be the end."

There is something too priceless to be lost in the "wide tombs of uncreated night." As Hugh Walpole puts it: "There is a kind of sniff of immortality in our love for one another." In one of Cowper's letters to a woman friend the poet says: "There is not time for friendship to unfold itself in such a nook of life as this!" Ah, no true and loyal love was ever fulfilled in this nook of life! And so a loved one departing feels the experience is not ended . . .

> Do not fear
> And do not grieve for me.
> I shall not die!
> I am like a forest oak
> Which many suns have seasoned;
> My body will be a little heap of ashes
> Upon a hearth,

But my soul will rise in flames
That leap and soar
And seek the stars.
Do not fear
And do not weep, my dear,
When death stoops to light the fire.

It is not egotism that leads our souls to demand immortality—it is the most self-less experience we know—love. One often feels one's own survival does not much matter, but these souls whose beauty we have beheld with love's quickening insights, if they are destroyed, then ruling the universe must be wild anarchic forces rejoicing in the destruction of their highest values.

Remember, love is a force of the universe—love with its hunger, its loneliness, its insatiable longing. We have no right to interpret life and leave this fact out of reckoning. What is this experience of life and whence comes it—this that cries out against the stupidity of annihilation of those whom it adores? A long time ago one who knew love and its meaning said this great word: "Now abideth love."

Think, too, of man's unfulfilled desires, of his noble outreachings never satisfied—"for there is not time in this little nook of life"—which we catch in Jesus when he said: "Let not your hearts be troubled." When the long evening is drawing on, the philosopher lays down his pen and says: "I had just begun;" the artist yields up his brush knowing that his masterpiece is a faint symbol of the flame of beauty his soul has seen; the saint is well aware that he has but learned the alphabet of saintliness. In every soul, withheld completions; masses of beginnings without endings; foundations laid and temples unbuilt; ships launched that shall never sail the sea.

It is this intuitive belief that their aspirations and their moral desires have meaning in the universe that keeps men struggling upward in what seems an alien world. I read of a Spanish girl, perhaps a refugee, who was in England for the first time, and approaching London in the train. Looking out on the sea of houses and factories and chimneys, she burst into tears and said: "Ah, these people, they have no view." What will happen to all our upward aspirations and longings when we have no view of eternity—when we know whatever we do we shall only add to some beginnings that soon shall waver to the dust? Says Macneile Dixon:

> Since I am not prepared to believe the fiery, invincible soul is a by-blow, a lamentable accident, I put my trust in the larger vision of the poets who know that man cannot support himself except by clinging to his intuitions—as a sailor clings to his raft in the angry seas—to his passion for justice, his trust in the affections of his heart, his love of the lovely, his lonely struggle for the best, however clumsy and mistaken he may be in his present estimate of what is best.

"It doth not yet appear what we shall be, but when he shall appear we shall be like him for we shall see him as he is."

I think of the motto of St. Catharine: "Come not to present a finished work to God who is infinite love and demands of thee only infinite desire." It was Browning's Grammarian, realizing that there was so much to be and do that he had never attained, who said: "But man has forever."

We must give up our lust of finishing, because if we

must finish our tasks they will be too small: if we set for
ourselves goals which we can reach they will prove not
worth the reaching.

If life is not made for a higher destiny, then the best of
it is mockery. We are here to make ships that shall never
sail the sea; to lay the foundations upon which shall rise no
cathedral groin and agonizing spire; we are here to love
and lose, and all our deepest longings are but the laughter
of a careless universe. But there is a better view. This con-
tinual craving for that which is not, this persistent anxiety
and pain which lies at the core of being, that deep-buried
concern which the pessimist interprets as the defeat of our
happiness—that, in reality, is the soul's loyalty to its own
goal, its underlying faithfulness to its destiny.

So Paul looked at life: "I count myself not to have attained, but this one thing I do, forgetting the things that
are behind and stretching forward to the things that are
before, I press toward the goal unto the prize of the high
calling of God in Christ Jesus."

Those who have lived before us have felt that the most
refreshing note of this promise is to be found in our experience of Christ. That is where the Christian teaching first
began. It is not as so many suppose, a development of the
Greek or Roman belief in a life in some world beyond. The
Christian hope was a new harvest springing from fresh soil.

There are in the Old Testament but a few gleams of this
faith. Then Jesus came. Some humble men walked with
him over the Galilean hills and camped with him on Gennes-
aret's lonely shores. They heard the words of grace as they
fell from his lips; their hearts' deepest loves were awakened
and united with his God-like love. For them life and the

world were utterly changed. Sublime significance crowned the commonest wayside flower and lingered like a golden halo about the head of the lowliest man.

Then they saw their friend die. For three days they were plunged into unutterable grief and despair. Then came Easter morning and they cried: "He is alive! His love and power are still with us; he guides and rebukes and inspires us—Christ is alive. Death cannot touch him! He is risen from the tomb. He lives!"

And then later, timidly at first: "Because he lives, we shall live too."

Then the memory of his holy words: "I am the resurrection and the life."

Interpret however you will, the belief in immortality for the Christian grows out of his experience of the love of Christ. And as those first disciples experienced Easter in their hearts, as we give out love and all our life to Christ and hear the whisper of his voice and touch him in life's throng and pain—we shall know that nothing in life or in death can separate us from the love of God which is in Christ our Lord.

That is the authentic Christian faith. In the mystic mountains of human experience, in the very nature of our world, in the life of Christ are the evidences that the promise he promised is true.

Prayer

Our Father, we come this day of Easter as worshipers, not as spectators. We come to bow before Thee—high and lifted up—and not to see or be seen. We come to seek Thy will so fully that no longer will we live by our own puny, selfish, narrow wills. We come that we might see the way and know the truth by which we may receive the gift of life eternal and share that life with others. We come to rediscover the purpose of our creation and here dedicate ourselves to that purpose, for we would not become broken links in history; we would not thwart the entire plan of creation.

We thank Thee for all the revelations of Thyself and Thy purpose; for all those in every generation who, catching Thy purpose, made plain the way to companionship with Thee and a life of helpfulness to humanity. We thank Thee for Christ and for all the stuff with which to build the world of which we dream.

Forgive us for living with so much plenty without gratitude, and without doing more for human misery. Forgive us for refusing the responsibility to make our republic truly Christian; for letting our children grow up believing in nothing and caring for nothing but the things of the flesh; forgive us for broken promises, for building houses but not homes, for letting love be cheap and all that is holy be desecrated. Forgive us for living without Thee until the end of life and then running to Thee like a whimpering child.

Let this morning be a time when we give our lives to Thee, and here and now accept the Christ and live his way. Use us to feed the hungry, to help the weak, to strengthen the forces of democracy and inspire all the leaders of the nations to follow the way of Christ. Amen.

—from PULPIT DIGEST *for April, 1950*

Gambling—Higher Style

BY GEORGE A. BUTTRICK

Pastor of Madison Avenue Presbyterian Church, New York City

TEXT: *And they crucified him, and parted his garments, casting lots.*—MATTHEW 27:35

THE DRUGSTORE clerk asked: "Mister, who won the third race?" We knew he meant a horse race and not the human race, but there our information ended. But his face was flushed: the question seemed almost a life and death concern to him. Times do not greatly change. The soldiers gambled for Christ's garments. Their action meant that He was as good as dead—and He saw them. It would be hard to imagine worse cruelty. He had five articles of clothing: a tunic, an outer robe, a turban, a girdle, and sandals—His whole worldly wealth. Who wore them afterwards?

The soldiers gambled. The clothes of a condemned man were then the perquisite of his executioners, and they cast dice for the booty. Plainly they were past feeling, or they would have waited until He had died. But is gambling

210

always wrong? Surely there is a harmless kind? Perhaps. But the harmless kind, if it exists, is still like a lion-cub in the house: the pet, if uncurbed, becomes a ravenous beast.

Then what *is* wrong with it? If a man win, he has no right to his gain, for a man is entitled only to earnings or free gifts. A certain student took a flyer on the market on the strength of inside information, and was bragging about his profits. An old Scotch professor asked quietly: "Did you earn it? Was it given?" Then he added yet more quietly: "Somebody lost it." If on the other hand a man loses he is guilty of waste, and knows it. So, winning or losing, he is in a bad light. Moreover the gambling soon becomes an absorbing passion, a fixed idea: the gambler is plainly warped. Moreover he warps other lives to the point of cruelty. You know the sorry story: defalcations at the bank, hunger in the home, and the disease still burning and burning. The money with which we gamble is not ours: the earth is God's, and we are only His trustees. What if all gambling is gambling for the garments of God? The soldiers gambled.

So much for that: we are concerned with vaster issues. Caiaphas and Pilate gambled. Perhaps that was inescapable in some form, for life is a venture for every man. Edmund Burke declared that "gaming is a principle inherent in human nature." It is fairly certain that racetrack betting will never be overcome by repressive measures or condemnation. Perhaps the victory will come through "sublimation"—if you like that modern jargon: through transforming a poor kind of gambling into a higher style. You cannot walk down the street without taking risks. Some witty person has said that in New York traffic there are two kinds of pedestrians—the quick and the dead. You cannot conduct a business without venture, for there is no infallible way of knowing if a policy or an investment will succeed. The farmer is a gambler, for how can he tell if the weather will destroy his crops or bring them to harvest? All discovery is by risk. Reasoned planning may carry us so far, but beyond that point we must venture. Wise people do not rebel against that rule; for if life had no uncertainties it could have no zest, and perhaps we could have no growth.

This necessity to venture holds in the high matters of the soul. Shall we live for the noisy world or for the "still small voice" of conscience? For the moment or for eternity? Reason offers some guidance. It is at least as reasonable to suppose that a universe that has brought forth personal life is governed by a Personal God, as to believe that all creation is a galvanized spasm. It is as intelligent to judge life by its best, namely, the spirit of Jesus, as to judge it by its worst, namely, a devilishness or deadness that gambles at the foot of the Cross. But reason cannot prove, either by logic or scientific demonstration, that conscience is a better treasure than cash. If it could, men might be good for common-sense advantage—in which instance real goodness would vanish. No, we must take the risk, on the body against the soul, or on the soul against the body.

So Caiaphas and Pilate gambled. On what? On the faith (if faith it can be called) that the sword rules, that death is the end of a man, and that selfishness brings joy to the selfish. They bet on the proposition that God is not watching, or that if He is He does not care. They could not prove their faith, but they took the chance. They would have told

you: "It is a sure thing, like money in the bank." Frank
Bets (appropriate name) has a poem about it, addressed to
Judas Iscariot:

> You sold Him and you thought Him slain,
> And the old proud game begins again,
> And Caesar plays with might and main.
> But a hidden Player has the Black,
> And the craft is foiled, and the White attack
> Move by move is beaten back,
> Iscariot.
>
> Knight nor Bishop can resist
> The pawns of this Antagonist
> Whose countenance is dark with mist.
> The game goes on and will not wait,
> Caesar is gripped in a deadly strait—
> What if the pawns should give checkmate,
> Iscariot?

Caiaphas and Pilate gambled. It seemed that they could
not miss. Was there a Hidden Player on the other side of
the board?

Let us say reverently that there was another gambler at
Calvary: Jesus gambled. While the soldiers were casting
lots for His garments, He ventured His soul on God for the
love of mankind. "I, if I be lifted up from the earth, will
draw all men unto me."

"Lifted up" means crucified in shame. What a hazard!
Someone may say: "But Jesus knew that God was on His
side." He knew by faith. He did not know by visible fact
or proven logic. His soul said "Yes," but His pain-racked
body still said "No." Golgotha is a word that means The
Place of a Skull. Perhaps the name was given because the

hilltop was littered with skulls, perhaps because it was shaped like a skull. In either event it declared silently that a skull is the last word about man's life. But Jesus made His venture, while other men cast lots for His garments. Jesus cried out on God: "Father, forgive them. Father, into Thy hands I commit my spirit."

His plea is that you and I should live in that self-same venture. He condemned the one-talent man, not because he had only one talent, but because he buried it in the earth instead of risking it in the traffic of the world. He bade His disciples: "Launch out into the deep!"—and had in mind more than their craft as fishermen. He constantly insisted, in crucial and cardinal teaching, that only "he that loseth his life shall find it."

Lose to win: there is the overturning of our human wisdom. Let a man lose his life in lowliness while others clamor for name and fame; let him lose his life in succoring human need while others seek the main chance; let him die like a seed dies in the dark earth. Thus Jesus ventured in the tremendous risk of the Cross.

When the Japanese first marched into China at the onset of the last world war, Heywood Broun wrote a column entitled "It Shall Come Back." Thus he prophesied that the ravaged land would be returned to the Chinese. At the moment the prediction seemed folly. China had fallen among thieves, and other nations were like the priest and the Levite in the story: they "passed by on the other side." There was no Good Samaritan. Our nation sold scrap iron to the aggressor. But it came back, and would have come back if no war had been fought. The Chinese have quietly absorbed the conqueror long before our time. "The mills of God grind slowly, but they grind exceeding small."

Could anyone have guessed on the first Good Friday that Jesus would "Come Back?" His death was more than death: it was an oblivion of shame. But Caiaphas and Pilate are now remembered, in pity or execration, only because of their victim. Jesus is not forgotten. The tragedy now is the revealing of the sorrow of God for the cleansing of our soul, and beyond the tragedy Jesus returned—because He hazarded His soul in death.

You and I must gamble—higher style. Donald Hankey has written: "Religion is betting your life there is a God." Perhaps he should have said: "High religion is betting your life there is a Christlike God."

It is not a blind bet. Reason gives as much support, and perhaps more, to faith as to unfaith. But God is not a theorem, and therefore cannot be proved. If He is a Person He can be known only in the venture of prayer and deed. How else? The Epistle to the Philippians has a fine sentence about a man called Epaphroditus who at risk aided Paul, when Paul was in prison for his Christian faith. Paul enjoins the Philippian church about the man: "Receive him therefore in the Lord with all gladness, . . . because for the work of Christ he was nigh unto death, staking his life"! Our version says: "not regarding his life." It means "having no regard for his life": the Greek word is one used of gamblers —"staking his life."

When all arguments are made and ended, if they are ever ended, you and I must stake our life. How are you betting? Like the soldiers? Have a care! That kind of gambling is at best the turning of life into a casual pastime, and at worst a destroying fever. Then how are you betting? Like Pilate?

It is an old game, and our world is still busy at it; Pilate's game,

> Whose game was empires, and whose stakes were thrones
> Whose table earth—whose dice were human bones.

Do not bet that money or fame will bring you happiness, let alone blessedness. Do not bet time against eternity. Do not bet that God is not looking, or that there is no heaven or hell: the skeptic may be very surprised the first moment after death.

Then how will you bet? Like Christ? You cannot: there is only one Christ. But you can bet that His suffering, as it cleanses you, is God's pardon; and you can venture your soul on Him for all eternity. You cannot prove the faith. If you could prove it you would be compelled to believe it; and then it would become, not a faith at all, but only a drab compulsion. There is enough evidence for Christ to provoke your venture, but never so much that you are spared the hazard.

A doctor friend in a quiet northern town heard one winter that there was an epidemic in a lonely island out in the lake. His methods as a doctor were hardly according to modern hygiene. The strips of adhesive tape stuck on the varnished door had been there a long time, and the scissors with which he removed bandages were more like rusty garden shears. But he had a great heart.

He must reach that island. But how? No boat could go through the ice those forty or fifty miles. Perhaps an aeroplane could make the trip. But the airport was poor enough in summer, and almost impossible in winter. Yet he persuaded a pilot to make the journey, and they did not crash.

Was it worth the risk? Reason could have been enlisted on the side of safety; a very plausible argument could have been advanced that there were plenty of sick and needy people close at hand. But a man's soul gathered to that venture. There is a telling fact: a man's soul is fevered by low gambling, but fulfilled in any Christian venture. Surely the world and time and eternity also gather when the soul gathers. But you could not prove it—thank God. It is proved in the zest of the venture.

Why gamble in a cheap way when you can gamble in noble soul? Race-track stuff is childish and petty: the world waits for men who still will hazard their lives, day by day or in early death, for the sake of Christ.

You have seen the colored squares on the counter of a game of chance in a country fair. The world is your coin. Your soul is the coin. What shall a man give in exchange for his soul? Now, on what color—Pilate or Jesus? You say that you have tried it, and have found that the Christian life does not pay off? It depends what is meant by "pay off." You will have zest of soul that no other venture can give you: that is rather better than some money-itch. The log of Columbus read night after night: "And this day we sailed on" . . . "And this day we sailed on" . . . "And this day we sailed on." There was still no sight of land. But you live in America. The man who sails by faith in Christ will reach his celestial country. Or will he? You can prove it only in the venture. High religion is "betting your life" there's a Christlike God.

—from PULPIT DIGEST *for April, 1950*

The American Home

BY HAROLD S. WINSHIP

Pastor of the German Congregational Church, Clinton, Massachusetts

TEXT: *Train up a child in the way he should go, and even when he is old he will not depart from it.*—PROVERBS 22:6

HOW WE thrill when we hear the word *Home*! Home is where the heart is! Home is the father's kingdom, the mother's world, and the child's paradise—the only place on earth where our faults and failings are hidden under the sweet mantle of love. A baby is a tiny feather from the wing of love, dropped into the sacred lap of a mother.

"Home, Sweet Home" was written by John Howard Payne, who was born in New York City in 1791. He went to work at an early age to help his father; later, he became an actor and went to England, where he was very successful in London. In the course of time he became our American Consul in Tunis, Africa. But he is remembered because he wrote "Home, Sweet Home." Because of that song, his body was brought back from Africa to be buried with high honors in the Nation's Capital. As his body was carried

218

down Pennsylvania Avenue, it was preceded by the Marine Band and followed by the President and Vice President of the United States and by members of the Cabinet. The Congress and the Supreme Court adjourned to honor the memory of the American who had written "Home, Sweet Home."

Our text is that wonderful piece of advice, given centuries ago by the writer of the Book of Proverbs: "Train up a child in the way he should go, and even when he is old he will not depart from it." How are things going in the American home? First, let us look at some American homes where the parents do not seem to train up the child in the way he should go. Today a tidal way of juvenile crime is sweeping America. Thoughtful persons ask, Is it because these young people are not brought up right by their parents? Have our public schools, our church schools, and our churches failed to train up this growing generation of Americans in the right way?

Most of us love beautiful flowers and we know that they require care and attention during their growing period. I often think of the boys and girls in certain American homes —in crowded sections of cities—growing up like weeds, rank and wild. Without care and cultivation how can these boys and girls become America's useful and successful citizens? In their ugly, unfavorable, congested surroundings it is almost impossible for them to grow and bloom into beautiful character and achievements, to become America's beautiful women and strong men!

Juvenile delinquents are boys and girls up to 16 who have come to the attention of the Juvenile Court. My experience has brought me into personal touch with about 200 of these boys and girls, in Hartford, Connecticut. The conditions in many homes drive the children out into the street, seeking an outlet for their pent-up energy—found, all too often, in mischief and deviltry, misdemeanors and crimes. Here are three actual cases.

A— had a father who was a drunkard. Losing respect for his father resulted in the loss of his own self-respect. He could not live down his father's reputation, so he decided that he would never amount to much himself, and he let himself go—falling in with boys of fast-growing criminal tendencies. Without spunk and strength to resist, he easily became an accessory in acts of vandalism and robbery. B— was a sullen, moody type of boy. He hung around with a corner gang instead of getting into something worth while. That is how he started toward reform school and a life of crime. C— did not have a fit place in which to play in his neighborhood, so he was out on the street most of the time. He became bolder, tougher, and quicker on the get-away from the cops.

I could give dozens more of these cases, all showing the unfavorable conditions in the surroundings of these juvenile delinquents. Right here, let us ask the question, who is to blame for these conditions? First, parents are to blame. Second, the family's spiritual adviser (minister, priest, or rabbi) is to blame. More and more I am convinced that parents and the family's spiritual adviser have failed, because, although they may have talked and pleaded and even threatened, they have not prayed with that boy or girl until he or she experienced a change of heart and will—a good, old-fashioned conversion, which can only be brought about through the Divine Power of Almighty God.

But not all the untrained boys and girls live in the crowded sections of cities. We will find them in the better residential sections of those same cities, in the towns and villages and countryside, in homes everywhere of the poor, the middle class and the rich. A boy or girl untrained in the way he should go—a boy or girl neglected—becomes a man or woman lost! A few weeks ago, over in Whitman, Massachusetts, one of the worst cases of vandalism ever reported in the town, evidently the work of juveniles, happened at the home of a kind old lady of 80 years. She was a great lover of flowers, and had a beautiful sunken garden in the back yard of her home, which contained rare lilies in a pool, and many varieties of plants in a rock garden. When she returned, after being away a week, she found the garden in shambles. The lily pond was filled with logs and trash; the buds and lily pads and plants had been ruthlessly ripped up, totally destroyed, and strewn around the yard. What kind of bringing up did the persons have who perpetrated this unspeakable, detestable wrong upon a lovely, kind old lady? In a case like this, the law should punish the parents as well as the children. The parents are largely to blame.

Here is another case. A certain public school principal found it necessary to expel a boy for stealing. There was no reason for the theft, as the boy had a wealthy father, and yet he stole $20 and gave it to a friend in payment for a debt. The boy's wealthy parents were summoned to the principal's office, and the door was closed. They were crestfallen, dumbfounded, and overwhelmed with grief, but not for their boy. They were fiercely angry with him and sorry for themselves because of the impending disgrace and public criticism. The principal asked them, "Who took that money?" "What do you mean?" asked the father. "You just called us here because our boy took the money." "Yes," said the principal, "your boy's hand took the money. I understand you taught him to gamble a little, and is it not true that you let him know that a gambling debt is a 'debt of honor' among gentlemen, and must be paid immediately?" "Yes," said the father, "I so believe, and have taught him so." "Well," said the principal, "he learned to gamble from you and with you. He made a bet last week and lost. He was dunned for the money, but he did not have it. It was a 'debt of honor' and must be paid immediately. And so, I ask you, who took that money?"

Now let us look at some American homes where the children are given training in the way they should go. Suppose your boy should come to you and say, "Dad, just what is the way I should go," what would you say to him? You would probably explain that the Christian way is the way he should go—the way Jesus lived and taught us to live. And your boy, who is growing in mind and heart every day, might press you further, by asking, "But why should I go in His way?" And then, father or mother, you would have a wonderful opportunity to tell your boy or girl that Jesus lived the most perfect life in all the world's history, that His teachings about daily life are the greatest in all the world's literature, that there is no better way known than the way Jesus lived.

Christian home training begins in infancy. The mother's heart is the child's schoolroom. As the twig is bent, the tree will grow. In a Christian home, how good it is to see such mottoes on the walls as "God Bless Our Home"; "As for me and my house, we will serve the Lord"; "Christ is the Head of this house, the Unseen Guest at every meal, the Silent Listener to every conversation."

The Bible says, "And all thy children shall be taught of the Lord." In the Connecticut State Library at Hartford, in the Supreme Court Room, there is a beautiful mural showing a child at his mother's knee. She is reading to him from the open Bible on her lap. She is guiding the first steps of his little feet in the gospel paths. Mothers and fathers should give their children Christian nurture, nourishing and feeding their mind and heart, opening their eyes, enlarging their point of view, their perspective, and their spiritual vision. They should train the mind, the heart, the will, the lips, the hands and feet for all the experiences of life ahead. They should prepare them for life, training them to improve their time and their opportunities. They should build those little Christian characters on the foundation of Jesus' life. They should love them into doing what is right. Years later, when you are grown up, you will remember that tender, devoted love of Mother and Dad, and you will not depart from your early Christian training.

> I took a piece of plastic clay, and idly fashioned it one day,
> And as my fingers pressed it, still it moved and yielded to my will,
> I took a piece of living clay—a little child—and day by day
> I moulded, with my teaching art, that tender, little childish heart.

During this war we have had, home is the source of all our men and women in the Armed Forces. Why should we not have a Christian Training Camp in the American Home, where Christian character is developed, built up, and made strong? Why should we not live under Christian Discipline in the American Home? Why should not Christianity actually be lived by the whole family—father, mother, and all the children?

In closing let me tell you about the king who had a dream. In his dream he saw a huge pair of scales, held in the hands of a gigantic figure, called Justice. The scales reached from the sky to the earth. In one side was a pile of gold, silver, precious stones and all the symbols of earthly material power and wealth. In the other side was a little nest of hay, just like the little nest in the Manger at Bethlehem. And in his dream the king saw the scales tip away down with all the valuable things of this world. Then, a beautiful angel brought a lovely little child and placed it in the little nest of hay, and immediately that side of the scales tipped down, and the king said to himself, "That means that the most valuable thing in this world is A Little Child."

Dear friends, that is why it is so important to "Train up a child in the way he should go."

—*from* PULPIT DIGEST *for October, 1945*

Is He Really Here?

BY TALMADGE C. JOHNSON

Pastor of First Baptist Church, Kinston,
North Carolina

TEXT: *And I will be with you all the time, to the very end*
of the world.—MATTHEW 28:20

IS He really here?

Vital religion depends upon the consciousness of the presence of God. No man can worship an absentee God; and no man can fail to worship a God who is present, if he is conscious of His presence. If God cannot really see us, hear us, and help us, there is no need for us to go through the formalities of worship. Elijah dealt a death-blow to Baal-worship when he demonstrated that Baal was not present and taunted his priests by suggesting that perhaps their god was too busy with other things to pay them any mind. But if God is really here, not to be aware of His presence is the very acme of human folly. To ignore a present God is as foolish as it would be for a man to blindfold himself and go stumbling in the dark when the sun is shining. It is as disastrous as it would be for a man to sit at a table,

225

richly laden with food, and starve himself to death by refusing to admit the presence of food.

Christianity as a religion could not have long endured without the Living Presence of Christ. The leaders of Judaism were right in thinking that they could destroy the new doctrines, which had proved so disturbing, if they could somehow banish Christ. So they had him crucified. Then were his disciples dismayed, scattered abroad, and ready to give up their faith in him. But something happened. They themselves claimed that he came back, and they acted as though he had come back and was truly present with them. There is no way of accounting for what happened in the first century of Christianity except by saying that these men believed, rightly or wrongly, that Christ was alive, and would remain with them, as he had promised, even to the end of the world.

Throughout the history of the Christian Church it has been true that strength, vigor, and power have been dependent upon a consciousness of the Living Presence of Christ. We may call it the Holy Ghost, or the Holy Spirit. But it is the same thing, for the function of the third person of the Trinity is to bear witness not of himself but of Christ. As often as the church has forgotten or ignored the Living Christ in its midst, and tried to generate its own power, it has degenerated like a branch cut off from the vine. Jesus knew whereof he spoke when he said: "I am the vine: ye are the branches. He that abideth in me and I in him, the same beareth much fruit; for without me ye can do nothing."

And the same thing is true for individuals as for the church. Whenever a person begins to doubt, or to forget, or to ignore the presence of a Living Christ, spiritual degeneracy sets in and the Christian life becomes for him an impossible ideal. If Christ be not with us, if he now dwells only in some remote and heavenly place at the right hand of God the Father, out of sight and out of reach, then you and I might as well abandon hope, forsake the church, and get whatever satisfactions we can from the world which is really here, even though it mean we shall ultimately go the way of all flesh and perish.

But is he really here?

Of such tremendous import is this question that we must face it frankly and honestly. We ought not to go on half doubting and half believing. He is really here, or he is not. And we had better find out for ourselves whether he is or is not. If he is really here, he can help us and save us. But if he is not here, it will do no good for us to deceive ourselves about it. Life is very real, and only that which is real has value for life. Illusions and hallucinations cannot possibly help us in the business of living. In fact, they will do us harm.

Now candor compels us to admit that people do sometimes suffer from illusions and hallucinations. Some people believe in ghosts. But you and I do not believe in ghosts . . . except maybe sometimes in the dark. Can it be that all of those who have said, since Calvary, that Christ is alive have simply been victims of their own imagination? It could be.

Dr. James Gordon Gilkey tells an interesting story about a recent experiment conducted by a famous American psychologist. Seven persons were blindfolded and seated in chairs with their backs toward a company of some twenty-five others. They were told that at any moment one of the company might step forward and stand nearby; and that if and when they sensed such a presence, they should raise their hands. A few moments later, three of the seven lifted their hands. One of them, later describing his experience, said: "I was suddenly conscious that someone was near me. I had no visual image of the person, but I was sure that it was a person and that he was standing about five feet behind my chair, and a little to the left. I had an uncanny feeling, and then an intense desire to turn around. I felt sure a conversation would soon begin and I wanted to be facing that other person when he started talking."

Was that feeling due to something real, or to something imagined? How many of you believe that someone had drawn near and was standing there? No. It was pure illusion. As soon as the experiment got underway, all of the other persons had quietly left the room.

Now is it something like that which accounts for all that has been said about the Living Presence of Christ? Were the first disciples victims of hallucination when they thought they beheld the Risen Lord? Was Paul deluded when he thought he saw Jesus on the Damascus Road, and was Festus correct when he said, "Paul, thou art beside thyself; much learning doth make thee mad?" Have the saints of the church, through all the centuries of Christian history, been the victims of suggestion and illusion? And if one dares to assert even now, even as I do, that Christ is alive and present, is he deliberately lying, or self-deceived, or bearing true witness to a glorious reality? Is he really here?

Two thousand years of Christian testimony is the balance when these questions are raised. Christ is alive and present here and now, or he has not been on earth since they crucified him at Golgotha and buried him in Joseph's lovely garden. Either he is now keeping his promise to be present unto the end of the world, or he was unable to keep it and never did return. Houdini, the magician, promised his friends and loved ones that he would return, if possible, after his death. But he never came back. Jesus promised to return, and he did not add, as did Houdini, "if possible." Did he, or did he not return? Thousands of people, widely separated in time and place, have declared that he kept his promise. Did he? Or have all these people been victims of pure illusion and hallucination?

Of course, it would be a bit strange that so many people through so many years would have had the same illusion. Most superstitions die out in time, and ghosts seldom appear generation after generation. Methods for checking errors of perception have been vastly improved. That which is false rarely stands for long the test of history. Indeed it is strange that there should be left in this twentieth century anyone to believe so ancient a story, must less to experience a repetition of the illusion, if illusion it be. Nevertheless, the fact of survival is not conclusive. Though fancies seldom survive, it could be that sometimes they do.

But it is wholly unreasonable to believe that so unreal and insubstantial a thing as a hallucination could be productive of the noblest kind of human character or could affect for good the course of human history. Yet that is exactly what this perceived presence of a Living Christ has done. It has repeatedly transformed human beings. By the presence of Christ, the first disciples were changed from discouraged, dis-spirited, and timid men into enthusiastic, crusading martyrs. Shrinking cowards became bold and aggressive advocates. By the presence of Christ, Saul of

Tarsus was made Paul the Apostle and counted all things but loss for the excellency of the knowledge of Christ. By the presence of Christ, the Christian Church did spread unto the uttermost parts of the earth, in spite of peril, fire, and sword. By the presence of Christ, men and women, in every age and in every land, have been lifted above the circumstances of life and made the masters of circumstances. Sinners have been transformed into saints. Drunkards have turned to sobriety, thieves and robbers to honesty, prostitutes and whoremongers to purity. Cruelty, selfishness, and greed have through that Living Presence, consciously recognized, been transmuted into kindliness, self-sacrifice, and philanthropy.

In our own times it remains true that no man can be aware of the Presence of Christ, without feeling his very soul burn within him, without being impelled to seek the highest and the best, or without discovering abundant grace and wisdom, sufficient for all the needs of life. If this felt Presence of Christ be only an illusion, it surely differs from all other illusions that men have ever experienced. If the living Lord of Life is merely a hallucination, it certainly differs from every other hallucination that human beings have thought they perceived. It is fantastic to think that an unreal shadow has effected real changes in individuals or in the social order.

The poor victim of the desert heat thinks he sees ahead of him a sparkling spring of water. He rushes to it, only to discover that the thing was unreal; and no mirage is capable of slaking his thirst. But he who moves into the Presence of Christ finds there Living Waters which can really satisfy his thirsty soul. The pitiable insane hear in their asylum cells voices that are not real and behold persons and things which are not present, but these poor creatures are never helped thereby to go out and live sanely, to integrate their personalities, to face reality with courage and strength, to conquer fears, and to achieve a life sublime. But he who hears the voice of Christ and beholds him as he is finds himself straightway made whole.

The ultimate test of reality is whether or not a thing produces results in a world that is real, whether or not it functions adequately in the vital processes of life. Even the physicists are agreed now that mere concreteness is no proof or quality of reality, that our universe is a universe of power. Where there is power, there is reality. The Living Christ must therefore be the most real thing in life, for nothing else has such power to determine the quality of life.

Indeed he is here! If you doubt it, you may test it for yourself. Come unto him, all ye that labor and are heavy laden, and ye shall find rest for your souls, and life everlasting.

—from PULPIT DIGEST *for May, 1944*

The Trinity

BY NELSON WAITE RIGHTMYER

*Professor of Church History, The Divinity
School in Philadelphia*

TEXT: *The grace of the Lord Jesus Christ and the love of
God, and the communion of the Holy Ghost, be with you
all.*—II COR. 13:14

THE PRIMARY requisite to a true religious life is a
sound idea of what God is like.

The practice of religion, the forms of worship, the principles of conduct of men or nations may do more harm than
good if they arise from false or harmful ideas of God. The
real meaning of idolatry and the reason it is so degrading is
that it represents devotion to an inferior god. And the more
vigorous, sincere, and consistent the idolatry, the worse the
result.

The doctrine of the Trinity which we honor today has
many aspects. Some of its aspects are most fully compre-
hended by the philosopher; some by the ordinary Christian
in the course of his prayers.

Critics of our religion, who assume that it is not necessary

232

to study theology before attempting to find fault with dogma, are apt to be superior concerning the doctrine of the Trinity because we say there are three *Persons* in the Godhead.

The doctrine of the Trinity means this—that in the Godhead there are three who are distinct, each something more than a mere aspect, yet not a separate individual.

This morning I should like to discuss two aspects of this doctrine. The first is: How did the Christian church reach the belief that God was, of His own nature, Three in One, and insist on this as a central Christian doctrine? The second: Why is it still necessary to maintain this doctrine?

First, no one, so far as we know, in apostolic times said in so many words that God is Three in One. Of course, they believed that there was only one God. At the same time they spoke of God as Father, as when they used the Lord's Prayer, they called Jesus the Son of God and worshipped him from the first: and they believed in the Holy Spirit as a definitely personal Being. They would have called both our Lord and the Holy Spirit "divine"; but they had not yet thought out the doctrine in its concrete form.

The two clearest references to the Trinity in the New Testament are the grace which I announced as my text, and our Lord's command to baptize "in the name of the Father, and of the Son, and of the Holy Ghost." Neither of these texts expresses the doctrine explicitly, though both apparently do so implicitly.

As a matter of fact it took Christians nearly four centuries to find the right words to express their meaning; St. Augustine in his famous work *De Trinitate* was the first writer to work out the doctrine with fullness. But the main thought of his argument is present in every writer from St. Paul onward. The Church had (in the first three centuries) to fight so hard to maintain the true nature of our Lord as both true God and true man that the doctrine of the Trinity remained practically unexplored.

One thing alone seems to have led Christians along in their definition of the Trinity—that one thing was their own personal experience. They knew how God had spoken to them in His Three Natures.

God was known to them as One who deals directly with souls in a personal way. He deals with us as individuals, from thorough knowledge of us. In all His dealings He displays love toward us, and demands a loving response from us. There could, of course, be no question of God's Oneness for those who reverenced the Old Testament. Yet their experience was that the personal relations with God of which they were conscious fell into three classes.

First there was the relation of the loving Creator to His creature, of the omniscient Potter to His Clay; the great Father above, powerful and transcendant, yet loving and merciful, to whom worship and service were the bounden duty of man. Next there was the relation of communion, in which the soul draws near to God yet remains distinct from God, and is not absorbed through its contact with Him. It was, no doubt, in the Sacrament of Holy Communion that this relation was most deeply felt by them.

Then, also, there was a third relation, quite distinct from that of communion—that in which the soul is possessed by God's "breath" or Spirit (the same word is used for both) or, in other words, the relation in which God's grace is poured into the soul to guide and inspire it.

Such a reflection by itself could hardly bring anyone to the doctrine of the Trinity; but taken in connection with the teaching of the New Testament it could hardly fail to do so. The New Testament makes it clear that our Lord stood in a unique relation to God. The Acts of the Apostles always speaks of the Spirit as God's own grace and power coming down to men: our Lord too promised that the Spirit would be sent from the Father to be the champion and helper of the disciples after His own departure.

The inference is not far to seek that it was in the nature of God Himself to exist in three relations: Father, Son, and Holy Spirit, since though one, He showed Himself to the soul in three characters. The word "Persons" means just this: that in the Godhead are these three which are not parts of God, but which is each fully God.

The doctrine of the Trinity grew out of the experience of Christians in developing the spiritual life and in reading the New Testament. But what value does this doctrine have for us? Why is it important to hold fast to it?

It is possible to err in two directions. You may over-emphasize the distinction of persons, and affirm that there are three gods; or else you may become a unitarian, by treating the persons as mere aspects of God—only ways in which He works. Both these points of view are harmful to religion; of the two the former is perhaps the worse, yet many people who mean to be quite orthodox fall into this difficulty.

They speak, for instance, of the Persons of the Trinity as though they were foils to one another. They describe the Atonement as a transaction in which the second Person pays a penalty to assuage the wrath of the first; or they represent the Son as holding discussions with the Father, such as Bunyan describes in his Holy War, which suggest nothing so much as the councils of the Olympian gods in Homer.

If we are to hold a right belief in the Incarnation and the Atonement, it is necessary to remember that God is one, and that you cannot contrast one Person in the Godhead with another.

The other error, though hardly less deadly, is more plausible. Those who reduce the Persons of the Trinity to mere names for the activities of God are fatally impoverishing the nature of God. First, God must be self-sufficient, and independent of the creatures He has made. We know that we are capable of love and fellowship with one another, and that these things are of absolute worth. If God has to look to us for them, and does not possess them in Himself, then He is not perfect; He needs us.

Unitarianism, though it may have a philosophy and an ethic, is not compatible with the facts and words of the Gospel. Yet after all, the Trinity remains ultimately a mystery, for the finite mind of man finds it difficult—nay, impossible—to comprehend the infinite mind of Deity.

Let us then see to it that we remember in all our worship, public and private, that fellowship, love, and every other personal relation which is ultimately good, exist eternally in the very being of the one God Himself. For if we forget this, the God whom we worship is something less than the God to whose service we are dedicated.

—*from* PULPIT DIGEST *for May, 1947*

Where Do We Go From Here?

BY JAMES A. PIKE
Chaplain of Columbia University

TEXT: *In the days that were before the flood they were eating and drinking, marrying and giving in marriage, until the day that Noah entered into the ark.*—MATTHEW 24:38

ADDRESSES at commencement time have changed greatly in their context since I first began to listen to them. That is because what was being "commenced" was different. The first ones I remember were in the late twenties, and they tended to run something like this:

There is unlimited opportunity ahead; you only need to grasp it. You are the potential leaders. Apply your talents and you will be rewarded with success and your industry will bring benefit to society in its upward march.

Obvious enough even in the pious idealism called for on such occasions was the general pattern of values by which this "success" was to be measured: the advance of science, the increase of material wealth, and (perhaps) the spreading of these benefits to a wider body of recipients.

At no commencement of mine was I able to bask in the

237

optimism which such sentiments displayed; hopes were held out with more restraint in the thirties when I was the more direct object of the remarks. No change in the world-view involved, mind you. The same values; but we were in an eddy in the onward tide which gave pause to the most hardened baccalaureate speaker. For example, I graduated from law school in a year when not the least reason I accepted a fellowship at Yale was the fact that the modest stipend afforded me a more reliable income than most of my fellow-counsellors could count on that next year. Society had the same aims; we were exhorted to "leadership" thereto; but the march was temporarily suspended; yet in "these changing times" we must be relied on to do better than our forebears—better, but in terms of the same scale of values.

Today—at the turn of this fateful century—the scene has changed again. There is no eddy in the tide. Wherever we are going, you can go along; indeed you can be out front. There'll be jobs for most of you, good jobs for quite a few of you. But a new factor, a factor in quite a different dimension, has entered the picture: we're not so sure we know where we are going. A brooding doubt about the whole enterprise hovers over every serious bit of planning. Over all the little securities hangs a large insecurity. It is as though around a most carefully balanced equation we had thrown parentheses and written a $\pm$ in front.

Now some of you are thinking that I am going to talk about the menace of nuclear physics and impose upon you who are here for a conventional collegiate exercise some preacher's rhetoric on some such theme as "Holiness or Hydrogen" or perhaps "Vision or Fission." I'm not—although actually we cannot preach or speak seriously about anything today without taking into account this obvious existential factor in every man's affairs. Far from unrealistic is the sermon title which formed the subject of a recent cartoon in *The New Yorker*: "Will the Atom Bomb Blow You to Heaven or Hell?"

But you have heard a good deal about all this, and I would rather use the few minutes allotted to me today to discuss another kind of *fission* which threatens all that you would now "commence" quite as much as atomic fission. Destruction by atomic fission is a depending possibility: the destructiveness of this other fission is already an actuality.

A fission in personal life is what we are faced with today: the break-up of community, the break-up of family, and the break-up of the individual. The atomization of our *community life* is such that we hardly know—or care to know— our fellow apartment-dwellers. The fission in *family life* brings one out of every four marriages to the courts, and in many of the remainder the deep cleavages justify T. S. Eliot's characterizations in *The Cocktail Party*:

> Two people who know they do not understand each other,
> Breeding children whom they do not understand
> And who will never understand them.

And finally there is the break-up of *the individual*: what Arnold Toynbee so penetratingly has called "schism in the soul"—a general condition of which schizophrenia is but the pathological expression.

The mention of Mr. Toynbee recalls the cosmic setting in which we should try to understand our times: each great civilization has had its "time of troubles" before its dissolution. And inner decay more than outward pressure has each time accounted for the ultimate downfall. But in our day it so happens that the outward threat—atomic fission— closely parallels the inner danger. It is, in a strange way, a sacrament of it—an outward and visible sign of an inward and spiritual *dis*grace—*i.e.*, fall from grace. Atomic explosion follows from the separation of the individual electrons from the nucleus, the center of their wonted order. So it is with the spiritual break-up of our common life: it is no wonder, for example, that statistics show 2 1/5 times as much divorce among couples without a common religious faith; destroy the transcendent center of life and life falls apart, stayed only by temporary conglomerations around false centers. In German intellectual life God had been discarded; it is no wonder that the universities were the first to render obedience to the Nazi false God, and that it was the Churches which resisted—a contrast which incidentally led Albert Einstein back to belief in God. And today Communism often serves as an integrating center for those who have lost the true focus. Nature—and personal life—abhors a vacuum.

Culture after culture, the same old story has been repeated. First the people believe in a center beyond themselves, be it the gods or God. On this basis life becomes so well organized and the people have such vigor and homogeneity, that they don't think they need any longer the source of their strength and order. At first the intellectuals, then the common people, discard the supernatural and worship the natural; as the confidence in their experiment grows, a sort of "cultural lag" keeps society relatively ordered and people relatively decent to each other. Though religion goes, the ethics based on the religion linger on for awhile; such ethics are what Elton Trueblood calls the "cut flowers" of religion. And cut flowers soon die. So in two or three generations the withering shows up and the symptoms of decay appear; the devaluation of all abiding realities; the consequent meaninglessness, the worship of false gods; divorce; neurosis; psychosis; increase of psychosomatic illness; fissiparous and divisive movements. These are the all too apparent signs of the times.

Now this is not just some abstract philosophy of history for armchair meditation. It is a realistic diagnosis of the society in which you are taking your place as adults; more specifically, it describes the real threats to your personal fulfillment, to your hopes of satisfying family life, to the maintenance of any society worth living in.

The state of our times should cause concern to you as ordinary individuals, potential fathers and mothers—just as people. But it is not on this level that I am seeking to challenge you today. One refrain from baccalaureate sermons in all decades I will endorse and repeat: You *are* the potential leaders, you are better equipped than most of your contemporaries. What you think, say, and do will leave vastly more impact than thoughts, words, and actions of those with a less extended or less thorough academic preparation. I fear it is true that most men are unaware of our inner perils. Only eight were ready to go into the ark; of the rest it could be said, in the words of the text:

> In the days that were before the flood they were eating and drinking, marrying and giving in marriage, until the day that Noah entered the ark.

Most men have learned nothing through two World Wars; Hiroshima has made no dent upon their consciousness; life goes on as usual. But let it not be so with you. If our fellow countrymen as a whole are to wake up before it is too late, it will be because people like you see the disease and can prescribe a remedy—and demonstrate it—in lives which, in the nature of the case, will be more conspicuous.

You can neither apply nor demonstrate the remedy if you don't know yourselves what it is. It is possible these days for a man to go through college and remain religiously illiterate—an adult in physics or psychology and still a child in religion and ethics (no wonder religious faith is so often discarded in college days; children's religion doesn't "rate" very well alongside adult learning); and all too often the colleges have provided little or no opportunity for the mature, intellectually honest but sympathetic study of the Judæo-Christian faith which has, in the main, furnished the roots of our culture. Studies limited to man's affairs and endeavors give many answers in realms which are of less importance than the highest reaches of human personality; but the problems of man himself remain unsolved until they are examined from a higher level. Man cannot lift himself by his own bootstraps (but how popular an exercise is the attempt!).

This is why at Columbia and Barnard we have developed an expanded curriculum in Religion covering every field of religious thought underlying our common culture, and in which each major tradition will be examined both critically and constructively by those standing without and within each faith. With a staff of fourteen full-time and part-time instructors offering thirty-six courses, it is the most comprehensive undergraduate program in religion in the nation.

Why all this now? Because the times are late, and we want an increasing number of the graduates of our three undergraduate colleges to go out as leaders in the realm of the spirit as well as in humane and mechanical skills. We want them to have a deep grasp of those things which make for integration and wholeness in man's life—both as a basis for their own personal and family life and as a basis for their communicating it—effectively and rapidly—to those whom T. S. Eliot has called the "hollow men" of our time: both to those who sense the danger but don't know the answers and to those (and these are the majority) who are not even aware that we are in peril—*as in the days that were before the flood* . . .

I hope as you begin to take your place in many different communities, and become co-founders of many new families, that you will focus your attention on this central— and determinative—realm. You may have already made a good start. There have been all along some opportunities in the curriculum for the systematic study of religion. Or perhaps you may have directed your private studies in that direction. But whether you have or not, make it a main focus now.

If you will be living in this area you would do well to come back and take some of these courses: through the School of General Studies most of them are available in late afternoon or evening, and a number of them yield graduate credit. Also many of the churches, aware of the religious illiteracy these days (even among their regular members), have developed adult study programs. If neither of these suggestions is feasible, we will be glad to supply to any of you who will write for it a reading list for private or family study of the most important fields of religious thought.

If you make religion a serious concern, it won't long remain an intellectual matter. There's no telling what changes it will make in your personal life. You will find your scale of values altering—when measured by eternity things look different. You will understand your own failings and inadequacies in a different way—you may learn the secret of how to have both genuine self-acceptance and honest self-criticism, in deeper understanding of the paradox of Divine judgment and forgiveness. You will come in touch with resources for the ordering of your unconscious life—for worship can project healing symbols into the inner life. You may even reassess how you want to use your life (when after eleven years of agnosticism I began to look at religion seriously, my collar got turned around—though the result for you may be less drastic, it will be equally important if it leads you to make a ministry out of whatever calling you are in, and any calling *can* be a ministry). True, many of you already stand in this larger perspective and have experienced these things; but it is important in this confused time that, in the words of St. Peter, you have *a reason for the faith that is in you*, that you are equipped to speak confidently to others in terms relevant to our time.

Truly you are the leaders, but *if the trumpet blow uncertainly*, who shall be prepared to follow?

What if they won't follow anyway—or more explicitly, what if enough do not follow soon enough? *As in the days that were before the flood they knew not until the flood came, and took them all away.* Well, in any event we are building an ark; we invite all who will to join us, not resting content till all our brothers join in building an ark big enough for our whole society. If they will not, the ark will be smaller. And should judgment come as it has many times, on an idolatrous, God-defying, fratricidal society, there may well be those who would not hear, would not change. Those who live for passing things will pass with them; and those who live for eternal things will abide eternally. In either event, God reigns. If we join our labors to bringing in His Kingdom, *God reigns*—and we with Him. If we decline to work with Him, *God reigns*—and without us. Such is His ultimacy.

Maybe not enough will change quickly enough. Maybe physical fission or spiritual fission—or both—will make an end of our culture. Nor do we know "the times or the seasons." *If the goodman of the house had known in what watch the thief would come, he would have watched and would not have suffered his house to be broken in.* Maybe a better society, maybe the end. But the interim task is clear enough if we see the issues. *Walk while ye have the light, lest darkness come upon you; for he that walketh in darkness knoweth not whither he goeth.*

In times in many ways similar to ours, when the Roman civilization had gone far toward decay within (though practically nobody suspected it but the little Christian underground—which was really the only spark of life in a dying Empire) when many men's *hearts were failing them for fear,* St. Paul wrote a letter to some of the little flock in Thessalonica, whose fear was in fact heightened by the new religious insight into their own times.

But as far as times and seasons go, my brothers, you don't need written instructions. You are well aware that the day of the Lord will come as unexpectedly as a burglary to a householder. When men are saying "Peace and security," catastrophe will sweep down upon them as suddenly and inescapably as travail upon a woman with child.

But because you, my brothers, are not living in darkness the Day cannot take you completely by surprise. After all, burglary only takes place at night! You are all sons of light, sons of the day, and none of us belong to darkness or the night. Let us then never fall into the sleep that stupefies the rest of the world: let us keep awake, with our wits about us. Night is the time for sleep and the time when men get drunk, but we men of the daylight should be alert, with faith and love as our breastplate and the hope of our salvation as our helmet. (I Thess. 5:1-8, Phillips' translation)

It is such a hope that is expressed in your Alma Mater's motto: *In Thy Light we shall see light*. Live by this light, spread it abroad. In these critical times let it not be said of you:

In the days that were before the flood they were eating and drinking, marrying and giving in marriage, until the day that Noah entered into the ark.

—from PULPIT DIGEST *for June, 1950*

The Problem of Freedom

BY ERNEST FREMONT TITTLE

*Late Pastor of First Methodist Church,
Evanston, Illinois*

IN 1863 Abraham Lincoln at Gettysburg made a five-minute speech which, contrary to his own expectation, the world has not forgotten. In fact what he said there is now become almost too familiar to quote. Every school boy knows that in 1776 "our fathers brought forth upon this continent a new nation conceived in liberty and dedicated to the proposition that all men are created equal," and that in 1863 it was an open question whether "this nation or any nation so conceived and so dedicated [could] long endure."

Well, the United States of America has endured. It survived the Civil War. It has come through two world wars with strength unabated. It is today the mightiest power on earth. But the question remains whether in today's world this nation or any other can long endure as a free people,

This sermon was included in a posthumous volume of Dr. Tittle's work, *A Mighty Fortress,* published and copyrighted 1950 by Harper & Brothers. Reprinted by permission.

247

cherishing a free press, a free radio, a free school, a free church, and free elections.

A future war waged with atomic and bacteriological weapons would almost certainly result in the spread of political totalitarianism over all the earth. You cannot build or maintain institutions of freedom on hunger, chaos, and despair.

We have, moreover, to reckon with an augmentation of the powers of government resulting from the interrelatedness of modern society and the present conditions of the world. We in this country do not like the idea of government interference in matters which until now have been regarded as personal and private. We deplore government intervention, unless we get into a jam and would be glad to have the government get us out. Yet even we Americans are coming to recognize that government must intervene in case the national economy as a whole is imperiled, whether by monopolistic practices or by strikes that threaten to paralyze the entire country. And among the peoples of Western Europe, including Britain, there is now general agreement that economic recovery and national welfare, at least in their case, call for a large measure of government control over natural resources, basic industries, banking, and foreign trade. In today's world no government would be tolerated that did not assume responsibility for the general welfare and appropriate to itself the power needed to discharge this obligation.

Hence one of the crucial problems of our time—the problem of providing adequate social control while at the same time preserving freedoms essential to a humane and civilized community and to the highest personal life.

Now, the thesis which I wish to present is that fundamental freedoms are rooted in a religious conception of the world and life and cannot possibly be maintained apart from the faith and concern of true religion.

In the Christian view, man is not merely an animal differing from the brute creation by having a somewhat superior brain. He is a child of God in the sense that he is a creation of God, is made in the image of God, and has value in the sight of God. He must, therefore, be treated with respect and given a chance to realize the divine possibilities within him. This involves that he will be given fundamental freedoms—freedom of religion and conscience, freedom of speech, press, and assembly, freedom of scientific inquiry and teaching, freedom of political opposition. These freedoms we Americans have enjoyed, thanks to the fact that the founding fathers of our nation were influenced by Christian beliefs and principles. They "brought forth upon this continent a new nation conceived in liberty" because they held that men are endowed by their Creator with certain inalienable rights—rights which governments exist to defend and must not take away.

Freedom can live in a world where man is regarded as a child of God, having dignity and worth. It cannot live in a world where God is denied and where, in consequence of this denial, human beings are thought to have no rights which governments are bound to respect. History in our time has conclusively shown that the denial and repudiation of the Christian view of man leads inexorably to the denial of fundamental freedoms.

On the Christian view, all men have worth—rich and poor, educated and ignorant, exalted and lowly, white and black and yellow and brown. All are children of God, and all must be treated with respect.

This teaching is in line with modern science, which recognizes the common origin of all peoples. And note its bearing upon the problem of freedom. In today's world freedom must be assured to all men, or it will not permanently be secure for any man.

This we may fail to see, especially we Americans who have come to take our traditional freedoms for granted. In some parts of the world, however, the fact that freedom must be for all if it is to be for any has been brought home by the logic of events. The German people now know that if fundamental freedoms are denied to Jews they will presently be denied to everybody. The Russian people now know that if freedom of political opposition is denied to any individual or group it will presently be found nonexistent in a one-party state exercising all but absolute control over the life of the people.

Time magazine, apropos of the current attempt to purge Russian music of bourgeois influence, tells of a Russian cartoon showing a man and a woman seated on a park bench while a bird sings overhead. Says she: "How do you like the nightingale's song?" Says he: "Until I know who wrote the melody, I can say nothing."

The irrefutable logic of events declares: If you wish to remain a free people you must not deny fundamental freedoms to any racial or religious group; you must not outlaw any political party, however much you may deplore its tenets; you must not deny to any minority the right to present its views and to win adherents.

It follows from the Christian view of man that the hungry

must be fed and the social causes of human misery removed
—a demand which bears directly upon the problem of
freedom. No people wants dictatorship. People everywhere
would like to be free, but they will consent to dictatorship
if it appears to be the only alternative to hunger and chaos.
Today, with the possible exception of Czechoslovakia, political totalitarianism is not to be found in any country
where the masses of the people live in tolerable conditions.
But where social conditions are shockingly bad and no
attempt is made to improve them, where age-old injustices
go unremedied and men and women, looking ahead, can
see no ray of hope for themselves or their children—there
Communism, with its rosy promise of food, work, education, and opportunity for all, can win adherents; there
dictatorship, under the guise of benevolent paternalism, can
be established.

Fundamental freedoms are inseparable from basic human
needs—food, work, education, opportunity. If freedom is
to survive, people everywhere must be delivered from
hunger and hopelessness. This is now entirely clear, or
should be.

Christianity at its best fits men and women for a free
society. To be fit for a free society, you must have faith
in man. This does not mean the naive belief that everybody can be trusted. It does not mean blindness to human
sin and folly whether in others or in yourself. But it means
the conviction that human beings the world over have
within them a spark of divinity, are capable of rising above
animalism and above ignorance and selfishness into some
attainment of dignity and moral worth. This conviction is
absolutely essential to the promotion and survival of free-

dom. Lacking it, we shall not even try to remedy social conditions, to bring into being a social environment in which freedom can live. We shall rationalize our failure by saying: "Human nature being what it is, it is utopian to expect any radical change and improvement in the conditions of the world."

To be fit for a free society, you must treat people with respect, regardless of race, color, creed, or condition. The Methodist General Conference of 1948 adopted a resolution calling for a non-segregated church and a non-segregated society. Well, I have received a number of letters protesting this resolution, letters so unreasoning, so steeped in prejudice, so bitter and violent that anyone reading them could hardly escape the thought: Here, alas! is a mentality more compatible with Hitlerism than with democracy. The writers of these letters would feel entirely at home in a society that sanctioned the doctrines and policies of Nazism. If such persons should come to be a majority among us, this nation would be ripe for dictatorship.

Even the telling of jokes at the expense of a particular racial or religious group is to be deplored. A joke told at the expense of Negroes or Jews may have no other intention than to produce a laugh. All the same, it may serve to undermine a respect for human personality without which freedom cannot endure among men.

To be fit for a free society, you must do on a voluntary basis things indispensable for the general welfare. If such things are not done on a voluntary basis, they will be done under government direction and control. No government these days is going to keep its hands off in a situation where the national economy as a whole is threatened. Business,

medicine, every vocation that is vitally related to the common life may be expected in our time to be regulated by
government unless it accepts responsibility for the general
welfare. In today's world the choice is not between regula-
tion and laissez faire. The only question is who is going to
do the regulating. If as a business man or a professional
man I do not regulate myself in moral regard for the welfare of my community, then government must and will step
in and regulate me.

To be fit for a free society, you must upon occasion stick
your neck out in the name of freedom. In Hitler's Germany
those were fit for a free society who protested outrageous
violations of human decency. What of those who kept silence? Our answer may be a condemnation not only of
them but of ourselves. Would we in the same or a similar
situation have spoken out, knowing that the price might
be a concentration camp? Did we speak out in protest
against the treatment administered to Japanese-Americans
when, after Pearl Harbor, they were condemned en masse
without trial to exile and imprisonment in concentration
camps? Are we now protesting the denial to Negro Americans of the right to vote and the right to equal opportunity
in housing, employment, education, and medical service?

Those are fit for a free society who, when freedom is
imperiled, do not keep silence but speak out at whatever
personal risk.

And here Christianity can make a world of difference.
Dr. Albert Einstein has confessed to a new respect and
appreciation for the Christian Church. When National Socialism in Germany threatened to destroy fundamental freedoms, he confidently expected protest and revolt to come

from the German universities. But the universities caved in. Men of international reputation in law, in history, in medicine and science consented to teach not science, medicine, history, or law, but propaganda. The revolt came from the quarter where he least expected it: it arose within the Christian Church. Well, he need not have been surprised. The human mind, even the scientific mind, unless it is under the control of something more reliable than fear or self-interest, can always find plausible reasons for staying out of a concentration camp. But you can neither bribe nor intimidate a man who recognizes an absolute for conduct—the righteousness of God revealed in Jesus Christ. To every command to act contrary to the teachings of Christ his reply is: "We must obey God rather than men."

I met recently a German layman who is mayor of his town in the Russian zone in Germany. In the early days of the occupation he went to the Russian authorities and said:

> We will obey every command of yours that is not in conflict with the teachings of our religion, but do not ask us to do anything contrary to the commands of Christ. That we will not do. You may starve us, imprison us, threaten to shoot us, but we will not do it. We will die first.

To be fit for a free society you must do the things that make for freedom, regardless of what other people do. We all know the temptation to hold back until enough people are doing the right and necessary thing to make it the safe thing to do. But, of course, no freedom ever was won in this world by people who cautiously waited for others to act. Nor can freedom now be kept alive in the world by anyone whose position is: "Well, I'll do my part if others will, but naturally I do not want to be the only one to take the rap." Somebody must stick his neck out and do it first. Somebody must stand up and say: "I know not what course others may take, but as for me, give me liberty or give me death." Somebody must say: "Here I stand, I can do no other, God help me. Amen."

To be fit for a free society you must pay the price of freedom, and this in the absence of absolute certainty that freedom will prevail in your time—perhaps the hardest test to which a man can be put. Will enough people in today's world start doing the things necessary for the preservation of freedom? As to that you cannot be sure. You only can be sure that freedom belongs to the divine purpose in the world.

Miss Muriel Lester tells of a German woman, a middle-aged Doctor of Philosophy, divorced by Hitler from her Jewish husband, also a Doctor of Philosophy, after having lived with him half a lifetime. This woman, when Miss Lester first met her, had just come from a luncheon with her husband. They had eaten together secretly, illegally, dangerously. She was suffering acutely from emotional strain; and thinking, perhaps, that her tears called for an explanation, she began to comment on the situation in which she found herself, and many others like her. She said:

> It's a new sort of human being that is evolving. Hitler thinks he will succeed where God has failed. He thinks he knows better than God. God wants people to be healthy, happy, and good. So does Hitler ... But Hitler thinks God made an initial mistake in giving His people a measure of free will. Hitler would do the opposite. He would take away the free will which

they had. He'd force them to be happy and healthy and good
. . . No one knows what sort of human being will evolve from
this training. It may be just a very beautiful healthy animal
free from inhibitions and complexes because freed from the
power of choice, free from conscience. Or on the other hand
it may develop into a brute.

Well, the answer is now clear. It is that the denial of
human freedom is the most terrible loss and hurt the human
soul can sustain. We can be entirely sure that freedom
belongs to the purpose of God; and trusting in God we can
resolve that whatever course others may take, we, to the
limit of our capacity, will pay the price of freedom.

—*from* PULPIT DIGEST *for June, 1950*

The Gospel and
Human Welfare

BY SARKIS PAPAJIAN

*Director of Social and Religious Welfare,
St. Paul's Orphans' and Old Folks' Home,
Greenville, Pennsylvania*

LABOR DAY emphasizes many questions that must be answered and problems that must be solved if we are to realize lasting harmony in the field of industrial activity, and security in our economic life. All of us are vitally interested in the subject before us, because it is definitely related to our common welfare, no matter what social or economic group we may personally represent.

It is fair to ask some pointed questions about Christianity in relation to our industrial and business world.

Is the gospel relevant to the problems presented by modern business and industry? Does it offer any solution to our social, economic and industrial difficulties? Can labor and management find in the pages of the Bible some guiding light which might lead them into a spirit of greater co-

257

operation, a deeper appreciation of their interdependence, and a stronger sense of responsibility on the part of both toward the welfare of the larger community?

Jesus offered no set of rules for the management of our present-day economic life. He drew no constitution to guide nations or industrial organizations. He did not live in a technical age. He lived during a period much less complicated in social and economic standards than our own.

Had he set specific rules for the business and economic conduct of his day, they would be meaningless for us. Laws set down for merchants, fishermen, and farmers would have little value for today's industrial empires, employing hundreds of thousands of workers, with immense wealth and machinery at their command. They would mean little in settling disputes or easing the strained relationships between conflicting interests, and in solving the knotty problems of finance and economics for the common welfare of all men.

On the other hand, the people of Jesus' day were human beings like ourselves, created in the spiritual likeness of God. They had to struggle for the same basic necessities of life; they were driven by the same desires; beset by similar temptations to be selfish, greedy, and callous; stirred by the same hopes and dreams as the men and women of our own age. They wanted freedom, security, and success, as most of us normal human beings desire these things today.

During his earthly life Jesus lived through a period of economic depression. He found people anxious and worried about their daily bread. They were groaning under the burden of heavy taxation. Inability to pay a bill meant prison or servitude.

Jesus constantly speaks about such matters. He speaks about debtors going to prison; about a man planning to build a tower, but not having enough capital to finish it; about people being desperately anxious concerning money, food, shelter, and clothing, and lacking these basic necessities; about widows losing their properties. He himself had no home.

But Jesus, looking upon all these problems, saw them as matters of human relationship. So his main concern was with human well-being, not directly with politics or economics. He knew that the right solution of most human problems depends upon the right attitude of men toward one another and toward God.

Therefore, he laid down some definite principles for our guidance—not to run machinery and finance, production scales and wages, but to help human beings live together as children of one heavenly Father, in the spirit of love, brotherhood, and cooperation.

These principles are eternally true. Political and economic systems will come and go, civilizations will rise and disappear, but the truths and the spirit of Christ will ever offer the only real and lasting solution to all human difficulties.

What are these truths? We may begin by recalling his two commandments: "You shall love the Lord your God with all your heart, and with all your soul, and with all your mind. This is the great and first commandment. And a second is like it, You shall love your neighbor as yourself."

Loving God with all our beings would solve all our personal problems. The beast in us would not ruin our souls. We would lose our fear of life. Our love for God would help keep our minds healthy and our hearts pure. Our love for our neighbor would solve most of our social problems.

Aside from these two commandments, Jesus has given us the Golden Rule in its most positive and helpful form: "Whatever you wish that men would do to you, do so to them." The Golden Rule is the keynote of mutual justice, confidence, and helpfulness in all human relations. In addition, through his parables and teachings, Jesus lays down some changeless guideposts, which alone can direct our confused age to a more harmonious and brighter day.

For one thing, Jesus emphasizes the supreme value of human life, as the most precious of all God's creation. All else is created for man's sake—for his welfare, happiness, spiritual development, and inward peace. "The sabbath was made for man, not man for the sabbath" applies to all life.

Machines are created to give man greater abundance in goods and services; man is not created to become just a cog in the wheels of the industrial machine, or just a Social Security number. Technical inventions are to be used to promote human comfort, safety, and well-being; men are not to be used as mere guinea-pigs to swell the profits of the producers. In all business and industrial activities human welfare must receive first consideration, while profits and personal gain become the by-products of such a healthy attitude.

In the light of his teachings, Jesus would approve the forceful statement of Sylvester Horne: "The essence of religious teaching is that the soul of man, whether a drunkard wallowing in the East End gutter, or a black man thrown on the human scrap-heap of the diamond mines of the

Rand, is worth more than the whole wealth of the world in the eyes of God." Any society that insists on ignoring this truth condemns itself to self-destruction.

Again, Jesus emphasizes the fact of human brotherhood. His idea of humanity is that of God's great family. God is the Father, all men His children, brothers therefore to one another.

No discrimination of race, class, or color can be justified. Men are brothers first, employers and employees afterwards. As members of a world-wide family, they must learn to share in all life's blessings, as well as in its hazards and problems. No group, no matter how exclusive it may try to be, no matter how privileged it may consider itself, can live unto itself alone.

We are all bound together by bonds stronger than class interests or group loyalties. Depressions, epidemics, wars curse us all together. Lasting peace, prosperity, security can be realized only when all men are willing to share them with each other. Paul's statement may be truthfully applied to all humanity: "We are all one body. If one member suffers, all suffer together; if one member is honored, all rejoice together."

Once again, Jesus maintained that human welfare requires a way of service and love. If humanity is a brotherhood, and if human welfare is the primary consideration of organized society, then the only way men can live together in security and peace is by mutual service and helpfulness.

Recall our Master's own statements: "He that is greatest among you shall be your servant."

"A new commandment I give unto you that you love one another, as I have loved you."

"The Son of Man came not to be ministered unto, but to minister and to give his life as a ransom for many."

The main purpose of life, Jesus would insist, is not to get all you can for personal gain, but to give and to do all you can in promoting the spirit and purposes of God among men; in helping to make this world a better, cleaner, safer, and more Christian place to live in. The ideal society is the one which does most, not in upholding the privileges of the few at the expense of the community, but in serving the common welfare of all in the self-sacrificing spirit of Christ.

Finally, Jesus would insist today, as he did in his own day, that privilege and responsibility go hand in hand. The larger our industrial capacity and power grow, the greater becomes the responsibility of the men who control them, toward those they employ and those whose livelihood and welfare depend upon the successful management of industry.

The wealthier a concern grows, the more it must feel responsible for the welfare of the community in which it operates. A representative leader of American business, Mr. Eric Johnston, blames the advent of socialism in western Europe on the failure of European businessmen to grasp this basic principle of human society. The stronger a labor union grows, the more responsible its leaders must become, not only in their dealings with management but also in their attitude toward the entire community.

"To whom much is given, of him much shall be required," is an eternal truth spoken by our Master. We are all God's stewards, called to use our power, capacity, wealth, and time to promote not so much our own selfish interests, but primarily the peace, security, and well-being of humanity, God's family on earth.

In the sharp struggle between conflicting ideologies of dictatorship and democracy, what matters most is not cheap, high-sounding, yet barren words and phrases, but the fruit of the Christian spirit practiced between management and labor, between rich and poor, employer and employee.

The greatest weapon against totalitarianism of any kind is the way and the gospel of Christ applied in all our industrial, financial, and business enterprises: loving our neighbors as we love ourselves; obeying the Golden Rule in all walks of life; considering human welfare more sacred than material gain or property right; treating others as our brothers; serving the common good and giving a full portion of our blessings back to the community from which we received them, and to God, their primary source.

The gospel of Jesus Christ alone can solve all our problems, heal our wounds, and answer all our questions.

—*from* PULPIT DIGEST *for August, 1949*

Why I Am a Catholic

BY HOWARD G. HAGEMAN

Pastor of North Reformed Church, Newark, New Jersey

TEXT: *All things are yours; whether Paul, or Apollos, or Cephas, or the world, or life, or death, or things present, or things to come; all are yours, and ye are Christ's and Christ is God's.*—I CORINTHIANS 3:21-23

FOR THE average person, by far the most puzzling phrase in the Apostles' Creed is the one which reads: "I believe in the Holy Catholic Church." It is no secret that the average person assumes that the word Catholic means Roman Catholic. To his way of thinking, it seems strange, to say the least that a Protestant should profess to believe in the Catholic Church from which his fathers fought and died to be free. And so the modern Protestant has lost consciousness of the meaning and the challenge of the Holy Catholic Church by quietly letting it be surrendered to one branch of the Church which has gleefully seized upon the chance to monopolize the word.

The Roman Church, of course, does everything which

it can to help further this illusion. For that Church realizes that the more it can monopolize the word "Catholic," the more surely it can put Protestantism in the unhappy position of being an upstart movement with no background and no future. A lot of silly Protestants, anxious to avoid everything even remotely connected with Rome, have played straight into their hands by themselves disavowing any part in the word. Happily, the Reformers themselves had no such notions. Never for one moment did they think of surrendering the grand old name of Catholic. Our friends may term themselves "Roman Catholics" if they choose. But our claim to catholicity is something which we dare not and will not surrender.

But why? Is it only stubborn prejudice, or is there something real at stake in our fight to claim the name "Catholic?" What are we claiming when we lay claim to this name? Were we to lose it, would we be giving up anything of any real importance, or would we merely be surrendering a title so empty of meaning as to make it hardly worth a fight?

It is common knowledge that the word catholic signifies universality or wholeness. Thus, we will say that Mr. A. is possessed of a catholic taste in music or in literature. That illustrates the basic meaning of the word, and it is within the idea of universality that we must look for answers to our question. But even within the meaning of the word, there are different applications of meaning which, taken together, contribute to the richness of the Holy Catholic Church.

I am a Catholic, first of all, because I believe in a Church for all mankind. That is to say, I believe in a Church which is inclusive rather than exclusive, a Church in which such things as race, color, social class, or economic standing mean nothing. I want no part of a Church that exists for Americans only, for white people only, for middle-class people only, for college graduates only, for ten-thousand-a-year men only. In Christ, all these distinctions mean less than nothing. In Him, there is neither Jew nor Greek, male nor female, slave nor free. His body is for all men, regardless of their color, their condition, or their race.

Need I tell you that we Christians could solve many of the problems that are confronting us today, if we took seriously this faith in the Holy Catholic Church? Everyone is worried, for example, about the problem of race relations, as we have it right here in our own country. Well, if we all were really catholic in our outlook, there would be no problem. The problem arises because we have been poor Catholics. This church, we say, is for white people only; this church for black people only. I suppose if we had green people, we should have a church for them, too. Can you imagine a Church for lawyers only? for businessmen only? Every time you say you believe in the Holy Catholic Church, you are saying that you believe that the Church of Jesus Christ is greater than our human distinctions and our human differences.

Or again, take our international problem. We experiment dangerously with Leagues of Nations and United Nations and all the rest. What is that but a confession that we have failed to realize the catholicism of the Church? If the Church were really Catholic, we would already have an international family held together by bonds so strong that nothing could break them apart. Frankly, I am a Catholic for selfish reasons, because I know of nothing else strong enough to cement this divided and shattered world together, save the power of Jesus Christ in His Church. Long ago, someone wrote: "It is the Christians who hold the world together." Unhappily, that is not true of us any longer. But it could be, if we were to take our Catholicism seriously. I am a Catholic because I believe in a Church for all mankind.

In the second place, I am a Catholic because I believe in a Church for the whole man. All too often our religion is something that affects only part of us part of the time. Most commonly, it is something for our souls on Sundays, and nothing more. But that is not the Catholic faith. The Catholic faith is a religion for the whole man all of the time. It is not just for his emotions, but also for his intellect; yes, also for his body. It is not just for his Sundays, but for his Wednesdays and his Saturdays. It is interested not only in what he does in Church, but in what he does in his job, in his family, yes, in what he does with his leisure time. It is a faith to which a man can respond, not just with a part of himself, but with everything that he has.

Here again we have crippled ourselves because we have not taken our Catholicism seriously. Do you remember what they used to say about the Pilgrims that they fell on their knees on Sundays and on their neighbors during the week? There has been too much of that about our religion. Particularly in this age of specialization, we have made religion just one department in our living. Then we wonder why our faith seems so remote and unreal when we need it. Every time you say that you believe in the Holy Catholic Church you are saying that you believe in a faith great enough to cover all of life, a faith that is relevant to your family life, your business relations, your job, your home, your recreation—to anything and everything that you do.

Here too we face all kinds of problems that we should not be facing if we had taken our Catholicism seriously. We have been such poor Catholics that we have divorced our educational system, our business life, our entertainment world from religion. We forced them apart, and now we are beginning to pay the price. Education, business, entertainment, and the rest have become secular and they are fast becoming pagan. And we don't know how to prevent this tidal wave of paganism that is rolling over the land from swallowing us and our children. Had the Church been Catholic, we should have been providing Christian principles for business, instructing in Christian education, giving opportunities for Christian entertainment and recreation. But instead the Church was content to take a little corner of life and specialize. And now we see the results. I am a Catholic because I believe in a Church for the whole man.

Finally, I am a Catholic because I believe in a Church with a whole faith. One of the curses of Protestantism is the fact that people will snip one thing or another from the Christian faith, just because it happens to appeal to them. They take this little fragment of truth and make it the be-all and the end-all of the Christian religion. Someone once said that a heresy is the revenge of a forgotten truth. How many of the sects can be explained in this way. They take one aspect of the Christian faith and play it up as though it were everything. The Christian Scientist seizes upon the fact of Christian healing and that becomes the whole of his religion. The Adventist fastens on the second coming of Christ and that is all he can talk about.

But within the Church, we all have the same dire tendency. We get hold of an idea and then ride it for all it is worth and more besides. How many Protestants think that the Golden Rule is the essence of Christianity! How many imagine that the Fatherhood of God and the brotherhood of man is the sum of the Christian faith! One fragment of truth is made to do duty for the whole faith.

Now it is the genius of the Catholic Church to give us the whole faith. A Catholic is never lopsided or fanatical. He never takes half a truth for the whole truth. He is never partial in his outlook. He is aware of God's love, but he also knows His justice. He knows man's hope and promise, but he also knows his sin. He realizes both the wickedness and the unselfishness of which the human heart is capable.

You cannot really deal effectively with a man unless you have this whole and balanced faith. Matthew Arnold once said of Sophocles, the great Greek tragedian, that he saw life steadily and saw it whole. Well, that's what the Catholic faith enables you to do. It saves you from a partial outlook. Through it you see life's misery and its grandeur, its shame and its glory, its ugliness and its beauty. It saves you from a false optimism, and from an equally false cynicism.

It is great enough and comprehensive enough to take all of the broken fragments of life and piece them together into a unified and meaningful whole. People complain nowadays that life has lost its meaning, that it is hard for them to find their way through it. That can only mean that we have been poor Catholics. That is why I am a Catholic, because I want and I need a Church which has a faith which is whole.

In all this I have said nothing about uniformity or even unity, for the very good reason that Catholicism is not directly bound up with any of these things. God does not expect us to think alike, to worship alike, anymore than He made us alike. Rigid conformity to a religious pattern has always been a fruitful source of trouble. The Holy Catholic Church is something far greater than that narrow kind of thing. In its simplest terms, it is this—the right to claim the fullest and richest heritage possible. A Church with a full faith for the whole man in every land, in every place, in every condition—that is the Holy Catholic Church to which, by the grace of God, you and I belong. For all things are yours, and ye are Christ's, and Christ is God's.

—*from* PULPIT DIGEST *for October, 1950*

Calvary's Armistice

BY CLARENCE E. MACARTNEY

Pastor of First Presbyterian Church, Pittsburgh, Pennsylvania

TEXT: *Having made peace through the blood of His cross.*
—Col. 1:20

PEACE! What a beautiful word it is; and when it comes after war, peace is a beautiful fact.

The signing of the Armistice in the Wood of Compiegne by the Allied and German plenipotentiaries brought to a close the most fearful war that the world had ever seen up to that time. It was a war in which the earth reeled, the sun was turned into darkness, and the moon into blood. Millions had fallen in battle, or died of wounds; millions had been left maimed and wounded; millions destitute and homeless, and millions were left brokenhearted. No wonder the earth rejoiced when the tidings were flashed around the globe that the cruel war had come to an end. Out of the blood and tears of humanity appeared the beautiful iridescent rainbow of peace.

The commemoration of the signing of the Armistice and

271

the conclusion of the First World War brings to our mind another war, the war of sin against God and against man, and the armistice which was signed on Calvary.

The peace of Versailles was signed in the famous palace of Louis XIV, which stands in the midst of rich gardens, with fountains flinging their silvery waters towards the sky. In the Gallerie des Glaces, with the representatives of all the great nations of the world assembled, the Treaty of Peace was signed. It was in the same hall that William I was crowned Emperor of Germany at the close of the War of 1870.

But the Treaty of Peace between God and man was signed on the Cross; signed not in ink, but in Immanuel's blood, while the heavens wondered and the earth shook and the sun veiled his face. The Treaty of Peace signed at Versailles affected all the nations which were at war with Germany; but the treaty of Peace signed at Calvary took in all ages, all races, all worlds, for, as St. Paul puts it, "It pleased the Father that in Him should all fullness dwell, and having made peace through the blood of His Cross, by Him to reconcile all things unto himself; by Him, I say, whether they be things in earth or things in heaven."

This war between man and God is as ancient as the fall of man, and as universal as the human race. When nations prepare for war, it occasions great excitement and rumor throughout the world. Newspapers display the tidings in flaring headlines. But the greatest and oldest and most widespread, most deadly, and most devastating of all wars, the war of sin, or man's war against God, receives hardly the slightest notice. This is because the whole human race is involved in this war, and has been involved in it throughout the history of the world.

Sin is the shadow cast by man wherever we find the human race. There is a reluctance on the part of men to face the deep facts of life, and one of the darkest and the deepest is this fact of sin. Sin is the breaking of the divine law, and therefore, the source of all human misery. What fact can be deeper and darker than this? What is it that casts so heavy a shadow across the path of man? What is it that poisons his cup, clouds the sky of his life, burdens his back, and fills his heart with sorrow? It is the fact of sin. The greatest of all delusions, the saddest of all self-deceptions, is that we have no sin. The faded sense of sin, and with it the feeling men have that they do not need a Saviour, that the Armistice signed on Calvary has no application for them, is only an evidence of the moral injury and decay which has overtaken man. Sin, or moral sin, is the fountain and source of the woes and sufferings of mankind. At war with God, man is at war with his fellowman, and at war with himself. "He that sinneth against God wrongeth his own soul." The earth has been devastated in the past, is being devastated today, and will be devastated in the ages to come by cruel and bloody wars. But there has never been a war, and there never will be a war which was not caused by this other war which underlies all wars and is the source of them, the war of man against God. Therefore, since men are engaged in this war against God, the world's great need is not education, or political organizations, or social amelioration, but reconciliation, peace with God.

In the midst of this war which takes in all nations and all ages, there come the tidings of peace to all men; an armistice has been signed on Calvary. Had peace not been offered, this war had destroyed mankind.

Earth has no spot so sacred as the place where the divine armistice was signed by Christ in behalf of God. Thousands have gone to the quiet spot in the midst of the dense forest at Compiegne where the representatives of Germany and the Allied Armies met and signed the Armistice. There is nothing there, save the inscriptions, to remind one of the cruel and devastating war which there came to an end. All that one saw was the beauty of the forest, and all that one heard was the song of the birds in the tops of the trees, as they moved in the summer wind. But the thoughts of mankind will ever halt at Calvary.

> There is a green hill far away,
> Without the city wall,
> Where our dear Lord was crucified
> Who died to save us all.

Here the representative of God and of man was the same Divine Person, the God-man, even Jesus Christ. In the Armistice of November 11th, 1918, Marshal Foch signed for the Allied Government and the delegated German representatives for Germany. But in the peace signed in Calvary Christ represented both God and man. God was in Christ, reconciling the world unto Himself.

"Couldn't anyone else have died for me just as well?" asked one to whom I was trying to explain the peace of Calvary. No; none other could have done what Christ did. In the first place, Christ died for man as a sinner. For a friend, for a good man, to save one from danger and peril, a man might lay down his life, but the marvel of Christ's death on the Cross was that He died for sinners. God commendeth His love towards us, in that while we were yet sinners Christ died for us.

The second reason why no one else could have died for us, and established peace between man and God, is that no one else could be what Christ was, and is, God in Christ. Therefore, what He did on the Cross has infinite value. He took on Himself as the representative of man all the responsibility of the war against God, and therefore all the guilt of the sinner; and as the representative of God, as the Son of God, and therefore truly God, Christ had the authority to make peace between God and Man. There is no Gospel, no message of redemption or of hope, in the mere fact that a good and noble man was tortured and crucified on the cross. But there is a Gospel, there is redemption, and there is hope in the fact that God was in Christ, and that Christ on the Cross bore in His own body the penalty upon sin, that is, the penalty which every sinner bears.

The problem of God was how to deal with sin, how to uphold the moral order of the world, to declare His righteousness and yet at the same time pardon the sinner. And not only pardon him, but make those who were the enemies of God His friends. In this great undertaking God did not deal lightly with sin. There was no ignoring of the fact of war and sin.

The world rejoiced when the Treaty of Versailles was signed. It seemed as if a new foundation had been built for the peace and welfare of the world. Now we know better. The peace of Versailles could not put an end to war among the nations.

But the peace of Calvary goes deeper. When Absalom

had murdered his brother, and was living in exile, it was not hard for Joab to persuade the mourning king and father, David, to be reconciled to Absalom and call him home again. But it was only a surface reconciliation. The heart of Absalom was not dealt with at all, and in a short time he conspired against his father and drove him from his throne. But the peace of God, signed on Calvary, went far deeper than that. It deals with the heart of man, the sinner and the exile, and makes him, once an enemy, and separated from God, now the friend of God.

It was to do this great work of making peace, of reconciling man to God, that Christ came into the World. God was in Christ reconciling man to himself. The heathen religions all were based upon the idea of attempting to reconcile God to man. Hence, all their altars, and all their dark and bloody rites. But the Gospel of Christ declares that God is reconciled to man, and now offers man the opportunity to be reconciled to God. God's enemies are to be made His friends.

That was the last thing Christ did in this world before He died. A thief and a robber who hung at His side on that awful day, and who at first had reviled Him and mocked Him, now prayed to Him, and asked Him to give them a place in His Kingdom. "Lord Jesus, remember me when Thou comest in Thy Kingdom." The enemy of God had become, through the reconciliation of Christ, the friend of God. That must be forever a picture of what Christ does for the soul of man.

Nothing but the Cross could bring about this reconciliation between man and God. Death sometimes has had reconciling effect. I have seen members of families who

were alienated reconciled by a death which came into the
family circle. When Abraham died, his sons, Isaac and
Ishmael forgot their feud, and buried him in the Cave of
Machpelah. A father and son who had become bitter
enemies were brought together by the bedside of the dying
wife and mother. The dying woman took the hand of her
son and placed it in the hand of her husband. Thus death
reconciled father and son. The death of Christ, the greatest
act of God's love and mercy, reconciles God and man. With
arms outstretched on the Cross, Christ lays hold upon man
and brings him to God.

Only the Cross can sound the depths of the human heart.
We have peace through the Cross. Only the Cross can take
away the stain of sin and the guilt of sin. Only the Cross can
still the tempest of conscience.

God is the Author of the great Armistice which was
signed by Christ on the Cross. But it is man who receives
it and benefits by it. It takes two to make a covenant, or
sign an armistice. When the agreement is signed, then there
is peace. If either of the belligerent parties had refused to
sign the armistice on that November day in 1918, there
would have been no peace. God has already signed the
Covenant of peace. Christ as His ambassador signed it in
the blood of the Cross. When by faith and repentance you
also sign it, then there is peace. Heaven's banners are flung
out and there is joy in heaven over the peace which has
come to a soul, for Christ would have come and died on
the Cross had there been just one soul at war with God.
Whenever by his repentance and his faith man accepts the
peace offered him by God, then God withdraws the armies
of His condemnation and His Judgment. Henceforth, there-

fore, there is no more condemnation to them that are in Christ Jesus.

This is the heart of the Gospel, the heart of Christianity, that Christ has made peace by the blood of His Cross; and all else is but the illustration, the expression, or the application of it.

Acquaint now thyself with God and be at peace with Him. Are you at peace with God? That does not mean: Are you satisfied with yourself? Are you enjoying life? Are you having reasonable success? All that may be true, and still you may be at war with God. Are you at peace with God? Have you accepted His terms? Have you signed the armistice? There is your Saviour's Name written for you in crimson colors of the Cross. Therefore, I beseech you, "Be ye reconciled unto God." When we answer the invitation of God's love and mercy, when we accept the pardon which Christ holds out to us with His pierced hand, then there is peace, peace with God, peace with the world, peace with ourselves. This is the peace about which Christ was speaking when He said, "My peace I give unto you."

It is the peace which the world cannot give, and which the world cannot take away.

—*from* PULPIT DIGEST *for November, 1946*

A Nation Gives Thanks

BY NORMAN E. NYGAARD

*Formerly Pastor of Westminster Presby-
terian Church, Steubenville, Ohio*

TEXTS: *Jesus said, Were there not ten cleansed? but where
are the nine? There are not found returned to give glory
to God, save this stranger.*—LUKE 17:17-18

*I thank Thee that I am not as other men are, extortion-
ers, unjust, adulterers, or even as this publican.*—LUKE
18:11

*Jesus took the loaves; and when He had given thanks,
He distributed to the disciples.*—JOHN 6:11

A NATION gives thanks. How? There are three attitudes
mentioned in the New Testament. There may be
others, but I think that these three sum up in a general way
the thanksgiving of mankind. They are expressed in our
three texts and in the incidents from which they come.

The first is the cleansing of the ten lepers recorded in the
eighteenth chapter of the Book of Luke. There is a miracu-
lous element in the story, but miracles are always happening,
even today; and the nub of the story is quite commonplace.
Ten lepers were made whole by Jesus. Nine of them rushed

279

away to exhibit themselves to the priest that they might be officially declared clean. Thereafter they hastened home at once to rejoin their families, without a word to their Benefactor. The tenth, after he had been pronounced whole again, one whom Jesus calls 'a stranger' to differentiate him from the other nine who seem to have been known by the Master, comes back to thank Jesus for his good offices.

The second incident is only a story, that which is called a "parable," a story cast down alongside of life, something we would term an "analogy," but so true to life that almost everyone can recognize himself in the picture. Two men went into the temple to pray. One was a Pharisee, a member of the exclusive first family group of the times, a religious leader of the people. The other was a despised publican. The Pharisee, in the carefully chosen words of Jesus, "prayed thus with himself." One might almost say—for it is implied—that he prayed *to* himself. He exalted in his prayer his own ego. The substance of his prayer was this: "I thank Thee, Lord that I am not as other men are, extortioners, unjust, adulterers, or even as this publican." The publican's prayer was not one of thanksgiving; it was an appeal for mercy—"Lord, be merciful to me, a sinner."

The third incident concerns the feeding of the five thousand. Five thousand hungry men with their wives and children are gathered on a hillside in Galilee. A lad with five barley loaves and two small fishes is touched by the needs of the people surrounding him, and he brings this lunch (it was not much more than that) to the Master and trusts it to Him. "And the Master took the loaves," the story records, "and when He had given thanks, He distributed to the disciples."

These three incidents, of course, have their modern parallels. Think of the nine lepers, if you will. Are they not typical of the great majority of the people of America? I venture to say that there will be comparatively few homes in which today, a day set apart for thanksgiving, even a moment will be spent in giving thanks to God for the meal which we shall eat.

I am not concerned, of course, about a merely formal word of blessing on our food. That is sometimes almost an insult to the Almighty. If we were to thank one who had given us something the way we thank God for the food that we eat, the hasty mumbling of a conventional and almost grudging thanks, the other individual would very likely say: "If that is your thanks don't bother to express it at all."

No! A conventional word doesn't suffice at all. I am sure that God Himself would rather have the warm and unconventional word which Lionel Barrymore used in "You Can't Take It With You" than any conventional and stereotyped mumbo-jumbo. You may remember the blessing: "Well, here we are again!" People smiled; some of them even laughed; some pious folks were shocked, in the first scene where such a blessing was given. But before the picture was over their hearts were touched with the warmth and the homeliness of those little messages of thanksgiving.

The great majority of Americans, at least, will sit down today to sumptuous repasts either with no word or a merely conventional blessing and thanksgiving.

So do we come to the second incident, the parable of the Pharisee and the publican. "I thank Thee, Lord, that I am not as other men," said the unctuous hypocrite. Certainly none of us are ever guilty of that, are we?

If we can answer "No!" to that question then ought we to remember Jesus' word of warning to His disciples: "Beware of the leaven of the scribes and Pharisees."

What was the essence of the Pharisee's prayer? Was it not a glorification of himself, his class, his group, his little inner circle of "good" people? There were prayers of that kind offered in Jesus' day. They have been preserved. There were prayers in which the pray-ers thanked God that they were not women, that they were not Gentiles, that they were not like other people.

Have we not been thanking God in press, and radio, and pulpit, in private and public devotions, that we were not Japanese, Germans, Italians? Yes, by our racial attitudes have some of us not thanked God that we were not negroes? By our economic and social attitudes have we not thanked Him that we were not born on the wrong side of the railroad tracks? By our religious exclusiveness and intolerance have we not thanked Him that we were born Presbyterians and not Roman Catholics, that we had come into the world intelligent Unitarians and not bigoted Southern Baptists?

A valued old friend of mine graduated *cum laude* at about seventy years of age from the active ministry. In the years that have followed he has been using his acute powers of observation to study two American communities. One is in Rhode Island, although I shall not name it; the other is in North Carolina, and it shall likewise be nameless. Either one of them might be this community.

The Rhode Island community is staunchly Republican, as you would expect. The North Carolina community is sturdily Democrat. The Rhode Island community is very liberal in its theological views; the North Carolina com-

munity is very conservative. The people would call themselves "fundamentalists." That which interested my old
friend was that the fundamental pattern was the same. In
Rhode Island it is fashionable to be Republican and theologically liberal. All the best people are. In North Carolina
it is fashionable to be Democratic and theologically conservative. All the best people are.

Both communities have certain attitudes toward the
people on the wrong side of the railroad tracks. They oppose any moves which will make the wrong side a "right"
side, which will raise the economic and social standards of
the wrong side. They would level off wages for those people
at a subsistence basis. They would feel that the working-
man, white or colored, ought to remain in his place. The
people on the right side of the tracks in both communities
by their attitudes have thanked God again and again that
He saw fit to bring them into the right social and ecclesiastical atmosphere.

To that large group who do not thank God at all must,
therefore, be added that other group who patronize God,
whom they regard really as their special friend, as One who
belongs to their class, their race, as One who espouses their
creed and believes, of course, as they believe.

Then do we come to this last incident. It is such a whole-
some one.

First of all, I like this little boy. He is nameless, as so
many of the great characters of the Bible are. But he has a
tremendous faith and a wonderfully warm heart. People are
hungry. He doesn't cut a little tail off the end of one of the
two little fish which he has. He doesn't break one of the five
barley loaves into two pieces, retaining the larger for him-

self and bringing the smaller to Jesus. Not at all; He brings
all five loaves and both fish to the Master. He resembles the
widow who cast her two mites into the treasury. She could
give no more. That was all she had.

I'd like to have seen the look on that lad's face as he
presented his store of food to the Master. If you will read
over the story in the Book of John you will note that it does
not say that Jesus took five loaves and two fishes and made
enough food to feed an army. We have often assumed that
that was the case. There is no statement in the Scriptures
themselves to that effect.

So do I like the explanation—which may not be true but
which does sound reasonable—to the effect that people did
have food along with them, plenty of food. But each was
afraid that he would have to bring it out, to share it with his
neighbor. They were like the "good" people at the beginning of the war who bought up all the sugar they could, all
the canned goods, all the foodstuffs that the community
would need. "The Lord helps him who helps himself," they
said.

This lad was different. It looked as if there were no food
in the crowd. If that were true then every ounce that he
possessed would be shared with everyone else. He might
have opened a black market there. He might have sold those
five barley loaves to people who were presumably hungry
for fabulous sums, depending upon the degree of hunger
of the purchasers.

He didn't do that. Instead he opened his heart and he
opened his pouch and out came every scrap of food which
he possessed. Five loaves and two fishes for a multitude!
Certainly the little scraps into which they would have to be

divided wouldn't satisfy anyone's hunger. That's true. But
he gave them nevertheless.

Then came the prayer. I am sure that Jesus must have
thanked God first for the heart of such a boy. He probably
gave thanks to His Father for the generous impulses which
He had implanted in the lad's heart, impulses which led the
boy to believe that his picayunish little store of food might
really be used to alleviate the hunger of such a multitude.
Then I am sure that He also thanked His Father for the
food, realizing that it had all come from Him.

There is an interesting picture in American life about
which jokes have been made immemorial, the picture of
the American boarding-house. Someone is saying grace, but
all the boarders have their eyes on the pork chops reposing
in the center of the table. Scarcely has the "Amen" been
concluded when the forks are stretched out in what is col-
loquially known as the "boarding-house reach" in order
that their wants may be supplied.

Something like that, but in reverse, occurred during
Jesus' prayer of thanksgiving. I believe that there was much
surreptitious reaching under voluminous garb for the food
which the owners had secreted there. And when the prayer
is completed a miracle is seen to have happened. Hard, selfish hearts have been touched, and there is food in abundance. And so generous have people become that they have
kept nothing for themselves. Twelve baskets of food are
left.

That, my friend, was really a great thanksgiving service.
They had started out as five thousand independent family
units. They ended up as one great family. Resources, fellowship, all were pooled.

How shall we give thanks? Shall we fail completely? Fail to recognize anything save our own personal welfare, our own desires, as did the nine lepers?

Or shall our thanksgiving be that complacent, self-right-eous "We thank Thee, Lord, that we are not as others?" That is the beautiful thanksgiving of "America First," of "America for White Protestants," of much of the current "God Bless America" thinking. Will that be our thanks-giving?

Or will our thanksgiving be instead the thanks of the mountainside, the thanks which is accompanied by sharing, the thanks that welled up in a generous boy's heart, the thanks that brought forth food intended for selfish consumption to make it instead food for general use?

That is the thanksgiving of Plymouth. That is the only true national thanksgiving. Let us give thanks.

—*from* PULPIT DIGEST *for November, 1947*

Is Bible-Reading Worthwhile?

BY LESLIE D. WEATHERHEAD

Minister of The City Temple, London, England

IT HAS always seemed to me a most valuable decision on the part of the Anglican Church to set aside the Second Sunday in Advent for the consideration of the Bible, and already this morning, in the Introit, you have had chanted to you the appropriate Collect for this day. There is no doubt that the Bible has played an immensely important part in the life story of our nation. There is no doubt that simple people, like Bunyan, for example, not only spoke and wrote in beautiful English, but built up their characters through meditation on the word of God. There is no doubt that Bible reading is largely neglected amongst us all, even those of us who were brought up, as I was, to hear it read in our childhood's home every morning. There is no doubt that no one can cut Bible reading out of his life without serious loss.

Let us first consider what we must bring to Bible reading. Let us be entirely honest and admit at the very beginning

287

that Bible reading sounds unattractive, dull, and boring.
The Bible is frequently printed in parallel columns and in
small type. Many of its passages are unintelligible to us,
and many of its passages would be useless to the modern
man, even if he could understand their significance. When
we have said that, we must go on to say that, even so, the
Bible is still a best seller. It has been translated into over a
thousand languages. In the phrase of Sir Arthur Quiller
Couch, it is "the most majestic literature in the world." And
although many parts of the Old Testament are unsuitable
for public worship today, yet the Old Testament was the
Bible of Jesus. One imagines Him, hardly out of boyhood,
pestering the Rabbi at Nazareth to give Him access to the
sacred roll, and one imagines Him poring over it and getting
it deeply into His mind. Again and again, in His hours of
distress and sorrow, it was the Bible that brought Him inspiration, the Bible that ministered to His comfort, the Bible
whose prophecies He Himself fulfilled. "These are they," He
said of the Scriptures, "which testify of Me."

Let us bring to our Bible reading the conception of the
Bible as a library and not as a book. It was written over a
period of almost a thousand years by over a hundred people,
and it is folly to be blind to the fact that it contains almost
every known form of literary expression, except the scientific textbook—which, indeed, rarely has any literary value
at all. The Bible contains myth, legend, fiction, allegory,
drama, poetry, parable, fable, history, biography, sermons,
mystic writing, letters, and philosophy, and yet the Bible
is unique. You could not possibly collect examples of these
literary forms and make a second Bible. The thread that

runs throughout the necklace and makes it a unity could be expressed in the phrase—*God matters*.

Every part of the Bible bears that refrain. For example, we have history which is obviously inaccurate. In the book of Kings, we are told that a certain king began to reign at one age, and in the book of Chronicles we are told that he began to reign at a different age. Whole reigns are passed over in a few sentences, but if a moral principle is involved, we have verses and verses to expound it. Clearly it is God Who matters.

Further, it is a tragedy that there ever was an argument about, shall we say, the days of creation. The editor of the book of Genesis is not concerned with scientific accuracy, though the order of creation is remarkably true to modern scientific findings. But he is only interested to show a wondering world that in the beginning it was God Who created the heavens and the earth.

Viewed ever as drama, the book of Job is one of the finest pieces of literature in our language, but the point of it is that God is the Hero. And right through both the Old and New Testaments it is the nature of God and God's ways with men, and man's response to God, in which the writers are interested. It is a thousand pities that a great parable like the story of Jonah should have been linked in so many minds with the story of a whale. By this trifling nonsense the point of the parable is lost, and we lose sight of a great preacher with a great message, bravely delivered in the teeth of hostility and opposition.

Having brought to Bible reading a great reverence and the conception of a great library, do let us bring, thirdly, an intelligible theory of inspiration.

Years ago Dean Burgon wrote: "The Bible is none other than the voice of Him that sitteth on the throne. Every book of it, every chapter of it, every verse of it, every word of it, every syllable of it, every letter of it, is the direct utterance of the Most High, supreme, absolute, faultless, unerring."

Such a sentence is, of course, nonsense. The words of our Lord for example, were spoken in Aramaic. The New Testament was written in Greek, and a colloquial Greek at that. It was then translated many times, and now even the Revised Version is left on one side by many students who turn to Moffatt, or to J. B. Phillips, or to the American Standard Version, in order to rest their minds, not on traditional and beautiful language, but on the real meaning of the text.

Many people think they believe in the verbal inspiration of the Bible, but no intelligent person has ever been able to defend that theory from attacks which can be made upon it on a dozen fronts at once. We must accept the fact that there are mistakes in the Bible. Actions of very questionable morality are praised in some parts of the Old Testament, and clearly the inspiration is unequal. It would be folly to suppose that there is more inspiration in some of the passages of Leviticus than in some of the poems of Browning. Let us remember that the expert in this matter of devotional Bible reading is not the scholar, but the saint, and if you pick up his Bible, you will find the pages of John's Gospel brown with use, and the pages of Leviticus white with neglect. This, in itself, is sufficient comment on the claim for the equality of inspiration.

The thing that amazes the student is that there slowly emerges so wonderful a picture of God. In the early parts of the Old Testament, God is a local storm deity enthroned on the top of Mount Sinai, but it is almost breathtaking to note the development of revelation in the Bible. Compared with the religions of the people who surrounded the Israelites, it is like watching a beautiful white water-lily, with stainless petals surrounded by and growing in some stagnant and filthy pond. The Bible closes with a God Who is the Father of all nations, the Ruler of all the earth, the Lover of every man's soul. And, of course, clearly the Bible exists to bring us Jesus. As someone has said, "Everything written before Him was preparation, and everything written after Him was comment."

I am going to suggest quite seriously that we ordinary busy people bring to our Bible reading a blue pencil. A great service would be done by anyone who could produce what I should like to call "The Busy Man's Bible." Let him cross out meaningless genealogies with his blue pencil. Let him cross out chapters of Leviticus and Deuteronomy which are merely directions to priests. Let him cross out prohibited degrees of marriage, for example, and the immoral stories which we find here and there in the Old Testament, and some of the foolish Proverbs, and some of the vindictive Psalms, which encourage the act, for instance, of taking the children of one's enemy and dashing their brains out against a rock.

Let him even cross out some parts of the last book in the Bible. He will not get much devotional help from the account of the beast with seven heads and ten horns, or the woman who swallowed the river which the dragon cast out of his mouth. Of course, when we read the Revelation of St. John, we are reading a book which only just found its way into the Bible at all. It is like reading a message written in

code when one has lost the key. The early Christians would
conceivably know what the last book in the Bible meant,
but without profound scholarship and the help of commentaries, for which we have no time, many of the verses must
elude us.

After we have used our blue pencil thoroughly, not only
crossing out, but perhaps sidelining passages of exquisite
beauty and agelong significance even for the modern man,
we should have, standing out from the Bible, a message of
relevance and power, of comfort and inspiration, the like of
which is not found in any other literature in the world.

The next thing I think we must bring to Bible reading is
imagination.

I must not dwell now on this, but I admired the way in
which Mr. Lewis read to you, at my request, the story of
Nicodemus visiting Jesus at night. When we have read such
a story, we should shut our eyes and try to see the picture.
The quiet, hushed streets; the shadow of Nicodemus gliding
through patches of moonlight hoping he will not be seen,
and stealthily waiting on the verandah of the house where
Jesus was staying. Then I imagine him going up to an upper
room; not on to the roof where he would clearly be seen by
others. I can imagine them sitting down in this upper room
in the lamplight, talking about the new birth. Perhaps the
night becomes intolerably hot in that close room, and they
hear the night wind moving the leaves of the vine that
climbs up the trellis on the wall outside. Then I can hear
Jesus saying: "The wind bloweth where it listeth, and thou
hearest the sound thereof, but cannot tell whence it cometh
and whither it goeth," and then, as He pushes open the
casement, saying: "*so* is he that is born of the Spirit." The

word "so" has no meaning unless we imaginatively see it
accompanied with the throwing open of the shutters and
letting the cool night air sweep into the stuffy room. What
a wonderful experience it must have been! The silly old
man thinks that rebirth means entering into his mother's
womb and thus being born again, and Jesus shows him that
it is a matter rather of opening all the windows of personality to the cleansing, healing, renewing breath of God that
longs to possess every room in the house of life. Yes, we
must bring imagination, and, in Ruskin's lovely phrase, "Be
present, as if in the body, at each recorded act in the life
of the Redeemer."

The sixth thing we must bring is the spirit of prayer. It
could well be the prayer we have offered already in our
opening hymn:

> Teach me to love Thy sacred word
> And view my Saviour there.

I have every sympathy with those who have found it difficult
to get anything at all from Bible reading, and clearly we
must bring the things I mentioned this morning to the reading of the Bible, or we shall get nothing out of it at all. But
do let us realize that whether we live an integrated life or
not depends on our sense of values. Our sense of values
depends on what we believe. What we believe depends on
our apprehension of truth, and truth streams from the Bible
in a way that is unique.

Now let me have a few minutes to expound those sentences. So many lives are unhappy and disquieted because
the mind is seething with moral conflicts. We should like to
do this, but we feel we ought to do that. A man only ends

these moral conflicts and begins to integrate his life when he has fixed very clearly in his mind his sense of values. Clearly, if I think that money is all important, I shall do almost anything, short of getting caught and found out and ostracized, in order to make money. My sense of values determines my actions, and my sense of values depends on what I believe.

I find it hard to understand the point of view of a person who asks the senseless question, "Does it matter what a man believes?" Who would enter even into a business transaction with a person who thought it does not matter what a man believes, and who, in fact, believed that dishonesty was the best policy, or that there was no value in completing one's contract, or keeping one's word, or standing by one's bargain? Further, what a man believes is never his mere choice of the most useful creed to possess, the one that will serve him best. If we take the word "belief" seriously, then that which is *believed* is only possible through a real apprehension of truth.

Notice how the word "ideology" has been bandied about of late years! Yet behind it lies an immensely important matter. Finally, it is our ideology that matters: the ideas which we believe to be true. Let me say it again: from our apprehension of truth come our beliefs; from our beliefs comes our sense of values; from our sense of values comes our integration, and from our integration our peace of mind and the happiness of our day-to-day living.

Let me read you a quotation and ask you to guess from whom it comes.

I am convinced that the welfare of mankind does not depend

on the State and the world of politics; the real battle is being fought in the world of thought, where a deadly attack is made with great tenacity of purpose and over a wide field upon the greatest treasure of mankind, the belief in God and the Gospel of Christ.

It might have been written yesterday. In truth it was written or spoken by Gladstone seventy years ago. Could any modern language more completely express the present situation? Once more the battle is in the world of thoughts. Once more a deadly attack is being made "with great tenacity of purpose over a wide field." Communism is said to be the creed of two hundred million people, covering one-fifth of the earth's surface, and it is all the time ceaselessly aggressive and militant. We can only meet it by an ideology, but instead of the flaming truths about God which make the Bible burn and glow, we, here in the West, are dull and apathetic about God. Few people believe in Him at all, if the word "believe" is given its real meaning. We suppose there may be something somewhere. . . . There may be a kindly grandfather in the sky who, after death, will pat us on the head and invite us home for Christmas, as it were. But He is remote, distant, unreal, and in tens of thousands of Western lives literally counts for nothing at all.

I believe that God matters more than anything else in the world. I believe that religion is the most important thing in the world. I believe that it is co-terminous with every part of life, with every phase of man's activities, and that this *laissez-faire*, tepid assent to religion, with no passionate conviction about it at all, an attitude which never allows religion to express itself in daily life, will, if not checked, bring down Western civilization to the ruin it deserves.

Now listen to the prophets as they tried to counteract that same deadly ennui in Old Testament days. "The lack of knowledge about God," they said, "is what brings ruin."

We hear Isaiah crying: "Hast thou not known? Hast thou not heard?" "My people," he cries, "have gone into captivity for lack of knowledge." "Israel doth not *know*; my people doth not consider."

We hear Hosea crying: "My people are destroyed through lack of knowledge." "I desire mercy and not sacrifice, and the knowledge of God more than burnt offerings."

And so on right down to Jesus crying: "O Jerusalem, O Jerusalem, if thou hadst *known* the things which belong unto thy peace . . . but now they are hid from thine eyes."

If only we would turn to the Bible, we might regain our sense of the importance of knowing God and of understanding His ways with men. The truth is that the world is God's, not ours. It was made for God, not for man. Any policy that leads away from God leads to disaster, however plausible and Utopian it may seem. Were ever words written in the whole of literature that were a more striking condemnation of mere humanism than Jeremiah's great cry? Listen to this!

Let not the wise man glory in his wisdom,
Neither let the mighty man glory in his might:
Let not the rich man glory in his riches:
But let him that glorieth, glory in this,
That he understandeth and knoweth Me—
For I am the Lord
Which exercise lovingkindness, judgment and righteousness in
　　the earth,
And in these things I delight, saith Jehovah.

When we turn from the nations to the individual, we find the same kind of thing. Life only works out successfully if it is in harmony with God's will. Pick up, if you like, one story, the story of David. I won't say: "You will remember." We say that too often in the pulpit, but people don't know their Bible well enough to remember. But the story is written of David looking lustfully from his roof one night at Bathsheba while she was bathing, and desiring her to satisfy his lusts. "The woman was very beautiful to look upon." But she was already married to Uriah, the Hittite, one of the finest captains in David's army. So what does this king, called "a man after God's own heart," do about it? He gives orders that Uriah is to be put into the hottest part of the battle that was raging, and when Uriah is slain, then David steals his wife and takes her to himself. But does he get away with it? Nathan the prophet saw to that. Does anyone ever get away with sin? I have never found anybody who did so. Turn to the fifty-first Psalm and let me read these verses to you.

Wash me thoroughly from mine iniquity, and cleanse me from my sin. For I acknowledge my transgressions: and my sin is ever before me. Against Thee, Thee only, have I sinned, and done this evil in Thy sight; that Thou mightest be justified when Thou speakest, and be clear when Thou judgest. . . . Purge me with hyssop, and I shall be clean; wash me, and I shall be whiter than snow. Make me to hear joy and gladness; that the bones which Thou hast broken may rejoice. Hide Thy face from sins, and blot out all my iniquities. Create in me a clean heart, O God; and renew a right spirit within me. Cast me not away from Thy presence; and take not Thy Holy Spirit from me.

David knows it is no good offering goats and oxen to put right a wrong like that. We can almost hear his sobs as he cries: "Thou hast no pleasure in burnt offering. The sacrifices of God are a broken spirit: a broken and a contrite heart, O God, Thou wilt not despise."

Who is there amongst us who has not done something and hated himself for doing it, found out how utterly alluring and attractive sin can be at the time, and then afterwards found it dust and ashes in the mouth and bitterness to the spirit?

We may turn from the rebuke and challenge of the Bible to its tender comfort. It is a moving thought that the twenty-third Psalm, for perhaps twenty-five centuries, has comforted the hearts of men and women, and latterly of every race under heaven. What minister has not sat on the death-bed of someone and seen the lips of some dying man or woman framing the words: "Though I walk through the valley of the shadow of death I will fear no evil, for Thou art with me"?

Or we may turn to the bewilderment that frequently falls upon the spirit, those times when we do not know which way to turn, when we cannot see any meaning, or beauty, or purpose in life. The Bible can speak to that need. Listen to this:

I sought the Lord, and He heard me, and delivered me from all my fears. They looked unto Him, and were lightened; and their faces were not ashamed. This poor man cried, and the Lord heard him, and saved him out of all his troubles.

Immediately the soul says, 'I, too, will try this way of

prayer. Perchance the Lord will comfort me and make *my* way plain,' and it happens.

Or turn to the question of sorrow and suffering, bereavement and trouble. Especially contemplate those hours when we have thought that we were confounded, that all our faith was a mockery; hours when the heavens seemed brass above us and there was no comfort in any voice of man, and then listen to this: "I know that my Redeemer liveth . . ." The words are familiar to you through Handel's great music, but I would beseech you not to be content with them in that very poor translation which entirely misrepresents the point of the original. Here is Professor Dodd's translation:

> I know One to champion me at last,
>   To stand up for me upon earth.
> This body may break up, but even then
>   My life shall have sight of God;
> My heart is pining as I yearn
>   To see Him on my side,
>   To see Him estranged no longer.

One could go on indefinitely, for the Bible is full of challenge to the careless and the complacent, comfort to the distressed, guidance for the bewildered, vindication for the doubting. We turn from our little outlook, from our life under the little bit of sky that we can see, into the wide open spaces of the Bible, and realize that we can never pass through any experience through which someone in the Bible has not already passed.

The Bible does not exist to hand out information. It is not a textbook of direction. It is rather in the category of art than science. It brings us to the place where we see truth for ourselves. We find the deep places of human personality stirred, and as pity and fear and love and trust are stirred within us, we find our nature purged, as Aristotle used to say tragedy purges the passion of those who watch it on the stage.

The Bible makes men turn to God, and in doing so they find life renewed within them. Moreover, they realize that "outside God there is only death." I only wish that I could persuade some young people of the truth of that last sentence before, in perhaps tragic circumstances, they realize it for themselves. If you are only going to remember one sentence from this sermon on the Bible, remember this. Write it down, if you wish to, on the back of an envelope and meditate on it: *Outside God there is only death.*

Men and women, the Bible has only one concern—to bring men into living communion with God. Its supreme achievement is to prepare for Jesus, then to show forth Jesus, then to draw us into fellowship with God through Jesus. He who through the Bible finds his Lord, knows what the Bible is for. He knows himself in the hands of a Love that will never let him down, never let him off, and never let him go.

—*from* PULPIT DIGEST *for December, 1950*

Christians, Wake Up!

BY O. E. GEISEMAN

Pastor of Grace Lutheran Church, River Forest, Illinois

TEXT: ROMANS 13:11-14

IF THE Spirit of God will let me bring to you the message contained in the words of our text as it should be brought, then you will be a more wide-awake and alert Christian than you have been in the past.

These words are designed to arouse us so that we will bestir ourselves to a finer kind of Christianity and a fuller measure of spiritual, moral living. Paul said to the Christians at Rome: "Awake." That exhortation needs to be addressed to us in like measure.

It is right, I think, to say that one of the greatest though perhaps least recognized tragedies of our day is the fact that Christians, professed sons and daughters of God, are asleep. This sleepiness and weariness, this want of alertness on the part of God's children, manifests itself in various ways. It is to be seen in our want of spiritual under-

301

standing, in our failure properly to analyze the meaning of what is happening all around us in our everyday lives.

If I were to ask this Christian audience, or any other Christian audience, why we became involved in a world war which was started thousands of miles from here, I am afraid a great many folk would resort to some political answer. They would find the solution in some political analysis of the situation. They would not be conscious that wars are a scourge of God and that people who do not live in God's way will be called by Him from their erroneous ways to the right way even though it must be by war. If I were to ask you why we have so many juvenile delinquents in our country, what would you say? Perhaps some of you would say that it is the result of the war. So many mothers went to work. So many children were neglected, and so we are getting all this behavior. Oh, I would not deny that it is a factor in the matter, but certainly that is not the real reason for it. The real reason for it is that the children's spiritual and moral training has been neglected. It was not boys and girls who were six, eight, ten, or twelve years of age who needed the attention of their fathers and mothers and have caused so much trouble. It was the older boys and girls, sixteen, seventeen, and eighteen years of age who should have known how to behave themselves but who didn't. We Christians certainly ought to understand why these things are happening, but we don't. We are asleep. We are not applying Christian understanding to the ways of life and to an analysis of human conflict.

Recently I received a questionnaire from the head of a Jesuit group of social students asking me to send them a 500-word answer to the question: "What in your opinion are the chief economic and social causes of the present day breakdown of the American home?" Well, it would not be difficult to enumerate certain factors in the economic and social conditions of our day contributing to this particular and very serious problem in American life, but when you look at that problem through the eyes of a Christian, in the final analysis it is not an economic problem. The reason there is such a widespread breakdown of the basic institutions in human life is that so many people have lost their regard for the binding quality of the holy bond of marriage. Others may not understand that, but you and I as Christians should awake to the fact and we should understand.

This admonition, "wake up!" is so important also because we let the hands on the clock of time go around and around and around, and act as though we had an eternity in which to accomplish the things that need to be done.

Today men's souls are being lost. *Today* men are going away from the pathway which God has outlined for them and destroying themselves eternally. It is *today* that humanity has its problem.

It is today boys and girls are growing up before our very eyes who must either be fashioned into God-fearing men and women now or never become such. It is today the hungry, empty stomachs of individuals are crying out for charitable help. It is today people are naked and cold and homeless and without hope. Today you have the opportunity of growing into something finer.

I do not know when you first came to believe in Jesus as your Saviour, when you first said that you were a child of God and a disciple of Christ, but I do know that you are closer to meeting your God than you were when you first began to believe. Time is fleeting. The clock does not stand still. It goes on. You and I have one life to live. Yesterday will never come again.

Well, what should we do? The Apostle tells us. *First*, he says: *"Put ye on the Lord Jesus Christ."* We don't get anywhere at all in spiritual matters until we do that.

This is to be taken seriously. Some of you who are here this morning may never yet have even professed to put on Jesus Christ. Certainly the great bulk of you *have* so professed. You have knelt at this altar or some other altar and said: "I believe in Jesus Christ as my Saviour. That is the One who is my Master and whose banner I intend to follow through life." But what are you doing about it? How serious a matter is it for you?

Wake up! The putting on of Jesus is not something which is to be taken lightly. It is something which you are to regard as the essential thing in life, without which you can achieve nothing. No matter how successful you will be in business, no matter how famous you may be, no matter how often you may strive to find joy and happiness in life, it will all fail you, leave you cold and dissatisfied, until you have the satisfying, peace-giving love of God through Jesus Christ to flood your soul and to put your heart at ease.

A Jewish rabbi wrote a book which bears the title *Peace of Mind*. Many people bought that book. Why, do you suppose? Because they are looking for peace of mind. You can look for peace of mind wherever you want. You will not find peace of mind until God gives you the answer to the soul and to its needs. And God has provided that answer in the sending of Jesus, your Saviour, your Redeemer. So don't be satisfied merely to know that once you learned a few catechetical truths. Make it the most serious part of your life, the steadfast concern of your every thought, every prayer, to be in Christ, to learn how to trust in Jesus, how to build the love of God in Christ into everything in your life, and how to look at all of life through the analysis of that Jesus and His love so that you understand life correctly, so that you can meet life face to face with courage and the assurance of ultimate victory.

If we do have some in our midst this morning who never yet have put on Christ, I certainly want to plead with you to do so. There is no other answer. There is no other way of getting real peace of mind. The psychiatrist can help you talk out the things that are on the inside of you. He can help you find out where your troubles are and what out of the past is preying on you and distorting your life, but when he has accomplished all of that he must send you to Christ to get the ultimate answer. It is only through Christ that you can get rid of the sense of guilt, that your inner tensions can be freed.

When we put on Jesus, then that must be followed by other things in life which are in harmony with this fact.

So Paul says: "Put off the works of darkness." He tells us what some of these works of darkness are. He says: "Rioting and drunkenness, chambering and wantonness" (debauchery and lasciviousness in more modern language) "strife and envying" (or as the more recent Revised Translation has it, "quarreling and jealousy").

These are the works of darkness. You and I have no difficulty in recognizing them, do we? They make up so much of our modern life. God will not allow the American people who want to swim in liquor to go on and on. God has given us many fine gifts, but He will not allow any of them to be misused. Why talk about that in a Christian Church? Need we fear that anybody in this church is going to be a drunkard or that we are going to live as the world lives? My friends, don't let us be simple! Let us at least be alert to the dangers in which we find ourselves.

Debauchery and lasciviousness—Paul says these are the works of darkness. Are they? Well, read the newspapers. I don't think there was anything in Sodom or Gomorrah or in any of the peoples of the past that surpassed anything that is being done now in the way of debauchery and lasciviousness. There is not a person in this audience this morning who can say: "Oh, that would never happen to me."

Wake up, my friend. Tomorrow it may be you. Maybe yet today, if you don't wake up. Not one of us but is capable of everything and anything any other human being anywhere in this world is capable of. It is not for a single one of us to turn up his nose and go through life as though he were immune. Wake up! Put on Jesus Christ and cast off the works of darkness.

Instead of doing as the world does, put on the armor of light. "Let us put on the armor of light." "Let us walk honestly as in the day." "Let us make not provision for the flesh to fulfill the lusts thereof," but let us walk as the children of God, and in reverent regard of the Holy Will of our Creator. That is how we should live.

This text stands in immediate relationship with some things which Paul said about Christian love and Christian life. Not quarreling, not jealousy such as is in the world and such as can very easily come into the life of a Christian Church or in a Christian home or any Christian institution, but love is to govern our lives, so that in our response to the Saviour who has loved us we try to express love in our relationship to God, to one another, to all our fellowmen.

Now, of course, we could speak for hours on that subject by itself, but you take it and you apply it to your life wherever you find yourself, whether you are a son, a daughter, a father, a mother, an employer, an employee. Whatever your position in life may be, apply to it the law of love.

If we will wake up, if we will put on Christ, if we will heed the warning of Christ and see that the night is far spent and that the day is at hand, then we will try to make the most of the opportunities we have now. And it is to this great adventure in Christian living, in the service of God, for the good of humanity; it is to this the Spirit of God would arouse us this morning, and to which I as His humble spokesman challenge and call you.

—from PULPIT DIGEST *for November, 1947*

From Bethlehem to Bikini

BY HAROLD A. BOSLEY

Pastor of First Methodist Church, Evanston, Illinois

TEXT: LUKE 2:1-20

SOME of you will want to know why we bring Bikini into this Christmas season when what we want to do is to center our attention in Bethlehem.

The answer to that one is easy enough. I am not bringing Bikini into the picture. It's already in! It cannot be left out of consideration at this or any other season of the year because it has invaded and stands as a central threat in every area of thought and life known to man. To ignore or neglect this fact is more than a bit of wishful thinking conjured up by the undoubted magic of the Christmas season; it is an intellectual and spiritual betrayal of the Christ that qualifies every man who makes it as a disciple of Judas Iscariot.

Hard words, you say. Yes, but not half hard enough. For mere words cannot do justice to the hard fateful choice before every responsible man and nation today. And, better

308

than anything else, Bethlehem and Bikini are symbols of the alternatives between which we must choose, if we have not already chosen. The spiritual pilgrimage of our generation is going to be to one or the other; it cannot be to both.

Certain characteristics of Bethlehem and Bikini invite comparison.

Both are small places, geographically. Bethlehem—one of the smallest cities in ancient Palestine when it stepped into the spotlight of history; Bikini—one of the smallest coral atolls in the southern Pacific, so small that only the professional geographer knew where it was before it became known to everyone. Yet something occurred in both places to propel them into the center of world interest.

In each case this tremendous "something" was a dealing in the elemental stuff of the universe. Each event unlocked a new dimension of meaning for life and history. Bethlehem's discovery lay in the spiritual basis of life, in the realm of Divine will and purpose. Bikini's discovery lay in the material and physical basis of the universe—in the area of atomic structure, particularly unstable atomic structure.

Bethlehem's revelation centers in a baby; Bikini's in a bomb. Bethlehem is the symbol of "Good tidings of great joy which shall be to all people. For unto you is born this day in the city of David a Saviour, which is Christ the Lord." Bikini is the symbol of the grim news of the stark menace which now confronts all people, for it shows man perfecting the power which actually can obliterate himself and his civilization.

Bethlehem is the symbol of God's mightiest effort to save the world. Bethlehem, celebrating the mystery of Divine love, exalts love as the central virtue in life. Bikini, celebrating the mastery of power, exalts power as the decisive factor in life. Bethlehem is the symbol of "Glory to God in the highest and on earth peace, goodwill toward men." Bikini is the symbol of the fact that man's life is rapidly becoming one long journey through fear, during which he will be separated from and finally lost to all he loves and seeks to save for himself and his children.

Bethlehem is the symbol of the beginning of a new era in human life and history. Bikini is the symbol of the beginning of the end of civilization.

That, I suppose, accounts for the fact that only a few people seemed to be aware of the meaning of the miracle of Bethlehem as it occurred, while the whole world watched Bikini with bated breath. A few shepherds, stirred by the angel's song, hurried to the manger in Bethlehem. But everyone else was quite unmoved by what seemed to be the ordinary fact that a girl from Galilee had given birth to a son. That was not even "news," let alone good news, when it occurred. But Bikini was quite different. For weeks and months it was anticipated by press and radio. Its awesome importance was hammered home to every thinking person. When it occurred, the news was flashed everywhere, and people were listening. I happened to be on a motor trip through Florida when the first bomb was dropped. I sought out a radio in a curio shop, hoping to hear the broadcast of the event. Business was at a standstill in the shop. Everyone gravitated toward the radio and we were chilled into silence by the tick, tick, tick of the metronome as the fateful moment approached. No fiction writer—not even Edgar Allan Poe—ever achieved such suspense as that! And when it was over one man, struggling to be optimistic, said to me: "Maybe it wasn't so bad after all."

Remembering the official report of what had happened at Hiroshima, I was not able to match his optimism, and replied: "It was probably a lot worse than we are able to imagine. We will never know how bad it really is until it hits us; then it will be too late to do anything about it."

He looked at me for a moment and then said: "Pessimistic, huh?"

Just so he wouldn't be in doubt on that point I said: "I wouldn't give a plugged nickel for our chances of using that bomb wisely."

The girl behind the counter added her bit: "After the first one hits us we won't care how many others come!"

If Bethlehem is the symbol of love, if Christina Rossetti is right when she sings:

> Love came down at Christmas,
> Love all lovely, love divine;
> Love was born at Christmas,
> Star and angel gave the sign,

then, in contrast, Bikini is the symbol of fear and despair: *fear* because we know now that we can make the inhabited places of the earth a sea of fire; *despair* because we are afraid that that is just what we are going to do.

This series of contrasts between Bethlehem and Bikini must make it clear that they symbolize radically different ways of thought and standards of value. They amount, actually, to two tragically different kinds of religion: a religion of the immeasurable love of God and a religion of the incalculable fear of each other.

No reconciliation between faiths like these is possible.

It's one or the other. We can no more worship at the manger of Bethlehem and the lagoon of Bikini than we can serve God and mammon—and we have it on good authority that that just cannot be done.

Yet many of us are trying to do it. We nod our heads approvingly over Oliver Cromwell's admonition to his embattled Puritan soldiers: "Trust God and keep your powder dry." And, like Cromwell, we are considerably more careful about keeping the powder dry than we are about cultivating a strong trust in God. That is why we feel double-business bound at this time of the year. For Christmas centers in Bethlehem; in the incomprehensible love of God; in the mystery of the incarnation; in the tremendous fact of Immanuel—God with us; in love as the fundamental law of life; in the Kingdom of God as the fitting goal for the good life. Whoever takes these amazing facts at anything like face value knows that they both open the door and lay him under the unlimited obligation to become "a new creation in Christ." They are the New Testament; they are the Gospel; they are the beating heart of the Christian faith.

But as we prepare like the Magi of old to make a pilgrimage to Bethlehem and kneel in humble adoration at the side of Christ, Bikini taps us on the shoulder and presents us with another set of fundamental facts and asks that we order our thought and life according to them.

How utterly different they are! *Power*—pride in power; mistrust of all others who may have or get this power; a determination to be ready to use it immediately and decisively, *i.e.*, ruthlessly, if and when the occasion should arise; a reluctant will to share the secret of the meaning of this power with any one, even our friends. *Fear*—the kind of

nervous, excitable fear that chips away at stable relationships of trust and cooperation until they weaken and break;
the kind of brooding, paralyzing feat that keeps us from
new adventures in trust and cooperation, and emasculates
existing organs for inter-communication. This is the way
of life to which Bikini calls. To follow it is to turn our back
on Bethlehem—not as a place but as the symbol of the hope
of the world.

It is not necessary for me to outline the claims of Bikini
or to list and consider the arguments which document them.
We can trust the daily press and radio to do that. Most of
the leaders in public thought and life are on pilgrimage to
Bikini today, both in word and deed. So we can count on
the fact that the case of Bikini both is and will continue
to be carefully presented.

But we may be sure that if Christian churches do not
present the claims of Bethlehem, they will not be presented.
It is desperately necessary and altogether appropriate for
us therefore to outline the claims of Bethlehem and to keep
them before ourselves and to present them to the world as
the only true and realistic appraisal of the conditions of
immediate survival and the hope for ultimate triumph.

The claims of Bethlehem grow out of what the Christian
faith believes occurred there. It was more than the birth of
a baby; it was the revelation in history of the love of God
for man. It was the clearest and the most persuasive presentation of that love that God had or has ever made.

The wonder of it all has amazed men from that day to
this. The writings of Matthew and Luke combine to give
us a vivid picture of how intimations of the importance of
the event ran everywhere even then. From humble shep-

herds who hurried to worship Him to haughty Herod who sent soldiers to slay Him; from unlettered men to learned men who shared the common assurance that in Him God was working a mighty work of fulfillment and redemption. For the human heart of Israel had longed for the day when God would fulfill their high hopes of seeing His Anointed come to usher in the Kingdom of God. And the human heart of all men longed for the moment and the One in whose life Heaven and earth would be united, man and God be reconciled. Hopes and longings like these echo through the great writings of Jew and gentile alike in the ancient world, giving them an air of expectancy and anticipation that is almost pathetic because it seemed to be so far from fulfillment. Then came Bethlehem with both fulfillment and redemption!

Is it any wonder the Gospel writers were sure the very angels in Heaven heralded the event? And that even the stars in the sky shone with a peculiar radiance in celebration of His coming?

Later Christian writers may have used less lyrical words in describing the meaning of Bethlehem, but they did not alter the meaning. The writer of the Gospel of John says that in Christ the love of God as an active, sacrificial concern for all men was revealed: "For God so loved the world that He gave His only Son that whoever believes in Him should not perish but have eternal life."

Paul, writing to the Corinthians about the meaning of the Christian faith, says: ". . . If anyone is in Christ, he is a new creation; the old has passed away, behold the new has come. All this is from God, who through Christ reconciled us to Himself and gave us the ministry of reconciliation; that is, God was in Christ reconciling the world unto Himself, not counting their trespasses against them, and entrusting to us the message of reconciliation."

Mr. T. S. Eliot, a modern poet, finds in the event of Christ's birth the only answer to the riddle of life and history:

> A moment not out of time, but in time, in what we call history;
> transecting, bisecting the world of time, a moment in time but
> not like a moment of time.
> A moment in time but time was made through that moment:
> for without the meaning there is no time, and that moment
> of time gave the meaning.

It is the firm and united conviction of the Christian faith that this is what actually happened in Bethlehem on that first Christmas Eve. For ancient and modern seers alike, Bethlehem is God's supreme effort to awaken man from his nightmare of selfishness, greed, passion, and hatred to his true destiny as a child of God. Not by whirlwind and fire but by His Son was the effort made. Paul grasps and sets forth this grand strategy of redemption in one vivid sentence. "In the fullness of time God sent forth His Son . . ."

And our religious forefathers knew, as every man must know, that this approach of God in love requires and deserves an active response from man. Just as a newly freed slave is both dazed and delighted in his freedom, so Paul and his comrades kept breaking into shouts of joy as they sought the proper response to God's effort. One of the great students of the life of Paul, casting about for an adequate explanation of his sudden conversion, settled on this: "It was this coming of God to meet him that utterly conquered him." And it conquered others besides Paul. The writer of First John could say with searching simplicity: "Brethren, if God so loved us, we ought also to love one another."

These men knew, as we must know, that the intention of God in Christ is not a theatrical spectacle to be gaped at; it is an invitation to be accepted or rejected by every man. An invitation to a new relationship with God which carries as an inseparable corollary the responsibility of seeking a new relationship with men. Not without good cause were the early Christians identified as "followers of the way"— for the Christian faith is not so much a private attitude as it is a public way of life. I could wish that in these latter days we spoke less about accepting Christ and more about following Him. He wanted and wants followers; He was and is in search of disciples; the final note in His appeal was not and is not "sit and think" but "go and do."

Go and do what? Live as citizens of the Kingdom of God! Conduct ourselves and our affairs as befit those who find in the Sermon on the Mount the guiding ideals for living, who find in Jesus Christ our clearest revelation of God's will for man. Cultivate a forgiving spirit toward any injury and indignity. Be prepared to help any and all needy people as best you know how and can. Center your life in the reality of the Kingdom of God, put it first in your thinking and planning for the present and future. Accept as your supreme vocation the call to be "co-workers together with God" in the further realization of that Kingdom of Love in the affairs of man.

We shall not need to be warned that Christians have never found it easy to make love the central motive and force for living. They have always subordinated it to or at best driven it in double harness with other values like justice, security, and freedom. But that is spiritual betrayal of the Kingdom of God. To do that is to turn from Bethlehem to Bikini. For in the Kingdom inaugurated in Bethlehem *love is central.*

The late William Temple put it exactly right when he said: "The Kingdom of God is the sovereignty of Love, and the subordination of power to Love is the principle of that Kingdom." There is a Christ-sized job for the Christian fellowship today: the subordination of power to love; the subordination of selfish concern to mutual welfare; the subordination of the luxuries of the few to the necessities of the many; the subordination of political, social, and economic conventions to the welfare of every hungry, dispossessed, disenfranchised child of God.

I'm glad the greatest living historian, Dr. Arnold Toynbee, said this: "Christianity places our conduct in this life on earth in its gigantic setting of infinity and eternity, and by opening our eyes to this vast spiritual vision it calls out our deepest spiritual energies." I'm glad one of our most thoughtful social scientists, Dr. Pitirim Sorokin, said this: "There must be a change of the whole mentality and attitudes of our day in the direction of the norms prescribed in the Sermon on the Mount."

Long before Bikini dramatized our devotion to power as the great god of life, men like these sensed the deep and desperate spiritual malady of our culture. They knew what Christian prophets have always known—that Bethlehem is the only true symbol of hope and life for mankind. To turn the face of civilization from Bikini to Bethlehem is the great spiritual task of our generation, and one of the greatest spiritual tasks to confront any generation.

I know. You wish we had a smaller or an easier job! And so do I! But no amount of wishing, much less whimpering, can lift the spiritual burden which rests upon us and our generation.

Strangely enough, there is one point of real agreement between Bethlehem and Bikini. When Mr. William L. Lawrence, science editor for "The New York Times," saw the bombs at Bikini he reached the conclusion that there was no defense against them and that "war must go." Mr. Bernard Baruch, elder statesman through two world wars, in the introduction to the report of the Atomic Control Commission said that the abolition of war represents the only real measure of safety against the bomb. Generals Eisenhower and MacArthur agree. Senator Carl Hatch, chairman of the President's Evaluation Committee, underscores this fact: *war must go*. Bethlehem is in complete agreement with this position. From that day to this men have believed in abolition of war and the dawn of a reign of peace and goodwill among men. So far as I know, no one has ever thought this task would be easy to fulfill.

But how is the curse of war to be lifted? Bikini's answer is through fear and power: Bethlehem's answer is through love and mutual service. Between these two methods there is a great gulf fixed. You choose one or the other.

The spiritual tragedy of western civilization can be put in a single sentence: It has not been able either to forget or to follow the vision of Bethlehem. With Bethlehem in its heart, its prayer, its art, its faith, it has nonetheless blundered along until it has found its way to Bikini. Needing above all else to kneel humbly at the manger in Bethlehem, finding thereby the true inspiration for human life and history, it has found itself watching a tiny lagoon in a faraway portion of the earth, conscious of the fact that there was being enacted the drama of its own destruction.

When Phillips Brooks, the great American preacher, was visiting the Holy Land he went on Christmas Eve to a height overlooking Bethlehem. It was there and then he wrote the poem:

> O little town of Bethlehem
> How still we see thee lie!
> Above thy deep and dreamless sleep
> The silent stars go by;
> Yet in thy dark street shineth
> The everlasting Light;
> The hopes and fears of all the years
> Are met in thee tonight.

What he saw we see; what he felt to be true we know to be true. "The hopes and fears of all the years are met in thee tonight."

We have reason to be fearful, for we are part of a mighty pilgrimage from Bethlehem to Bikini. It will take a tremendous faith in the reality of God and the leadership of Jesus Christ to turn the face of our generation from Bikini to Bethlehem. But the star of hope continues to shine— over Bethlehem and nowhere else.

—*from* PULPIT DIGEST *for December, 1946*